D0848164

Joyce's politics

Dominic Manganiello
Department of English
University of Ottawa

Joyce's Politics

ROUTLEDGE & KEGAN PAUL
London, Boston and Henley

First published in 1980
by Routledge & Kegan Paul Ltd
39 Store Street, London WC1E 7DD,
9 Park Street, Boston, Mass. 02108, USA and
Broadway House, Newtown Road,
Henley-on-Thames, Oxon RG9 1EN
Photoset in 10 on 12 Bembo by
Kelly Typesetting Ltd, Bradford-on-Avon, Wiltshire
and printed in Great Britain by
Redwood Burn Ltd, Trowbridge and Esher
© Dominic Manganiello 1980

British Library Cataloguing in Publication Data

Manganiello, Dominic
Joyce's politics.
1. Joyce, James, b. 1882 – Criticism and
interpretation
2. Politics in literature
I. Title
823'.9'12   PR6019.092/   80–40571

ISBN 0 7100 0537 7

Ai miei cari genitori Francesco e Lucia

Contents

Acknowledgments

This book began as a doctoral dissertation at Wolfson College, Oxford, under the supervision of Professor Richard Ellmann. I cannot thank him adequately for his guidance. I am indebted to him for letting me see the list of books in Joyce's library before publication. I also wish to thank Dr John Kelly for discussing various issues with me and for making helpful suggestions. Professor S. E. Finer kindly let me see his unpublished notes on Guglielmo Ferrero, and Mr Denis Mack Smith also helped me with information on Ferrero. I am grateful to Mrs Nina Ferrero-Raditsa and Mr Jacob Schwartz for kindly writing to me. In Ireland, I wish to thank Dr John Garvin and Mr Gerard O'Flaherty for discussing Joyce with me. I would also like to thank the staffs of the Bodleian Library, the National Library of Ireland, the Biblioteca Civica di Trieste, and the Biblioteca Universitaria di Napoli for their assistance in making available to me various books and newspapers.

The author and publisher would like to thank The Bodley Head and Random House Inc. for their permission to quote from *Ulysses*; Jonathan Cape Ltd for their permission to quote from *A Portrait of the Artist as a Young Man* and *Stephen Hero*; Faber & Faber Ltd for permission to quote from *The Critical Writings of James Joyce* (edited by Ellsworth Mason and Richard Ellmann) and *Letters of James Joyce*, vol. 2 (edited by Richard Ellmann); The Society of Authors as the literary representative of the Estate of James Joyce for its permission to quote from *A Portrait of the Artist as a Young Man*, *Stephen Hero* and *Ulysses*; and Viking Penguin Inc. for their permission to quote from *A Portrait of the Artist as a Young Man* (Copyright 1916 by B. W. Huebsch, Copyright renewed 1944 by Nora Joyce), *The Critical Writings of James Joyce* (edited by Ellsworth Mason and Richard Ellmann, Copyright © 1959 Harriett Weaver and F. Lionel Monro,

Administrators for the Estate of James Joyce) and *Letters of James Joyce*, vol. 2 (edited by Richard Elmann, Copyright © 1966 by F. Lionel Monro, Administrator for the Estate of James Joyce) – all the above titles by James Joyce. They would also like to thank Michael Yeats and Macmillan for their permission to quote from *Uncollected Prose by W. B. Yeats*, vol. 2; and Eyre Methuen for their permission to quote from *Peer Gynt* by Henrik Ibsen.

Notes on the Text

Abbreviations

JJ   Richard Ellmann, *James Joyce* (London: Oxford University Press, 1966).

I, II, III   The three-volume edition, *Letters of James Joyce*, ed. Stuart Gilbert and Richard Ellmann (London: Faber & Faber, 1957–66).

CW   *The Critical Writings of James Joyce*, ed. Ellsworth Mason and Richard Ellmann (New York: Viking Press, 1959).

MBK   Stanislaus Joyce, *My Brother's Keeper* (London: Faber & Faber, 1958).

SF   *Sinn Féin*.

UI   *United Irishman*.

JJMU   Frank Budgen, *James Joyce and the Making of 'Ulysses' and Other Writings* (London: Oxford University Press, 1972).

References

Bracketed page references following quotations from *Ulysses* are to the two standard editions, the one published by Random House, New York (1961) and the other by The Bodley Head, London (1960), cited in that order in italic. References in the text to Joyce's other books are to these editions:

1 *A Portrait of the Artist as a Young Man: Text, Criticism, Notes*, ed. Chester G. Anderson (London: Jonathan Cape, 1968) (New York: Viking Press, 1968, in italic).
2 *Dubliners: Text Criticism, and Notes*, ed. Robert Scholes and A.

Walton Litz (London: Jonathan Cape, 1968) (New York: Viking Press, 1969, in italic).

3 *Stephen Hero*, ed. John J. Slocum and Herbert Cahoon (London: Jonathan Cape, 1969) (New York: New Directions, 1963, in italic).

4 *Exiles* (Harmondsworth: Penguin, 1973) (New York: Viking Press, 1961, in italic).

5 *Finnegans Wake* (New York: Viking Press, 1969).

6 *Giacomo Joyce* (London: Faber & Faber, 1969).

Chapter 1

Old Ireland

1 A Portrait of the Artist as a Young Parnellite

I

The tenor of innumerable critical statements about Joyce is that he was indifferent to politics. From the earliest reviews to the more recent ones, we are told of his 'fanatical neutrality' on political matters, and of the divorce of his art from social issues.[1] Such views rest on impressions of Joyce as an apolitical writer conveyed by his friends. Yeats, when he was trying to obtain a grant for him from the Royal Literary Fund, informed Edmund Gosse by letter in 1915 that Joyce 'had never anything to do with Irish politics, extreme or otherwise, and I think disliked politics.'[2] In Zürich, at the end of the First World War, Frank Budgen marvelled at Joyce's reticence to discuss politics: 'On one subject he was more uncommunicative than any man I know: the subject of politics.'[3] In the charged atmosphere of the 1930s, Louis Gillet found Joyce remarkably aloof: 'I do not remember, during all those years, that Joyce ever said anything on current events.'[4] And when at his last meeting with his brother in Zürich in 1939 Stainslaus Joyce was eager to talk about the Fascist regime in Italy, he was rebuffed, 'For God's sake don't talk politics. I'm not interested in politics. The only thing that interests me is style.'[5]

From such statements it would be possible to construct a picture of Joyce as a writer totally detached from his century. To regard Joyce as a dweller in an ivory tower, however, does not jibe with the attempt to picture totally the situation of man and woman. The portrayal of Bloom and Molly, for instance, can hardly be said to be idealised or sentimentalised. Joyce insisted that we must accept life 'as we see it before our eyes, men and women as we meet them in the real world, not as we apprehend them in the world of faery'.[6] The material he worked with is the common, the average, the everyday. To treat actuality in all its aspects in a truthful manner presupposes that art affords a degree of interaction with society, or indeed that it reflects its society. Such an artistic aim, therefore, must necessarily include a concern with politics.

If by politics we mean campaigning for votes, or for particular candidates, Joyce took no part. If by politics we understand attempting to get new laws passed through legislatures, Joyce never participated in such activity either. He did not make himself a champion of causes, however noble. By refusing to do so Joyce did not discountenance political awareness, but rather indicated his conviction that an active role in politics would compromise his position as an artist. To be an artist entailed a sense of civic responsibility greater than that of the ordinary citizen, but not necessarily expressed at ballot boxes or in caucuses.

In the literature of the nineteenth century, in so far as it was political, an artist had only to show compassion towards the lower classes and the oppressed as a sign and measure of a responsible social conscience. Adherence to a political line was not expected, although some novelists, like Disraeli, were obviously partisan. The idea of having to choose between political parties, as far as the novel is concerned, is a problem which has been posed only in this century. Scrutiny of the political orientation of writers has come about only recently, especially since the Russian revolution. Only since the 1930s has the question of whether a writer was fascist or communist, whether he belonged to the right or left wing, been a matter of crucial concern.

Joyce has remained a somewhat enigmatic figure because he does not present a vision of the social order in accordance with a strict ideological line. His reluctance to inculcate a rigid political view can be explained, in part, by his hatred of didacticism. The didacticism used by previous writers was, on the one hand, in the service of a tradition, that of the Church, the State, or of social conventions. Joyce's refusal to commit himself to this tradition was not a sign of political indifference; rather he exercised his right to make a positive choice. His objection to being dictated to was an assertion of personal freedom, an unwillingness to reduce the role of the artist to that of a priest or politician. Other writers, like Tolstoy, on the other hand, had launched their attacks on such institutions violently and openly. Joyce interpreted this didacticism of 'revolution' to be equally repugnant. He believed that the artist, whether progressive or reactionary, would lose his credibility by browbeating his readers into accepting his point of view. To embrace a dogmatic political outlook would limit the effectiveness of his art, and expose him to the charge of presenting a *parti pris* about society. Joyce's dismissal of didacticism, then, was itself a political act. The political statements he made were often ironical, and cannot always be taken at face value; that is, they were not exhortations but criticisms of helplessness, or of situations that offered no cause for hope. If he was reserved in his principal writings, he was less so in others. Some of his minor works, for instance, deal with political questions with acerbity. In whichever mode he chose to express himself, he demonstrated a constant awareness of Irish politics. For Joyce the great question in literature is not allegiance to any particular party or platform. The writer must marshal the feelings and events of the time, political in their implication, into a possible order, and interpret day-to-day issues in the light of the loftier struggles of ideals, and the puncturing of delusions.

The first work Joyce ever wrote was political. This was the poem (now lost), 'Et Tu, Healy',★ which he composed at the age of nine shortly after Parnell's death on 6 October 1891. The poem was a diatribe against Tim Healy, leader of the clericalist faction in opposition to Parnell. In denouncing Healy as a traitor, Joyce was inspired by the invective of his father, an ardent Parnellite, against the 'Bantry gang'. This epithet, by which John Joyce meant Healy and his uncle T. M. Sullivan as well as other relations who hailed from Bantry, is recalled by Stephen in *A Portrait of the Artist as a Young Man* (233) (*228*): 'His father's jibes at the Bantry gang leaped out of his memory.' John Joyce admired his son's poem and had it printed and distributed among his circle of friends. Parnell's fall from power stamped itself indelibly on Joyce's imagination, and he concentrated mainly on this aspect of the Parnell era when he sat down to reconstruct its events about two decades later in *A Portrait*. Parnell's fall possessed that dramatic quality which other events did not, and produced those polarised attitudes and divisions in Irish society which helped to shape events in the early twentieth century.

Joyce described the Protestant, English-educated Charles Stewart

---

★ Stanislaus Joyce remembered that the poem ended with the dead Parnell, likened to an eagle, looking down on the grovelling mass of Irish politicians. For the few surviving fragments of the poem see *JJ*, p. 33 and fn.

Parnell as 'perhaps the most formidable man that ever led the Irish'.[7] When he came to prominence in the 1870s, Parnell mounted a fierce campaign for Home Rule which proved to be the touchstone of Irish politics up to the First World War. He did so, as Joyce pointed out, by uniting 'behind him every element of Irish life and began to march, treading on the verge of insurrection'.[8] These disparate elements were the constitutional nationalists and the Fenians or physical force advocates. On the floor of the British House of Commons Parnell with a handful of his supporters made a concerted effort to block government business by opposing every important English or Scottish bill under parliamentary debate. By initiating the technique of the filibuster the small Irish Party would eventually succeed in holding the balance of power between the two major English parties in 1886. Parnell kept in the forefront of political activity at home too. As President of the Land League founded by Michael Davitt, he pressed for land reform and was instrumental in creating a movement more or less along the lines of passive resistance. For those buying the farms of evicted tenants Parnell advocated the morally coercive but essentially non-violent policy of social ostracism or boycotting. A parliamentary campaign of obstructionism coupled with the land agitation gave the 'Irish question' the predominance in the Commons it had hitherto lacked. Writing almost thirty years later about the second Home Rule Act, Joyce, alluding to this period of ferment in his country's history,* described the Irish as 'a people who, poor in everything else and rich only in political ideas, have perfected the strategy of obstructionism and made the word "boycott" an international war-cry'.[9]

Joyce was aware that Irishmen were also capable of misguided gestures of political extremism. In 1882, his birth year, the British Undersecretary and the new Chief Secretary were assassinated in Dublin's Phoenix Park by the Invincibles secret society. This incident disrupted the non-violent programme of Parnell, and forced Joyce to take a stand against political violence and against the physical force tradition in Irish history. In this attitude Joyce is represented in *Ulysses* by Bloom as well as by Stephen. The cabman's shelter, which they visited in 'Eumaeus', is reputedly owned by Fitzharris, or Skin-the-Goat, the man who allegedly

---

* In the 'Ithaca' episode of *Ulysses* (*716; 843*), we are told that Bloom had supported 'the agrarian policy of Michael Davitt' and the 'constitutional agitation of Charles Stewart Parnell'.

drove the getaway cab for the Invincibles. When the discussion veers towards the murders, Bloom, although fascinated by revolutionary activity, registers his disapproval:

> He disliked those careers of wrongdoing and crime on principle. Yet, though such criminal propensities had never been an inmate of his bosom in any shape or form, he certainly did feel, and no denying it (while inwardly remaining what he was), a certain kind of admiration for a man who had actually brandished a knife, cold steel, with the courage of his political convictions though, personally, he would never be a party to any such thing. (*642; 744*)

Joyce indicates that however just a political cause might be, violence can never provide a solution.

Parnell rebounded from the politically dangerous acts of terrorism to gain some measure of support for the concept of independence within the next few years. In 1886 the English Prime Minister, William Gladstone, dramatically introduced the first Home Rule Bill only to have it defeated on second reading by two dissident groups within his own Liberal Party. Gladstone's conversion to Home Rule was taken in good faith by Parnell and by the Irish people, but Joyce suspected the purity of his motives. In *Ulysses* (*716; 843*) we are told that Bloom at one time supported Gladstone's programme for reform. Joyce, however, denounced Gladstone as a 'self-seeking politician', and classified his brand of liberalism as

> an inconstant algebraic symbol whose coefficient was the movement's political pressure and whose index was his personal profit. While he temporised in internal politics, contradicting and justifying himself in turn, he always maintained (as much as he was capable of it) a sincere admiration for liberty in the house of others.[10]

Joyce stressed the 'elastic quality' of Gladstone's liberalism in order to highlight the magnitude of Parnell's achievement. A prominent example of this elasticity or duplicity was Gladstone's opposition to Daniel O'Connell's efforts to repeal the Union. Joyce apparently overlooked the fact that it was the Fenian rising of 1867 which had first stirred Gladstone to change his position. If political calculation alone had dictated his final move for Home Rule, Gladstone would have been aware of the split within his own party that the measure would precipitate. Rather, some credit must be given him for recognising that under Parnell Ireland was ready for self-government. It was Gladstone's role during the future Parnell crisis that coloured Joyce's view of him and explains why he painted Gladstone as a villain.

Joyce continued to be dazzled, moreover, by Parnell's personality. His coldness in the face of outbursts of public approval, for instance, was remarkable. After being vindicated in a devious attempt by the London *Times* to blackmail him, Parnell re-entered the House of Commons and was greeted with a standing ovation from all its members, starting with Gladstone. 'Is it necessary to say', Joyce asked admiringly, 'that Parnell made no response to the ovation with a smile or a bow or a gesture, but merely passed to his place beyond the aisle and sat down?' He added that Gladstone was probably thinking of this incident when he called Parnell an 'intellectual phenomenon'.[11]

Both parties now courted Parnell. At a meeting in Brighton in 1890, John Morley, who had been Chief Secretary in an earlier Liberal administration, now boldly proposed that Parnell should hold that post in the next Liberal government. 'Parnell not only refused it,' reported Joyce in perhaps overstating the case, 'he ordered all his followers as well to refuse ministerial duties, and forbade the municipalities and public corporations in Ireland to receive officially any member of the royal house until the English government should restore autonomy to Ireland.'[12] Joyce would remember bitterly Parnell's stricture when Queen Victoria and King Edward VII visited Dublin in 1900 and 1903.

Parnell's fall came at the peak of his popularity 'like lightning from a clear sky', as Joyce put it. On Christmas eve in 1889 Captain William O'Shea, a former member of the Irish Party, filed a divorce suit citing Parnell as co-respondent. Parnell had met O'Shea's wife, Katharine, in 1880 and shortly afterwards began living with her. Their affair was an 'open secret' in political circles at least as early as 1886. O'Shea admitted in the court proceedings that he cast suspicion on their relationship at this time, but claimed he had been deceived all along. Since neither Parnell nor Mrs O'Shea defended themselves at the hearing – their one hope was to get married as quickly as possible – O'Shea received his decree of divorce on 15 November 1890. What impressed Joyce was Parnell's indifference to moral convention in Catholic Ireland, and his severe reticence or unwillingness to express any remorse about it.

Gladstone, meanwhile, came under intense pressure from powerful elements within his party to break the alliance with

Parnell. He became increasingly convinced that if Parnell did not step down the Liberals would lose the next election, and Home Rule be indefinitely postponed. The alternatives posed by Gladstone, Home Rule or Parnell, obliged the Irish Party to make an agonising choice. The alliance with the Liberals seemed vital since only Gladstone of all the English leaders had embraced Home Rule in a manner acceptable to most Irishmen. On the other hand, Parnell had gained more success for this measure than any previous Irish politician. To depose him now at the bidding of an English politician when Home Rule was within reach was to court charges of betrayal from those who viewed the man and the cause as inseparable. Originally the members of the party pledged their loyalty to Parnell but a second meeting proved inconclusive with the result that another meeting was scheduled. Parnell, meanwhile, had sized up the growing forces against him and issued a 'Manifesto to the Irish People' in which, as Joyce said, he 'denied the right of a minister to exercise a veto over the political affairs of Ireland.' He also referred unwisely and inaccurately to a meeting he had had with Gladstone in 1889, and accused the Liberals of formulating a policy against Irish interests. The manifesto forced Liberals to part company with Parnell once and for all, and infuriated members of his own party as well as the Irish delegation in the USA. At the same time, it allowed the bishops to enter the fray. The vote in Committee Room 15, therefore, ended with 45 against and 27 for the retention of Parnell's leadership. But Parnell fought the combined forces against him literally to the death. When the dust had settled, Joyce could say with bitterness that Parnell was brought down 'in obedience to Gladstone's orders' and that the 'high and low clergy entered the lists to finish him off.'[13]

To proceed in this manner, however, entails the risk, to the historian's eye, of oversimplifying the intricate aspects of the Parnell crisis. Irish history is still highly controversial. The degree to which Parnell was a genuine leader and the degree to which he forsook his position are difficult to measure. An astute modern historian, F. S. L. Lyons, has argued that to dwell exclusively on the last phase of Parnell's life is to misinterpret and to minimise the part Parnell played in his own downfall.[14] In other words, Parnell betrayed himself as much as he was betrayed by others. He became so distracted by his love affair that after 1886 he absented himself frequently and regrettably from Parliament. Oblivious to adverse political repercussions, he prolonged for nearly ten years his relationship with Katharine O'Shea. This course of conduct might have been pardonable in an ordinary man; but for Parnell, entrusted with the national interests, it endangered and finally destroyed his capacity to lead.

The interpretation of these events by Joyce, as a very young contemporary, was quite different from this later one. A great deal of what Joyce presents is the attitude of his father and that of his father's friends. Joyce adopted it out of sympathy or family loyalty, and out of shared anticlericalism. If the Church was wrong, then Parnell presumably was right. We now know that the Church itself was divided between admiration for Parnell's leadership and reproach for his liaison. Despite these differences in interpretation, the Christmas dinner scene in *A Portrait*, as will soon appear, crystallises Joyce's political position. If his Parnell is not the whole man, his prominence in Joyce's work exculpates Joyce from the charge of indifference or detachment from the explosive political world in which he had grown up. The Parnell crisis was the pivot from which Joyce viewed the rest of Irish history. The central theme of 'betrayal' in his work takes its origin from *the* political event of his youth.

Beyond Parnell lay seven centuries of Irish struggle for Home Rule. Like his fellow countrymen, Joyce considered this long-sustained English presence in Ireland an occupation. He would have agreed with Robert Dahl's standard definition of 'political', that it treated 'any pattern of human relationships that involves, to a significant extent, power, rule, or authority'.[15] In his lecture on 'Ireland, Island of Saints and Sages', delivered in Trieste in 1907, Joyce dealt with the seven centuries of English rule and searched for evidence of the Irish character, and the character of Anglo-Irish relations.[16] Oppression was not an English innovation. 'Anyone who reads the history of the three centuries that precede the coming of the English must have a strong stomach,' he maintained, 'because the internecine strife, and the conflicts with the Danes and the Norwegians, the black foreigners and the white foreigners, as they were called, follow each other so continuously and ferociously that they make this entire era a veritable slaughterhouse.' These nordic invaders, whom the native Irish called the 'Lochlanns', took control of the island and established a kingdom in Dublin. They were finally vanquished in the tenth century by Malach II, King of Meath, and later by Brian Boru at the battle of Clontarf in 1014. In 'Proteus' Stephen stresses his feeling of kinship with these ancestors who resisted the Lochlanns. He affirms that he is an Irishman even if his views, as will later appear, lead him to quarrel with his homeland.

The Anglo-Norman invasion was, as Joyce remarked, an accursed day in the national calendar 'according to the patriots'. He challenged nationalist belief on this point:

> But the fact is that the English came to Ireland at the repeated request of a native king, without, needless to say, any great desire on their part, and without the consent of their own king, but armed with the papal bull of Adrian IV and a papal letter of Alexander. They landed on the east coast with seven hundred men, a band of adventurers against a nation; they were received by some native tribes, and in less than a year, the English Henry II celebrated Christmas with gusto in the city of Dublin.[17]

The native king who invited the English to Ireland was Dermot MacMurrough, King of Leinster. In 1152 he eloped with Devorgilla, wife of Tiernan O'Rourke, Prince of Breffni.* MacMurrough was deposed in 1167 when Roderick O'Connor, High King of Ireland, joined forces with O'Rourke against him. MacMurrough fled to England and solicited the aid of Henry II. Henry was preoccupied with urgent affairs of State in England and in France, but gave MacMurrough permission to recruit. MacMurrough's plea paved the way for the invasion of 1169 led in part by Robert Fitzstephen and the earl of Pembroke (better known as 'Strongbow'). Henry at first gave his token consent to the enterprise, but before he could finally decide against it, Strongbow gave him the slip. Henry sent envoys to Ireland with the clear warning that if Strongbow and his band of adventurers did not desist and return home, forfeiture of their lands in England and in France would be the penalty. Henry's fear was that Strongbow and the other barons would escape liability for service in the wars on the continent.[18] So when Henry landed in Ireland in 1171, the adventurers paid formal homage to him. Three papal letters and a papal privilege of Alexander III, which conferred on Henry dominion over the Irish people, confirmed English control of Ireland.

---

* Mr Deasy confuses the two men in 'Nestor' (*34–35; 43*). 'A faithless wife first brought the strangers to our shore here, MacMurrough's wife and her leman O'Rourke.' Joyce's view is reiterated in 'Cyclops': 'The strangers . . . Our own fault. We let them come in. The adulteress and her paramour brought the Saxon robbers here' (*324; 420*).

Joyce traced the root of Ireland's problems to an alleged political gesture of Adrian IV, Nicholas Brakespear, the only English Pope. By virtue of the bull *Laudabiliter*, it is claimed that he had already commissioned Henry II to invade Ireland in 1155. Joyce complained that throughout history the Papacy had never lent a word of support to her most Catholic domain, yet Ireland remained faithful to the Papacy. He exploited this theme to the full in 'Oxen of the Sun', where the medical students engage in an intricate wordplay on 'bulls'. To Dixon's proclamation that the first bull was sent to 'our island by farmer Nicholas', Lynch adds crudely and ironically that 'a plumper and portlier bull . . . never shit on shamrock.' Nicholas then bids the Irish bull to do 'all my cousin german the Lord Harry tells you' (*399–400; 522*). In other words, the English King, Henry II, was invested with full powers over Ireland by the Vatican. Joyce interpreted MacMurrough's treachery to be a native Irish growth, a charge he would level consistently at his countrymen and some of his friends.

Every Irish revolution – those of 1798, 1848, and 1867 – Joyce pointed out, had its informer. He filled the pages of *Ulysses* with verses from the ballads about the rebellion of 1798, 'The Croppy Boy' and 'The Boys of Wexford' in particular. Wolfe Tone, a leader of the rebellion, had formed a secret, oath-bound society called the 'United Irishmen', comprising both Catholics and Protestants, pledged to republican aims or complete independence. The British took strong measures to check the growing conspiracy. It was the government's intelligence system, based on informers, which proved to be the most devastating ploy. Leonard MacNally, a lawyer who had introduced William Jackson, a French agent, to Tone, turned traitor. Thomas Reynolds was another prominent informer. He joined the provincial directory of the United Irishmen, which included most of the leaders of the movement, and eventually had all of its members arrested in 1798. Only Lord Edward Fitzgerald, a French envoy, escaped, but his hiding place was disclosed by Francis Higgins, known as the 'sham squire'. (In 'Wandering Rocks' (*241; 309*) Tom Kernan remembers this incident.) Joyce, in a letter to Stanislaus of 1906, predicted that his nemesis, Oliver St John Gogarty, would play the part of MacNally and Reynolds.[19] For Joyce there is no distinction between personal feeling and the nature of Irish society. A personal judgment is by extension a political judgment.

The immediate consequence of the rebellion was that William

Pitt, the English Prime Minister, was determined to avoid at all costs a similar uprising aided by the French. He proposed a legislative union of the British and Irish parliaments as a solution. The Act that united the kingdoms of England and Ireland in 1800 was the other 'ill-omened' day on the national calendar. Joyce again brought the question into focus:

> There is the fact that parliamentary union was not legislated at Westminster but at Dublin, by a parliament elected by the vote of the people of Ireland, a parliament corrupted and undermined with the greatest ingenuity by the agents of the English prime minister, but an Irish parliament nevertheless.

The Irish Parliament can hardly be said to have represented the whole of Ireland, as Joyce claims, since its members were Protestant. It is undeniable, however, that Pitt 'bought' the Union. When the measure was first introduced in Dublin in 1799, Henry Grattan, head of the 'Patriot Party', led the opposition and it was defeated by a majority of five. The Lord Lieutenant, Cornwallis, undeterred, proceeded to achieve his end through devious means. He offered compensation to the owners of pocket boroughs, and gave peerages to twenty-eight Members of Parliament. Through promises of positions, pensions, and threats of dismissal, Cornwallis garnered the necessary votes to secure a majority for the Union. At the same time to appease the Roman Catholics, Pitt managed to convince the clergy that total emancipation* could only come about in the British parliament. As Gladstone was to say in 1886 on the floor of the House of Commons, 'we obtained the Union against the sense of every class of the Community, by wholesale bribery and unblushing intimidation.'[20] For Joyce political expediency did not justify the loss of national self-respect.

The two facts which coloured Joyce's view of Irish history, that 'at the time of Henry II Ireland was a body torn by fierce strife and at the time of William Pitt was a venal and wicked mess of corruption', did not deter him from stating his firm belief that 'When a victorious country tyrannizes over another, it cannot logically be considered wrong for that other to rebel.' On the other hand, he had no

---

* Catholics were excluded from Parliament and the professions, as well as being prohibited from attending their own public schools and to own a horse worth more than five pounds. Catholics were also barred from purchasing land, obtaining a mortgage, or renting land on a lease over thirty-one years.

sympathy for pointless resistance to British rule. He judged Robert Emmet's rebellion in 1803 to be a 'foolish uprising', a belated flash out of 1798 ending in dismal failure.[21] Emmet could scarcely have hoped for success with a handful of men and erratic strategy when Ireland was under the control of a large British army and an Insurrection Act which granted extensive powers to local magistrates to search for arms. Yet the idealistic and sacrificial nature of Emmet's action and his subsequent execution was to generate a powerful emotional appeal to leaders of the Easter Rising of 1916, such as Patrick Pearse.* Joyce found sentimentality in all of life's aspects, including the political, to be equally distressful.

The 1848 uprising was inspired by 'physical force' men who advocated the aims and principles of 1798. This group of men, led by Thomas Davis, John Blake Dillon and Charles Gavan Duffy, started the *Nation* in 1842 and soon became known as 'Young Ireland'. The *Nation* devoted itself to creating a national consciousness, and Davis defined nationality as embracing all creeds, races and classes in Ireland. The idea was not entirely new, since Wolfe Tone and Daniel O'Connell had held the same belief. The Young Irelanders drew inspiration from the cultural and historical past, from the time of the Gaels and Normans, and national motives usually dominated their writings. A notable exception, who won Joyce's praise, was James Clarence Mangan. In an essay read at University College in 1902 and later, in a lecture delivered in Trieste in 1907, Joyce singled Mangan out as 'the most significant poet of the modern Celtic world'.[22] Mangan's contemporaries, Joyce emphasised, were surprised to find literary merit in his poetry since it lacked patriotic fervour. Mangan succeeded (though not always) in not subordinating his art to the national cause. This distinction between the demands of nationalism and those of art which Joyce preserved placed him at odds, as will be subsequently shown, with the literary movement of his own time. Joyce, in effect, considered the 'impassioned movement' of Young Ireland to be as futile as Emmet's rising.[23]†

---

* See below, pp. 162–3.

† The founders of the *Nation* were initially supporters of Daniel O'Connell, to whom Joyce claimed his paternal grandmother was related.[24] In 'Ithaca' (*716; 843*) we are told that Bloom had apparently supported 'the collective and national programme' advocated by James Fintan Lalor (who saw land reform as the key issue in Ireland), John Mitchel (who was in favour of complete separation from England by physical force), John Fisher Murray (another radical Young Irelander) and J. F. X. O'Brien (a Fenian involved in the 1867 rising).

The Irish Republican Brotherhood, or Fenian society, on the other hand, fascinated Joyce. When 'the last Fenian', John O'Leary, died in 1907, he wrote an article on 'Fenianism' for *Il Piccolo della sera*. Joyce was primarily impressed by the Fenians' method or organisation: 'Under the leadership of James Stephens, head of the Fenians, the country was organised into circles composed of a Sergeant and twenty-five men, a plan eminently fitted to the Irish character because it reduces the possibility of betrayal.'[25]* For Joyce averting betrayal had become the key political factor in revolutionary Irish history. Unfortunately, the 'circles' proved vulnerable and were frequently infiltrated by informers and secret agents.

Joyce was overoptimistic about the progress of the Fenian movement up to the rebellion of 1867. 'Everything seemed to go well,' he wrote, 'and the Republic was on the point of being established (it was even proclaimed openly by Stephens), when O'Leary and Luby . . . were arrested.'† The Fenians, however, represented only a minority within the national movement, and the Republic was never on the verge of being established. Joyce attributed the disintegration of the movement to informers, but the rising of 1867 was, in effect, as desperate and futile an attempt as that of the Young Irelanders. Joyce disagreed. He claimed that the Fenianism of 1867 was not self-defeating, not 'one of the usual flashes of Celtic temperament that leave behind a darkness blacker than before'.[26]‡ He was thinking in particular of how Fenianism had inculcated in the minds of the future generation the doctrine of separatism.

Although Joyce drew attention to the role the indigenous population and the Church had played in the Anglo-Norman invasion and in the series of betrayals against the revolutionary patriots, he did not condone English misdeeds in Ireland. 'A conqueror cannot be casual', he stated ironically, 'and for so many centuries the Englishman has done in Ireland only what the Nipponese dwarf will do tomorrow in other lands.' Joyce's indictment telescopes several centuries. In feudal times England kept the Irish barons divided

---

* Bloom concurs in 'Lestrygonians' (*163; 207*): 'James Stephens' idea was the best. He knew them. Circles of ten so that a fellow couldn't round in more than his own ring.'

† Joyce was also intrigued by Stephens's escape from prison, and how 'he left the capital in a gig, disguised as a bride (according to legend) with a white crepe veil and orange blossoms' (*CW*, p. 189). In *Ulysses* (*43; 54/68; 83*), both Bloom and Stephen remember this apocryphal version of Stephens's escape.

‡ Cf. Joyce's attitude to Easter 1916, pp. 162–3.

among themselves, while her own barons forced King John to sign the Magna Carta. The English then proceeded to exploit Ireland's land and wealth. Joyce mentions Shane O'Neill, son of the first earl of Tyrone, who was the fiercest opponent of English rule in the sixteenth century. O'Neill resisted the feudal machinery installed by Henry VIII in 1541 whereby Gaelic lords would give up their lands to the crown and receive them back as feudal grants. His downfall came about not on account of his quarrel with the English, but in a battle against another Gaelic chief, the O'Donnell. Other instances of English perfidy which Joyce adduced were the penal laws enacted in 1695 and carried through the first decades of the eighteenth century, and the Great Famine. The penal laws discouraged Irish commerce and hurt the Protestants, in whose hands trade and industry lay, more than the Catholics. In 1699 Irish woollen goods could be exported only to England, where heavy duties were then imposed on them. Consequently, the Irish woollen industry was demolished. In 1847 and 1848 the Great Famine and the emigration that followed reduced the population by about two millions. In a vitriolic attack in 'Cyclops' (*326; 423; 329–30; 427–8*), the Citizen blames England for the collapse of the Irish economy at this time, and for allowing the poor to starve to death. This was Joyce's point of view too, for he asserted in 'Ireland, Island of Saints and Sages' that 'Ireland is poor because English laws ruined the country's industries, especially the wool industry, because the neglect of the English government in the years of the potato famine allowed the best of the population to die from hunger.' Joyce was to keep this constant awareness of his country's impoverishment when analysing the contemporary Irish scene. Joyce's reading of Irish history always had a crucial bearing on his politics.

II

The great débâcle did more than provide Joyce with a way to view his countrymen and their past. Its political magnitude brought into focus those powers which Parnell resisted heroically but unsuccessfully and against which the artist would muster his own forces, although in a totally different manner. In *A Portrait of the Artist*, political consciousness matures simultaneously with artistic consciousness. Joyce is not only concerned with the individual but with how society impinges upon his consciousness. Stephen acts as a kind of sounding-board for Joyce's reactions to those forces that at once shaped and threatened his artistic integrity. Although it can be argued that other characters 'are too little individualized' in comparison to Stephen,[27] they nevertheless embody the various positions that could be taken up. At the earliest stage of development, Stephen's mind is exposed to the Irish world of politics in the form of Dante's brushes representing Michael Davitt and Parnell. As he grows older and the scene shifts to Clongowes Wood College, Stephen is seen meditating on the story of Hamilton Rowan (10) (*10*), an associate of Wolfe Tone. He then mentions the 'Liberator' without further identifying Daniel O'Connell (26) (*26*), thereby tacitly indicating his steady indoctrination into Irish history. He always lent an ear, we are told, whenever his elders spoke of 'Irish politics, of Munster, and of the legends of his own family' (64) (*62*). The Parnell question in particular preys on his mind continually:

> He wondered which was right, to be for the green or the maroon, because Dante had ripped the green velvet back off the brush that was for Parnell one day with her scissors and had told him that Parnell was a bad man. He wondered if they were arguing at home about that. That was called politics. . . .
>   It pained him that he did not know well what politics meant. (16–17) (*16–17*)

So politics holds its fascination for Stephen and means simply debate about the moral dilemma of right and wrong.

The political crisis surrounding Parnell, moreover, inspires Stephen's first attempt at poetry and, consequently, his artistic consciousness: 'He saw himself sitting at his table in Bray the morning after the discussion at the dinnertable, trying to write a poem about Parnell on the back of one of his moiety notices' (72) (*70*). This artistic activity, as Stephen says, is precipitated by the heated discussion at the Christmas dinnertable. The initial part of the exchange hinges on the role of the Church in politics, with Dante clearly asserting the Church's supremacy in political matters dealing with morals: 'It is a question of public morality. A priest would not be a priest if he did not tell his flock what is right and what is wrong' (32) (*31*). Dante's statement reflects the tension that existed between Church and State since Fenian times. The Church now seized the opportunity to reassert its authority and leadership which it felt had been weakened by Parnell's ascendancy over the Irish people. Mr Casey, a Fenian, and Simon Dedalus, however, deny the Church this prerogative, and oppose any intervention in the realm of politics: 'Let them leave politics alone, said Mr Casey, or the people may leave the Church alone' (33) (*32*).

The separation of Church and State powers becomes crucial when it involves acquiescence to a foreign ruler. 'Were we to desert him at the bidding of the English people?' asks Mr Dedalus pointedly. And Mr Casey finally condemns outright the Church's part in Parnell's downfall:

> The priests and the priests' pawns broke Parnell's heart and hounded him into his grave. . .
> — Sons of bitches! cried Mr Dedalus. When he was down they turned on him to betray him and rend him like rats in a sewer. Lowlived dogs! And they look it! By Christ, they look it! (35) .
> (*33–4*)

Dante counters by proclaiming that 'The priests were always the true friends of Ireland.' Mr Casey responds by citing examples from the time of the Union onwards to prove his point that the bishops and priests were actually traitors to the Irish cause. Dante is led to exclaim, in that case, 'God and religion before the world!' which provokes Mr Casey's vehement rejoinder 'if it comes to that, no God for Ireland!' (39–41) (*38–9*)

In what way has Stephen absorbed the points raised in this fierce dispute? His remarks to his peasant friend Davin clearly indicate that Stephen, like Joyce, interpreted the lesson of Irish history to be that any man attempting to solve the national question risks betrayal. When Davin urges him to join the nationalist ranks and to fight for Ireland's freedom, therefore, Stephen responds coldly:

> No honourable and sincere man . . . has given up to you his life and his youth and his affections from the days of Tone to those of Parnell but you sold him to the enemy or failed him in need or reviled him and left him for another. And you invite me to be one of you. I'd see you damned first. (207) (*203*)

He refuses to serve a nationalist tradition that has always been infiltrated by what he calls 'the indispensable informer' (206) (*202*), many of whose prototypes Stephen claims can still be found among their college friends.

Nationalism, for Joyce, exemplified political delusion in the secular sphere. But Irishmen were submissive to a spiritual creed as well: 'Ireland prides itself on being faithful body and soul to its national tradition as well as to the Holy See', Joyce argued in

'Ireland, Island of Saints and Sages'. The Pope, however, and not the British monarch, posed the greatest threat to Irish liberty, a view affirmed in *Stephen Hero* (57) (*53*): 'The Roman, not the Sassenach, was for him the tyrant of the islanders.' As a result, Joyce insisted, 'I do not see what good it does to fulminate against the English tyranny while the Roman tyranny occupies the palace of the soul.'[28] For this reason Joyce was embittered against the Church that smashed Parnell, and evinced sympathy for the Fenian cry of 'No priests in politics!' echoed by John Casey and Simon Dedalus.

Joyce did not exonerate the English for their role in Parnell's downfall either, and accused Gladstone of having committed 'the moral assassination of Parnell with the help of the Irish bishops'.[29] Joyce's statements on the whole seem to support Parnell's view of the political crisis, especially that expressed in his 'Manifesto to the Irish People'. In it Parnell ignored the divorce issue altogether, and pleaded with the Irish people not to throw him to the 'English wolves now howling for my destruction'. In other words, as Simon Dedalus argued, the Irish were not to abandon him at the bidding of the English people. If the Irish were disposed to sacrifice him, however, the party should at least make the Liberals pay the price by conceding certain points in the projected Home Rule Bill. What Simon Dedalus, Mr Casey, Stephen, and even Joyce ignore, however, is that the party *complied* with Parnell's request. In early 1891 William O'Brien, and later John Dillon, met Parnell in France in an effort to have him retire temporarily. Considerable progress was made in gaining the kind of concessions for Home Rule which Parnell himself had proposed in Committee Room 15. But Parnell changed his mind and refused to withdraw from public life even for a short while and broke off the negotiations.[30] In 'The Shade of Parnell', however, Joyce wrote with cruel irony that Parnell's countrymen did not fail him in his final appeal: 'They did not throw him to the English wolves; they tore him to pieces themselves.'[31] Joyce alluded again to Parnell's entreaty in 'The Home Rule Comet', where he claimed that Ireland had 'betrayed her heroes, always in the hour of need and always without gaining recompense'.[32]

So far Joyce had modestly compared Parnell to Caesar and his conspirators to Brutus. In 'Home Rule Comes of Age' he enlarged this perspective on the theme of betrayal by associating Parnell's plight with that of Christ. The Irish Party is accused of having sold their leader to 'the pharisaical conscience of the English Dissenters without exacting the thirty pieces of silver'.[33] Joyce carries this image over into 'Ivy Day in the Committee Room' which ends with the poem 'The Death of Parnell'. It is again an angry denunciation of the 'coward hounds' who betrayed the Chief to the 'rabble-rout of fawning priests'. The Christ-Caesar parallel is yet enriched by an allusion to Moses in 'The Shade of Parnell' where Joyce claims that Parnell 'led a turbulent and unstable people from the house of shame to the verge of the Promised Land'.[34] This Mosaic imagery, also employed in 'Aeolus', supplies an ironic reference to Healy who, at the inception of the crisis, urged that the leader should not be abandoned 'within sight of the Promised Land.'[35] (It was Healy too who had first hailed Parnell, in a phrase previously used of O'Connell, as the 'uncrowned king of Ireland' at a meeting in Montreal in 1880.)

For Joyce, the artist and politician seemed doomed to share the same fate in an Ireland 'where Christ and Caesar are hand and glove'.[36] Joyce had ascribed the melancholy of Parnell's final year, when he went about 'like a hunted deer', to the 'profound conviction that in his hour of need, one of the disciples who dipped his hand in the same bowl with him would betray him'.[37] Richard Rowan in *Exiles* (52) (*44*) tells Robert Hand that 'There is a faith still stranger than the faith of the disciple in his master. . . . The faith of a master in the disciple who will betray him.' Joyce clearly identified and paralleled his own situation with that of Parnell in his broadside of 1912, 'Gas from a Burner', inspired by his contract disputes for the publication of *Dubliners*. In 'The Holy Office' he cast himself in the same image of the 'deer' he used for Parnell, 'I flash my antlers in the air',[38] an image to be repeated in *Stephen Hero*. Yeats was fond of quoting Goethe's statement, 'The Irish seem to me like a pack of hounds, always dragging down some noble stag.'[39] Joyce probably also blended this image of the politician with that of the artist in *Michael Kramer*, where Arnold is described as having 'thought himself pursued everywhere', seeing 'nothing but enemies all around him' hiding 'their claws and fangs'.[40]

Some critics have disputed some aspects of Joyce's charges of betrayal of Parnell. Conor Cruise O'Brien, for example, takes issue with the argument presented by Mr Casey that Parnell's followers deserted him at the command of the Catholic bishops because of the divorce verdict. As long as the case against Parnell centred on the 'moral' question, Ireland stood by him. The divorce verdict was given on 17 November, and on the following day the *Freeman's Journal*, politically the most important newspaper in Ireland, came out in favour of Parnell in an editorial, and argued that the question of leadership was a political one, not moral or religious. The divorce verdict did not deter the Irish representatives from reinstating Parnell as leader at a party meeting in London on 25 November.[41] Davitt, in fact, was the sole voice opposing Parnell when the verdict for O'Shea was declared, and even Davitt desired that Parnell retire only temporarily. Parnell had assured him that the divorce proceedings would not damage his reputation (which Davitt took to mean that Parnell was innocent of the charge of adultery), and he took action independently of the bishops before Gladstone's letter was published. It cannot be denied, however, that the Church's role in Parnell's downfall ultimately was a crucial and decisive one.

Joyce reserved fierce scorn in particular for Archbishop Walsh, referred to as 'Billy with the lip' by Simon Dedalus (34) (*33*). The Reverend William J. Walsh, Archbishop of Dublin from 1885 to 1921, was a nationalist. He became an authority on the land question and was consulted by Gladstone about the working of the Land Act of 1881. The Archbishop's incessant interference in Irish politics forced some of his fellow bishops to lodge complaints at the Vatican.[42]

The Archbishop's reputation has tended to distort the truth about his actual role in the deposition of Parnell. He hoped that Parnell would for a while voluntarily retire, and encouraged his fellow bishops to refrain from making any public pronouncements before the Irish Party met in Committee Room 15 on 1 December to consider the leadership question for the final time. To speak out before then might split the party ranks, and he hoped the Irish members would decide the issue themselves. Accordingly, a meeting of the Episcopal Standing Committee was arranged to take place on 3 December, after the party had started its own deliberations. In other words, the bishops did not want to act before the battle lines had already been drawn. These precautionary measures were taken precisely to save the hierarchy from those bitter accusations of clerical interference which soon followed. Such accusations, however, overlooked the fact that sooner or later in such a case as Parnell's clerical interference was bound to come.[43] The Archbishop's move was also influenced by his precarious standing in Rome. The Vatican had in the past shown displeasure at the way the Irish hierarchy had defended Parnell, and now the English Cardinal Manning wrote to Archbishop Walsh that the present moment was opportune to 'convince Rome that you do not put politics before faith and morals'.[44] Joyce's couplet in 'Gas from a Burner', that 'Everyone knows the Pope can't belch/Without the permission of Billy Walsh', although according to F. S. L. Lyons it probably expressed accurately the general popular sentiment,[45] reversed the truth about what was happening.

There is no doubt, however, that after the bishops made their public declaration they threw their full weight against Parnell. They were largely responsible for Parnell's defeat in the crucial by-election of April 1891 in North Sligo,[46] and were instrumental in effecting the change of policy of the *Freeman's Journal*. Archbishop Walsh's views were always well received by the Dublin daily, but since the outset of the crisis it had openly sided with Parnell. The Archbishop became so incensed by its reporting that he had considered making an episcopal pronouncement against it. He hit on a more subtle way of making the newspaper withdraw its support for Parnell, however, by exercising his influence on the chief shareholder, Edmund Dwyer Gray.[47] This web of affairs provides the background to 'His grace's' easy access to the columns of the *Freeman's Journal* in 'Aeolus', where Joyce obliquely accuses Archbishop Walsh of meddling in politics.

The aftermath of Parnell's catastrophe was a decade of internecine strife within the Irish parliamentary party. The party broke up into three separate groups, headed by the Parnellite John Redmond, Healy, and Justin McCarthy, later replaced by John Dillon. The momentum for Home Rule, for which Parnell had been sacrificed, came almost to a standstill. Gladstone's second Home Rule Bill of 1893 passed through the House of Commons but was overwhelmingly rejected by the House of Lords. The Irish Party was finally reunited, under Redmond's leadership, in 1900 and still managed to top the polls in Ireland during subsequent elections. But even when Home Rule seemed a real possibility for a brief moment between 1912 and 1914, the ultimate failure of the measure exposed the inadequacies of the Liberal alliance which had been deemed indispensable for success.

Joyce, like many historians, dismissed this period after Parnell's death as a political vacuum. He characterised the Irish representatives at Westminster as corrupt, self-seeking politicians, whose sole interest was improving their own lot.[48] Redmond he described as a 'fatuous leader' and William O'Brien, leader of a dissident faction, had become 'what every good fanatic becomes when his fanaticism dies before he does'.[49] In effect, post-Parnell politics signified for Joyce the futility of working for Home Rule within the framework of English parliamentary democracy.

This political paralysis is conveyed in 'Ivy Day in the Committee Room'. F. S. L. Lyons objects, maintaining that the years of the 'split' were ones of 'movement, if not actually renaissance'.[50] The revival of political extremism and the rise of Sinn Féin were imminent. Lyons admits that his observations are after the fact, and that the evidence for his view may have been hidden from contemporaries. The Sinn Féin Policy actually came into being in late 1905, and by this date Joyce had already begun writing his story. 'Ivy Day' is probably set in 1902 or 1903, at the time of King Edward VII's impending visit to Dublin.* Still, as will later appear, Joyce perceived the importance of Sinn Féin as early as 1906. That there existed a lull in political activity and efficacy after the fall of Parnell, however, is indisputable.

Joyce's distrust of the parliamentary methods advocated by the Irish Party is made explicit during the proceedings of the Committee Room on Ivy Day on 6 October, when Parnell's death is commemorated. Joe Hynes, supporter of the labourite Colgan, voices his suspicions about the Nationalist candidate:

> – Don't you know they want to present an address of welcome to Edward Rex if he comes here next year? What do we want kowtowing to a foreign king?
> – Our man won't vote for the address, said Mr O'Connor. He goes in on the Nationalist ticket. Won't he? said Mr Hynes. Wait till you see whether he will or not. I know him. Is it Tricky Dicky Tierney?
> – By God! perhaps you're right, Joe, said Mr O'Connor. (136) (*122*)

Hynes's point is brought home when John Henchy, a canvasser for Tierney, answers Mr O'Connor's question, 'Why should we welcome the King of England? Didn't Parnell himself . . .' with the cold, blunt retort, 'Parnell . . . is dead' (148) (*132*). Joyce's complaint that Irish politicians at Westminster were motivated by self-interest is recalled in the argument used by Henchy to secure the Conservative vote: '*He* [Tierney] *has extensive house property in the city and three places of business and isn't it to his own advantage to keep down the*

---

* See below, pp. 126–7 for a discussion of 'Ivy Day' with reference to Arthur Griffith.

rates?' (147) *(131)*. Again, Henchy reveals that the main reason for welcoming the English King is that 'It will mean an influx of money into this country.' Henchy's comments sound all the more ironic since he had earlier confided to Mr O'Connor that he suspected half of the labourites, whom he calls 'hillsiders and fenians', of being in the pay of the Castle and willing to sell their country at the first opportunity *(139–40; 125)*. Joyce's point seems to be that the Nationalist party, as during the Parnell crisis, is still subservient to the British government and that national politics are still haunted by the 'shade of Parnell'.

Bloom continues the indictment of the Nationalist party in *Ulysses* when he describes Parnell as a 'born leader of men', whereas his successors, 'Messrs So-and-So who, though they weren't a patch on the former man, ruled the roost after their redeeming features were very few and far between' *(649; 754)*. He draws a simple moral from the Parnell story, that of 'the idol with the feet of clay'. Bloom's approach strikes a new note in the Joycean canon, for it tempers the inflammatory rhetoric of Mr Casey. Bloom looks at Parnell's death close-up in a homely and humorous fashion:

> Either he petered out too tamely of acute pneumonia just when his various different political arrangements were nearing completion or whether it transpired he owed his death to his having neglected to change his boots and clothes after a wetting when a cold resulted and failing to consult a specialist he being confined to his room till he eventually died of it amid widespread regret. *(649; 753–4)*

Even Joyce's own rhetoric in his essay on Parnell seems to be deflated. When the subject in the cabman's shelter switches to Katharine O'Shea as another cause for Parnell's fall, as Deasy had argued earlier in the day, Bloom once again provides a realistic approach:

> Whereas the simple fact of the case was it was simply a case of the husband not being up to scratch with nothing in common between them beyond the name then a real man arriving on the scene . . . falling victim to her siren charms and forgetting home ties. *(651; 756)*

If ivy day is dying out Bloom nonetheless remains aware of the culpability of the Church and Parnell's own adherents in his deposition (*649; 754/651; 757*).*

2 Literature and the National Consciousness

Joyce was not the only young man in Ireland to experience dis-illusionment after Parnell's death or to turn his back on the party politics of Home Rule. While parliamentarians at Westminster were engaged in political backbiting, at home small groups of Irishmen were forming literary societies to revive the national consciousness. Literature was to fill the political vacuum left by Parnell's death. The key figure in this new literary movement was William Butler Yeats. In *The Trembling of the Veil* he described how

> A couple of years before the death of Parnell, I had wound up my introduction to those selections from the Irish novelists with the prophecy of an intellectual movement at the first lull in politics, and now I wished to fulfil my prophecy.[51]

He explained, in the lecture delivered to the Swedish Academy in 1925, how 'A disillusioned and embittered Ireland turned from parliamentary politics; an event was conceived; and the race began, as I think, to be troubled by that event's long gestation.'[52] He always maintained that the Irish literary revival began with the break up of the political movement of Parnell: 'The fall of Parnell had freed imagination from practical politics, from agrarian grievance and political enmity, and turned it to imaginative nationalism, to Gaelic, to the ancient stories, and at last to lyric poetry and drama.'[53] It was the literary and cultural aspect of the same nationalistic impulse.

---

* Joyce adds his own footnote to Irish history, for Bloom apparently came into personal contact with the Chief. This was on the occasion of the 'historic *fracas*' over the *United Ireland*, and 'as a matter of strict history' Bloom returned Parnell's fallen hat to him in the scuffle (*654; 761*). Joyce probably inserted this detail after having read R. Barry O'Brien's biography of Parnell in which he states that 'A description of the scene has been given to me by a gentleman wholly unconcerned with politics'. (*The Life of Charles Stewart Parnell* (London, 1898), vol. 2, p. 293. This book was in Joyce's library in 1920 which is listed in full in Richard Ellmann, *The Consciousness of Joyce* (London, 1977), pp. 97–134. Whenever a book from Joyce's library is mentioned it refers automatically to this list unless indicated otherwise.) The fact that the observer was unnamed allowed Joyce his unstated and modest claim that Bloom – though he is not apolitical – could have been the original narrator.

'Can we not unite literature to the great passion of patriotism and ennoble both thereby?' Yeats asked.[54] (The new movement was to be in some ways similar to that of Young Ireland.) The true voice of Irish nationalism could be heard among Parnell's loyal followers and not the anti-Parnellites who had betrayed their allegiance to Gladstone and were becoming Anglified in the process. The literary movement would emancipate Ireland from English cultural domination.

With this purpose in mind, Yeats, along with Douglas Hyde, founded the National Literary Society in 1892. At one of its early meetings Hyde, in a lecture entitled 'The Necessity for de-Anglicising Ireland', set the tone for the new cultural orientation. He pleaded with Nationalist and Unionist alike to stop imitating the English in their names, music, and even dress, and to assert their national self-respect. He also claimed that the Gaelic Athletic Association, which had been formed in 1884 to revive Gaelic sports, had benefited the country to a greater extent that the speeches of politicians. Hyde's plan for Irish cultural independence culminated in 1893 when he founded, with the help of Eoin MacNeill, the Gaelic League. Its aims were to preserve Irish as the national language and to extend its use as a spoken language, as well as to cultivate a modern literature in Irish. The League was to be politically neutral and Hyde hoped that both Irish and Anglo-Irish would work together in this common cultural objective. He was realistic enough to know that such aims could not be realised overnight, and recognised in the Anglo-Irish literature of men like Yeats a ready substitute.

Some, however, like D. P. Moran, felt that the Anglo-Irish tradition was a threat to the ideal of a distinct Irish nationality. He viewed Irish history as a battle between 'two civilisations', the Pale versus the Gael, or the Anglo-Irish versus the Irish. He called the Anglo-Irish 'West Britons', and claimed that their loyalties lay with England. He also attacked 'shoneens', persons of native Irish stock who imitated English or West Briton manners and customs. Moran decried to the point of absurdity all nationalist activity from Tone to Parnell as a victory for the Protestant ascendancy and not for the 'Irish' nation. Moran's aim was to bring Hyde's language drive into the political sphere.

The *Leader* was exerting a tremendous influence on the undergraduates of University College, particularly those who had joined the Young Ireland branch of the United Irish League headed by

Joyce's friend, Thomas Kettle.[55] Joyce was among the few who resisted its influence. In 'The Dead' Miss Ivors taunts Gabriel Conroy with being a 'West Briton'. Joyce, like Gabriel Conroy, indicated that writing for the Unionist *Daily Express* did not necessarily make him pro-English. He considered attacks on Protestant Irishmen to be equally misguided. In 'Ireland, Island of Saints and Sages' he claimed that

> to exclude from the present nation all who are descended from foreign families would be impossible, and to deny the name of patriot to all those who are not of Irish stock would be to deny it to almost all the heroes of the modern movement – Lord Edward Fitzgerald, Robert Emmet, Theobald Wolfe Tone and Napper Tandy,* leaders of the uprising of 1798, Thomas Davis and John Mitchel, leaders of the Young Ireland movement, Isaac Butt, Joseph Biggar, the inventor of parliamentary obstructionism, many of the anticlerical Fenians, and finally, Charles Stewart Parnell.[56]

For Joyce the battle of the two civilisations was, in effect, pointless.

The *Leader's* policies were almost entirely negative. The principal aim was to expose and destroy *rameis* or cant. Other aims were 'to kill the "stage Irishman"; to kill bigotry; to dethrone "Bung" – to reduce the influence of the Liquor Trade; to sweep away the Irish Party at Westminster; to industrialize Ireland, as far as possible; to make Ireland Irish; to make Ireland Catholic; and to make Ireland fit for freedom'.[57] Joyce may have been sympathetic to a few of these points, but the purely destructive force in them he ascribed to his Irish Cyclops. The Citizen is modelled on Michael Cusack, the man who, in Joe Hynes's words, 'made the Gaelic sports revival' (*316; 410*). Hynes and the Citizen discuss 'Irish sport and shoneen games the like of lawn tennis and about hurley and putting the stone and racy of the soil and building up a nation once again.' Bloom deflates these high-sounding aims by claiming that over-strenuous exercise damages the health. When Hynes makes 'an eloquent appeal for the resuscitation of Gaelic sports and pastimes', Bloom opposes the move (*317; 411*). The Citizen rudely answers one of Bloom's later statements with '*rameis*' (*326; 423*). Attempting to make Ireland Catholic means denying religious freedom, for Bloom is at once a

---

* Napper Tandy (1740–1803) helped to found the Dublin section of the United Irishmen.

'bloody freemason' and a 'bloody jewman'. Killing bigotry by pig-headedness, according to Joyce, only results in further bigotry.

At this time, too, a literary clique was forming around the *United Irishman*. As James Stephens, Joyce's 'rival',[58] reported, 'all the poets in Ireland were then solid for Mr Griffith.'[59] Yeats, George Russell (A.E.), Padraic Colum, George Moore, Stephens, W. K. Magee (John Eglinton), Alice Milligan and Gogarty all wrote for the *United Irishman*. This weekly paper was founded by Arthur Griffith in conjunction with his friend William Rooney in 1899. The name Griffith chose for the paper bound it to the tradition of John Mitchel. This did not mean approval of the abortive revolution of '43, but rather it looked beyond parliamentary campaigns and armed resistance to achieve repeal of the Union. In the very first issue Griffith stated his separatist ideal:

> To be perfectly plain, we believe that when Swift wrote to the whole people of Ireland 170 years ago that by the law of God, of nature, and of nations they had a right to be as free a people as the people of England, he wrote commonsense.

He also laid down the terms by which independence was to be achieved:

> Lest there might be a doubt in any mind, we will say that we accept the Nationalism of '98, '48, and '67 as the true Nationalism and Grattan's cry, 'Live Ireland — Perish the Empire!' as the watchword of patriotism.[60]

Although Griffith was forceful, he seemed to be linking revolutionary nationalism with parliamentarianism.

Griffith, however, like Joyce, thought Parliament would never enact Irish independence. Although he joined the Irish Republican Brotherhood, he did so, like Yeats, in sympathy with its aims rather than with its methods.[61] Resort to arms was in any case inadmissible for the present:

> The *United Irishman* . . . has never advocated armed resistance because – and only because – it knows that Ireland is unable at the present time to wage physical war with England. But it has maintained and always shall maintain the right of the Irish nation to assert and defend its independence by force of arms.[62]

Joyce later surveyed the trends which influenced Griffith's statement in his article on 'Fenianism':

Anyone who studies the history of the Irish revolution during the nineteenth century finds himself faced with a double struggle – the struggle of the Irish nation against the English government, and the struggle, perhaps no less bitter, between the moderate patriots and the so-called party of physical force. This party under different names: 'White Boys',* 'Men of '98', 'United Irishmen', 'Invincibles', 'Fenians', has always refused to be connected with either the English political parties or the Nationalist parliamentarians. They maintain (and in this assertion history fully supports them) that any concessions that have been granted to Ireland, England has granted unwillingly, and, as it is usually put, at the point of a bayonet. The intransigent press never ceases to greet the deeds of the Nationalist representatives at Westminster with virulent and ironical comments, and although it recognizes that in view of England's power armed revolt has now become an impossible dream, it has never stopped inculcating in the minds of the coming generation the dogma of separatism.[63]

Griffith solved the dilemma of the two irreconcilable traditions in Irish history by hitting upon a scheme that was at once constitutional without being parliamentary, and coercive without adopting physical force. This was the plan for an abstentionist assembly in Dublin and the advocacy of a policy of passive resistance.

Griffith and his associate Rooney had grasped at once the political utility of the literary movement, and they were willing to accept Anglo-Irish literature because of their belief that the Irish nation could not speak Gaelic overnight. Griffith, however, disliked its mysticism, as exemplified in Yeats's 'Celtic Twilight', which failed to incite the political fervour he deemed essential for Ireland's nationalistic ambitions. Yet Griffith greeted warmly *The Countess Cathleen*, the play which inaugurated the Irish Literary Theatre in 1899, and told Yeats that he had brought 'a lot of men from the Quays and told them to applaud everything the Church would not like'.[64] In his play, Yeats represented his heroine selling her soul to the devil in order to obtain bread for Ireland's starving population. Griffith shrewdly recognised the play's value as propaganda for the Irish cause.

---

* The Whiteboys were organised Catholic groups of the 1760s who reacted to oppressive measures and abuses, such as rackrenting and the collection of tithes for the Protestant Church, with agrarian violence.

Joyce too applauded *The Countess Cathleen*, but not for the same reason as the patriots. In *A Portrait* Stephen recalls how his fellow-students denounced the play's heretical or blasphemous sentiment, and how they claimed it was 'A libel on Ireland' (230–1) (*226*). When a letter of protest was drawn up by Francis Sheehy-Skeffington and other friends, Joyce refused to sign it. He perceived a discrepancy between resisting foreign oppressors and striving for national independence while, at the same time, submitting to the more subtle thraldom of the spirit, that of Catholicism.* *The Countess Cathleen* provided a prime example for Joyce of how artistic consciousness could combat external authorities like the Church.

Although Joyce welcomed Yeats's initiative, by 1901 he began to fear that the theatre, in dealing solely with Irish themes and producing only Irish plays, ran the risk of becoming 'all too Irish'. He felt Ireland would cut itself off from the mainstream of European culture. He preferred the tradition of the 'old master' Ibsen and the universal appeal of Tolstoy's plays about the peasantry (such as *The Power of Darkness* and *The Fruits of Enlightenment*) to those of Lady Gregory on the same topic. In *The Day of the Rabblement* (published together as a pamphlet with Skeffington's plea for equal status of women in education after both articles had been censored by the university authorities), Joyce accused the Irish theatre of being 'the property of the rabblement of the most belated race in Europe'. He claimed that Yeats and Moore were paying lip-service to Gaelic, although they could not speak it. 'If an artist courts the favour of the multitude he cannot escape the contagion of its fetichism and deliberate self-deception, and if he joins in a popular movement he does so at his own risk', he warned. By allying itself to Griffith's political movement, by its 'surrender to the trolls', the Irish Literary Theatre had 'cut itself adrift from the line of advancement'. If a man wants to be an artist, Joyce asserted, he must free himself from the mean influences which beleaguer him, that 'sodden enthusiasm and clever insinuation and every flattering influence of vanity and low ambition'. The freedom embraced by the Irish Literary Theatre was delusive: 'the most seeming-independent are those who are the first to reassume their bonds.' Joyce allowed that the artist may employ the crowd, but he must be careful to isolate himself.[65]

This attack was intended as a cultural directive, but the nationalists, steeped in an Irish-Ireland philosophy, objected to its

---

* Skeffington did in fact give up Catholicism later.

élitism and snobbery. Similarly, when Stephen reads his essay on 'Drama and Life' in *Stephen Hero* he is denounced as a 'renegade from the Nationalist ranks' for professing 'cosmopolitism'. His opponents argue that 'a man that was of all countries was of no country – you must first have a nation before you have art' (108) (*103*). Griffith too ascribed a different purpose to literature, as will shortly appear, claiming that it should channel itself into national-istic currents. But he could not be accused of obstinate narrow-mindedness. When Skeffington and Joyce published their 'Two Essays', they drew Griffith's attention and he reviewed them under the pen-name 'Cuguan' in the *United Irishman*.[66] This review has been overlooked, but it must have caught Joyce's eye. Griffith endorsed the plea for equality of the sexes, which he attributed to a 'Miss Skeffington'. Although he disagreed with Joyce's attack on the Irish Literary Theatre, Griffith found no 'heresy, blasphemy, or sedition' in its contents. He also expressed bewilderment as to 'why we should grow Censors at all'. 'Turnips would be more useful', he claimed. Griffith concluded by saying he hoped the pamphlet would enjoy wide circulation, 'if only to convince blooming Censors and budding Censors that this is the twentieth century, and that it is a holy and wholesome thing for men and women to use the minds God gave them and speak out the things they think'. The cultivated rabblement was not, as Joyce had imagined, totally unreceptive. This was Griffith's first attempt at conciliation with Joyce.

Griffith, however, soon discovered that Joyce was not a man to be won over easily. Joyce challenged the *United Irishman*. The issue was William Rooney's *Poems and Ballads*, published posthumously by the *United Irishman* in 1902. The preface was written by Arthur Griffith, and he made it clear that he considered Rooney to be 'the destined regenerator of his people', and that had he lived Rooney would have become perhaps 'the greatest leader Ireland had known'.[67] Yeats had dedicated *Cathleen ni Houlihan* to Rooney, with perhaps something of the same conviction. Joyce, on the other hand, attacked the poems for their use as national propaganda and their lack of literary merit in an unsigned review in the *Daily Express*:

> They are illustrative of the national temper, and because they are so the writers of the introductions do not hesitate to claim for them the highest honours. But this claim cannot be allowed, unless it is supported by certain evidences of literary sincerity. For a man who writes a book cannot be excused by his good

intentions, or by his moral character; he enters into a region where there is question of the written word, and it is well that this should be borne in mind, now that the region of literature is assailed so fiercely by the enthusiast and the doctrinaire.

He indelicately referred to the collection as being 'issued from headquarters' (that is, from the *United Irishman*), but conceded that Rooney might have written well had 'he not suffered from one of those big words which make us so unhappy'. Griffith, piqued by the reviewer's strictures, responded by publishing an advertisement for the book in his paper. He quoted much of the unsympathetic article, but inserted the bracketed word 'Patriotism' to indicate what Joyce thought Rooney had suffered from.[68] Joyce seemed to have overlooked the fact that Griffith himself had conceded in his introduction that Rooney, like Thomas Davis, 'wrote verse merely to rouse his countrymen' rather than to achieve artistic excellence.[69] Still, patriotic fervour did not make up for poor writing, and to exploit national and racial themes for political propaganda constituted 'a false and mean expression of a false and mean idea'. Such writing assailed the integrity of literature and its paramount virtue of literary sincerity. Joyce was no prey to the delusion that to be patriotic, an artist must propagandise. What Ireland needed was not more patriotic verse, but verse of better literary quality.* For it was good writing, not patriotism, that would attune literature to the moral necessities of Irish life.

Coupled with his unholy views on nationalistic poetry, Joyce found Griffith's provincial outlook to be equally deplorable. When the Irish Theatre staged John Synge's play, *In the Shadow of the Glen*, in 1903, Griffith attacked its portrayal of an errant wife in Wicklow as a slur on Irish womanhood† as well as on Irish peasant home life. Joyce considered this view to be naive and sentimentalised. In *A Portrait* Stephen sees the peasant woman who invited Davin inside her home as

> a type of her race and his own, a batlike soul waking to the consciousness of itself in darkness and secrecy and loneliness and,

---

* Cf. *Stephen Hero* (151) (*146*), where Stephen acknowledges to himself in 'honest egoism that he could not take to heart the distress of a nation, the soul of which was antipathetic to his own, so bitterly as the indignity of a bad line of verse'.

† One wonders what Griffith would have said of the portrait of Molly Bloom!

through the eyes and voice and gesture of a woman without guile, calling the stranger to her bed. (186–7) (*183*)

Joyce also rebuked Lady Gregory for glorifying the peasantry in his review of her *Poets and Dreamers* in the *Daily Express*.[70] He preferred instead a less stereotyped, more down-to-earth portrait of the peasant such as the old man in Stephen's journal at the end of *A Portrait* who speaks first in Irish for his visitor, Mulrennan, but then in English, as if to indicate the pointlessness of the language revival. In the prolonged controversy over Synge's play, Yeats, who was not as insular as Joyce made him out to be, protested against Griffith that there were limits to nationalism. Griffith replied sternly that 'Cosmopolitanism never produced a great artist nor a good man yet and never will. . . . If the Irish Theatre ceases to reflect Irish life and embody Irish aspirations the world will wag its head away from it.'[71] Joyce interpreted this as a wrongheaded attitude. In his Italian lecture on Mangan, he reiterated his view that

> Poetry considers many of the idols of the marketplace unimportant – the succession of the ages, the spirit of the age, the mission of the race. The poet's central effort is to free himself from the unfortunate influence of these idols that corrupt him from without and within.[72]

The autonomy of the artist in his activity, his motivation and the exercise of his liberty was paramount.

Joyce's declaration of artistic independence contained unmistakable political overtones. He indicted Ireland's art *and* politics for admitting only narrow sympathies. In *Stephen Hero* we are told that Griffith only looked abroad to report 'any signs of Philocelticism which he had observed' to the circle of irreconcilables gathered in Cooney's tobacco-shop presided over by Michael Cusack (66) (*61*).* Stephen keenly observes that

> By all this society liberty was held to be the chief desirable; the members of it were fierce democrats. The liberty they desired for themselves was mainly a liberty of costume and vocabulary: and Stephen could hardly understand how such a poor scarecrow of liberty could bring serious human beings to their knees in worship. (66) (*61*)

---

* In *A Portrait* (184) (*181*), Stephen says of Davin, 'of the world that lay beyond England he knew only the foreign legion of France in which he spoke of serving.'

Stephen claims that the patriots' lives are governed by the sole motive of political independence, which is marked by the exclusively Gaelic sports they play, or by the violent slogans in favour of their cause. Their lives consist in worshipping the idol of patriotism, and Stephen distrusts their alleged aim of a non-violent revolution. He puts Madden (the Davin of *A Portrait*) on the spot by puncturing the beliefs of the patriots:

> – You consider the professions of arms a disreputable one. Why then have you Sarsfield Clubs, Hugh O'Neill Clubs, Red Hugh Clubs?
> – O, fighting for freedom is different. But it is quite another matter to take service meanly under your tyrant, to make yourself his slave.
> – And, tell me, how many of your Gaelic Leaguers are studying for the Second Division and looking for advancement in the Civil Service?
> – That's different. They are only civil servants: they're not. . . .
> – Civil be damned! They are pledged to the Government and paid by the Government.
> – O, well, if you look at it that way. . . .
> – And how many relatives of Gaelic Leaguers are in the police and the constabulary? Even I know nearly ten of your friends who are sons of Police inspectors.
> – It is unfair to accuse a man because his father was so-and-so. A son and a father often have different ideas.
> – But Irishmen are fond of boasting that they are true to the traditions they receive in youth. How faithful all you fellows are to Mother Church! Why would you not be as faithful to the tradition of the helmet as that of the tonsure? (68–9) (*63–4*)

Griffith's movement professed non-violence but, as Stephen notes, it named its clubs after Irish military heroes. Its violent rhetoric was bound to lead to violent action, as Joyce clearly foresaw. By the time Joyce reconstructed this scene in *A Portrait* he has Stephen taunt Davin for having signed a petition for universal peace but for being unwilling to burn his Fenian 'copybook' or manual of arms: 'That's a different question, said Davin. I'm an Irish nationalist, first and foremost' (206) (*202*). Stephen also suspects that today's radicals are tomorrow's reactionaries, a suspicion which crosses Bloom's mind in 'Lestrygonians': 'Silly billies: mob of young cubs yelling their guts out . . . Few years' time half of them magistrates and civil servants. War comes on. Into the army helter skelter' *(163; 206)*. Revolutionaries can be time-servers who simply want to get ahead in a future Irish society.★ Stephen, therefore, finds an element of shamness in democratic freedom.

Madden for his part needles Stephen about his politics and his supposed anti-Irishness:

> – So you admit you are an Irishman after all and not one of the red garrison.
> – Of course I do.
> – And don't you think that every Irishman worthy of the name should be able to speak his native tongue?
> – I really don't know.
> – And don't you think that we as a race have a right to be free?
> – O, don't ask me such questions, Madden. You can use these phrases of the platform but I can't.
> – But surely you have some political opinions, man!
> – I am going to think them out. I am an artist, don't you see? Do you believe that I am?
> – O, yes, I know you are.
> – Very well then, how the devil can you expect me to settle everything at once? Give me time. (60) *(55–6)*

The political opinions of the artist must await their period of gestation in the same manner as a new work of art. Enthusiasms must be tempered in the crucible of art, and must be judged in perspective.

Emma Clery, like Madden, attempts to induce Stephen to learn Irish and to join the Gaelic League: 'She seemed on her part to include him in the general scheme of her nationalizing charm' (51–2) *(46–7)*. In 'The Dead' the nationalistic Miss Ivors similarly tries to persuade Gabriel Conroy to go to the Aran Islands to learn Irish, but Gabriel refuses. Stephen also refuses to be tantalised by his Maud Gonne, and condemns the siren charms of her nationalism. He objects in the first place to the use of Gaelic because he considers it to be a devious instrument of the priests. (Yeats himself had stated that the literary societies had been formed to oppose 'the vulgar books and the vulgar

---

★ Stephen reiterates this view of his classmates in *Stephen Hero* (238) (232): 'They have eyes only for their future jobs: to secure their future jobs they will write themselves in and out of convictions.'

songs that come to us from England'.)[73] Stephen then discusses his
reservations about the intellectual and political movement with
Madden who acts as a spokesman for Griffith's 'young irreconcilables under his charge' (66) (*61*):

> – Do you not see, said Stephen, that they encourage the study of
> Irish that their flocks may be more safely protected from the
> wolves of disbelief; they consider it is an opportunity to withdraw
> the people into a past of literal, implicit faith?
> – But really our peasant has nothing to gain from English
> Literature.
> – Rubbish!
> – Modern at least. You yourself are always railing. . . .
> – English is the medium for the Continent.
> – We want an Irish Ireland.
> – It seems to me you do not care what banality a man expresses so
> long as he expresses it in Irish.
> – I do not entirely agree with your modern notions. We want to
> have nothing of this English civilisation.
> – But the civilisation of which you speak is not English – it is
> Aryan. The modern notions are not English; they point the way of
> Aryan civilisation.
> – You want our peasants to ape the gross materialism of the
> Yorkshire peasant?
> – One would imagine the country was inhabited by cherubim.
> Damme if I see much difference in peasants: they all seem to me as
> like one another as a peascod is like another peascod. The
> Yorkshireman is perhaps better fed.
> – Of course you despise the peasant because you live in the city.
> – I don't despise his office in the least.
> – But you despise him – he's not clever enough for you.
> – Now, you know, Madden, that's nonsense. To begin with he's
> as cute as a fox – try to pass a false coin on him and you'll see. But
> his cleverness is all of a low order. I really don't think that the Irish
> peasant represents a very admirable type of culture.
> – That's you all out! Of course you sneer at him because he's not
> up-to-date and lives a simple life.
> – Yes, a life of dull routine – the calculation of coppers, the weekly
> debauch and the weekly piety – a life lived in cunning and fear
> between the shadows of the parish chapel and the asylum! (58–9)
> (*54–5*)

Joyce took his contemporaries to task for being weak-kneed in conviction or, as Stanislaus Joyce says, for being 'extremely heterodox in thought, politely orthodox in action, and revolutionary only at the beer-table'.[74] As an artist, Joyce would betray no such infirmity of purpose. He came to the conclusion that he could not write patriotic art, that he could not engage in what Stephen calls 'flag-practices with phrases' in *Stephen Hero* (88) (*83*), and for this reason:

> The programme of the patriots filled him with very reasonable doubts; its articles could obtain no intellectual assent from him. He knew, moreover, that concordance with it would mean for him a submission of everything else in its interest and that he would thus be obliged to corrupt the springs of speculation at their very source. He refused therefore to set out for any task if he had first to prejudice his success by oaths to the patria. (81) (*76–7*)

This statement marks the breaking-point between Stephen and the patriots. Joyce felt that to call oneself a nationalist in the Dublin of his day was to demote art, to advance one's country before everything else.* He must keep himself unaffiliated so that he could effect what *A Portrait* (250) (*246*) calls that search for a mode of life or art through which the artist's spirit might express itself in unfettered freedom.

Joyce had to maintain this sense of artistic freedom in the face of challenge not only from belligerently patriotic classmates, but also from those who endorsed peaceful, social emancipation. Joyce was not the only young Irishman to rebel against some aspects of the society in which he lived. Skeffington, for instance, had already earned the reputation of being an iconoclast on account of his support for vegetarianism and pacifism as well as for feminism. His heterodoxy was as repugnant as the others' orthodoxy, and in *Stephen Hero* and *A Portrait* Stephen delights in riddling Skeffington's (or McCann's) progressive views with 'agile bullets'. (Skeffington in turn would often bait Joyce with discussions on politics or philosophy.)[75] For his originality McCann is dubbed 'Knickerbockers'. In *A Portrait* he is presented as a 'propagandist', speaking fluently of the

---

* As Davin tells Stephen in *A Portrait* (208) (*203*), 'A man's country comes first. Ireland first, Stevie. You can be a poet or mystic after.'

Csar's rescript, of Stead,* of general disarmament, arbitration in
cases of international disputes, of the signs of the times, of the
new humanity and the new gospel of life which would make it the
business of the community to secure as cheaply as possible the
greatest possible happiness of the greatest possible number. (201)
(*196*)

When Stephen refuses to sign the universal peace petition and
McCann taunts him with the epithet 'reactionary', the former,
unperturbed, responds 'Keep your icon. If we must have a Jesus, let
us have a legitimate Jesus' (202) (*198*). McCann snaps back,
'Dedalus, I believe you're a good fellow but you have yet to learn the
dignity of altruism and the responsibility of the human individual'
(203) (*198–9*). A voice is then heard branding McCann as an
intellectual crank. Skeffington would have replied, 'A crank is a
small arm which creates a revolution.'[76] By refusing to sign the
petition Stephen is not being apolitical, as is frequently maintained,
but, on the contrary, he is recognising political realities for what they
are. We all know the way the best are often taken in by mock-
idealism, and Czar Nicholas was not the apostle of peace he
pretended, any more than Edward the Peacemaker was. His crusade
for peace in 1898 proved to be an ironical prelude to the Russo-
Japanese War of 1904–5. Accordingly, Joyce spurned the tendency to
Schwärmerei, the enthusiast's vulgar sentimentality about the future
and freedom, replacing it with a toughminded art that exposed, and
was not easily swayed by, illusory measures. Joyce's refusal to accept
political shibboleths constituted a political act.

Skeffington's passion for social reform sometimes verged on the
fanatical. When the editor of the *Freeman's Journal* received
Skeffington's small column on 'Rats', for example, he promptly
returned it, saying 'You have written about rats as if they were an
oppressed nationality.'[77] Excessive enthusiasm also led 'McCann' to
misrepresent the artist's role. His comment to Stephen underlines
the irony of being carried away by political slogans: 'Dedalus, you're
an anti-social being, wrapped up in yourself. I'm not, I'm a
democrat: and I'll work and act for social liberty and equality among
all classes and sexes in the United States of Europe of the future' (181)
(*177*). The attempt to embrace 'all' leads to a patent absurdity. A false

---

* William Thomas Stead (1849–1912), the English journalist and editor of the *Pall
Mall Gazette* from 1883 to 1899, was an avid supporter of the peace movement.

dichotomy is created between the social democrat, a man of the people, and the artist who allegedly withdraws from social concerns. When Joyce arranged in 1903 to start a newspaper, the *Goblin*, to offset what he considered to be corrupt Dublin journalism, he asked Skeffington to collaborate with him. Although it was to be primarily literary, Joyce anticipated that Skeffington would discuss his pet issues.*[78] Joyce's impatience with Skeffington did not arise from total disagreement with his views. Temple, another of Stephen's classmates in *A Portrait*, proclaims that he believes in universal brotherhood and in freedom of thought (201) (*197*), aims not uncongenial to Joyce. But as employed by Temple these aims become mere watchwords, and require the special pleading which Joyce as an artist was not prepared to engage in. Similarly, the liberation of women might be desirable, but it had to go with a liberation of men (as that which Richard strives for in *Exiles*), of the human consciousness generally. Liberation had to come from within not without, and literature served the purpose of liberating, of unlocking secrets from the heart, 'secrets weary of their tyranny' as Stephen says in 'Nestor' (*28; 34*), 'tyrants willing to be dethroned'.

The tyrannies that kept the heart prisoner, in Joyce's view, came from several directions. In the first place there was the Church which, through its ministers, imposed a rigid sexual morality. In *A Portrait* Stephen is riled by Emma's custom of whispering her 'innocent transgressions' in the secrecy of the confessional to a priest: 'To him she would unveil her soul's shy nakedness, to one who was but schooled in the discharging of a formal rite rather than to him, a priest of the eternal imagination' (225) (*221*). Art, as Joyce conceived it, would open the doors of the heart, would affirm what was frowned upon: 'He hoped that by sinning whole-heartedly his race might come in him to the knowledge of herself.'[79] Writing required candour and moral courage, qualities which Joyce found wanting in his literary compatriots, and for which he taunted them mercilessly in his broadside, 'The Holy Office',[80] in 1904. He now accused the 'mummers' (Yeats, Russell, and their coterie) of self-deception, of inhabiting a world of ethereality:† 'That they may dream their

---

* Nothing came of this venture however.

† Bloom concurs with this appraisal of the literary revivalists in *Ulysses* (*166; 210*) when he spots A. E. with Lizzie Twigg: 'Her stockings are loose over her ankles. I detest that: so tasteless. Those literary ethereal people they are all. Dreamy, cloudy, symbolistic. Esthetes they are.'

dreamy dreams / I carry off their filthy streams.' The movement towards formless spiritual, yet in some way national, essences was a falsification since it renounced the life of the body. Accordingly, he spurned their hypocritical ideals: 'I must not accounted be / One of that mumming company.'

As if such strictures did not expose the whole truth, Joyce rebuked his contemporaries, in addition, for their moral cowardice, for resisting 'enlightenment'. Joyce felt his judgment was vindicated on two occasions. When George Russell asked him in 1904 to write a short story that would not 'shock' the readers of the agricultural paper, the *Irish Homestead*,[81] Joyce complied with 'The Sisters', and later with two more stories, 'Eveline' and 'After the Race'. The editor accepted them but asked Joyce not to submit any more because of complaints from shocked readers.[82] It is no wonder that Stephen anathematises the *Irish Homestead* as the 'pigs' paper' in 'Scylla and Charybdis' (*193; 247*). Earlier in 1904, Joyce had anticipated that another Dublin magazine might prove more amenable. This happened to be *Dana*, edited by John Eglinton and Fred Ryan. In opposition to the inflamed rhetoric of the *Leader*, the rationalist perspective of *Dana* provided a moderate plea for independence. In the very first issue Ryan urged as a national ideal the twin forces of political and intellectual freedom. *Dana*'s aim of fostering 'independent thought' appeared to Joyce as 'an amusing disguise of the proselytizing spirit'.* Joyce was referring to the utter solemnity of the new magazine, which probably reminded him of Skeffington's over-earnest efforts at proselytism. Ryan, in any case, was a socialist and freethinker and, according to Constantine Curran,[83] not very far removed from Joyce in outlook. It was no accident, then, that Joyce submitted his socialistic first draft version of 'A Portrait of the Artist' to *Dana* for publication.† That the editors rejected the essay for the 'sexual adventures' of the hero probably proved to Joyce that their brand of intellectual freedom evaded what he considered to be the real issues.

For Joyce, then, the emancipation made possible through

---

* Eglinton recalled how Joyce accosted him on the street one night and endeavoured 'with a certain earnestness, to bring home to me the extreme futility of the ideals represented in *Dana*, by describing to me the solemn ceremonial of High Mass' (*Workshop of Daedalus*, p. 199). Joyce was twitting Eglinton for rejecting authority in religious belief only to replace it with an equally doctrinaire atheism. He detected a kind of fanaticism turned inside out.

† See below, pp. 67–72.

literature transcended those notions of freedom embraced by nationalists and socialists. Literature operated as an instrument for altering men's minds. The transformation of institutions does not depend on force, lobbying for peace, or pleading for social justice, but can only follow upon this unsuspected process of changing basic attitudes and prejudices.

In *A Portrait of the Artist* Stephen perceives his role as that of a martyr for his art as Parnell was a martyr for the national cause,* and he considers his choice to be no less patriotic than Parnell's. The Parnell case presented him with a first instance of Church and State in collusion. In the first place, he interpreted their compliance in thwarting the movement towards Home Rule as a betrayal of Irish political interests. That Irishmen should have deposed Parnell at the bidding of the English for reasons of immorality and yet condone the similar conduct of King Edward VII (as 'Ivy Day in the Committee Room' ironically underlines)† proved to Joyce that Irish political and social life fed on hypocrisy. Irishmen were all too ready to submit to conventions imposed by the Church and enforced by the State. The Parnell who stood his ground against attacks from all quarters provided a model of defiance which Joyce deemed imperative for the artist. Stephen's acceptance of the artistic vocation as opposed to holy orders, then, is an act replete with political connotations. The priest as 'natural leader' of his flock holds sway not only in spiritual matters but also in Irish temporal affairs. The director who makes Stephen the offer describes the 'awful power' invested in the priesthood: 'No king or emperor on this earth has the power of the priest of God' (160–1) (*158*). In other words, the spiritual order transcends and dominates the temporal. Stephen, however, disowns the 'proud' claim of the Church urged upon him because 'an instinct subtle and hostile . . . armed him against acquiescence' (164) (*161*), and asserts that 'His destiny was to be elusive of social or religious

---

* In 'Eumaeus' (*660–1; 769*), Bloom sees the ironical implications of the legend that Parnell is not dead and that his coffin was filled with stones, since 'it was in fact a stoning to death on the part of seventytwo out of eighty odd constituencies that ratted at the time of the split.' Parnell is now a martyr dying for the national cause as St Stephen was for the sake of Christ.

† '– But after all now, said Mr Lyons argumentatively, King Edward's life, you know, is not the very . . . . – Let bygones be bygones, said Mr Henchy. I admire the man personally. He's just an ordinary knock-about like you and me. He's fond of his glass of grog and he's a bit of a rake, perhaps, and he's a good sportsman. Damn it, can't we Irish play fair?' (148) (*132*)

orders' (165) (*162*). He would dedicate himself unstintingly to his art, mindful of the consequences arising from defiance of Church authority.

Stephen makes a concerted effort to hit the conscience of the 'patricians' of Ireland and cast his shadow over the imagination of their daughters 'before their squires begat upon them, that they might breed a race less ignoble than their own' (242) (*238*). His art would now supplant a religious conscience which he thought paralysed and stifled the will to live. Joyce viewed his contemporaries as 'dead souls' (in contradistinction to Gogol's serfs who were merely dead bodies), who abdicated their individuality by going through the motions of living. To foster and affirm one's individuality required a combative spirit, as he informed Lady Gregory by letter: 'I shall try myself against the powers of the world . . . I want to achieve myself . . . for I know that there is no heresy or no philosophy which is so abhorrent to my church as a human being.'[84] In *A Portrait* Stephen tells Davin:

> The soul is born . . . first in those moments I told you of. It has a slow and dark birth, more mysterious than the birth of the body. When the soul of a man is born in this country there are nets flung at it to hold it back from flight. You talk to me of nationality, language, religion. I shall try to fly by those nets. (207) (*203*)

Accordingly, Joyce set out to embody and ensoul Ireland in his works by giving birth to the individual, alerting him to those secular and spiritual snares which aborted that growth, and preparing for his release. With this purpose in mind, he had stubbornly dedicated his first play, *A Brilliant Career*, 'To My Own Soul'.[85]

In order to see why Joyce insisted vigorously on the free development of the individual against the backdrop of national authorities, we have to investigate the implications of the comparison he drew between *Stephen Hero* and Lermontov's *A Hero of Our Time*.[86] In a personal note to the hero's journal, Lermontov justified publication of his 'innermost secrets' by maintaining that 'the story of a human soul, even the smallest of souls, is hardly less interesting and useful than the history of a whole nation.'[87] This was a principle Joyce abided by and stoutly upheld in all his works. It was not a selfish principle, since the keys to freedom were offered to all through his art. An instance of Joyce's approach may be witnessed in the dream recorded in Stephen's journal:

Strange figures advance from a cave. They are not as tall as men. One does not seem to stand quite apart from another. Their faces are phosphorescent, with darker streaks. They peer at me and their eyes seem to ask me something. They do not speak. (254) (*249–50*)

The 'strange figures' must be the 'ignoble race' referred to earlier. A reason for their stunted growth is the tyranny over mind and body exercised by Church and State, and their blind devotion to the 'troll' nationalism then rampant. Their eyes seem to ask Stephen something, probably an unspoken plea to provide a viable alternative to their 'sleek' lives. Stephen complies with their request by providing a possibility of choice through his art. His conception of the artist, it should be duly emphasised, involves the usurpation of priestly powers and functions in order to dethrone tyranny and to forge the uncreated conscience, thoughts and aspirations of his race. As he tells Almidano Artifoni in *Ulysses* (*228; 293*), his decision to become an artist is a '*sacrifizio incruento*', a bloodless sacrifice. It is important, therefore, that in *A Portrait* a priest, the dean of studies, should be the first to recognise Stephen as an 'artist' (190) (*185*). Stephen's early flashback to Parnell's funeral and his innocent comment, 'But he had not died then. Parnell had died' (96) (*93*), is equally significant. Although Ireland's political hopes were buried with Parnell, Stephen's mission of ennobling his country holds a new promise of freedom, since the artist asserts that the individual is more important than institutions such as Church and State.

In setting himself against Church, fatherland, family and friends Joyce was not being apolitical. Exile did not mean escape but a widening of political consciousness; it did not mean indifference but preserving his intimacy with his country by intensifying his quarrel with her. It may be argued from Stephen's discussion with Lynch, on the other hand, that the primary principle of Joyce's aesthetics is that of impersonality: 'The artist, like the God of creation, remains within or behind or beyond or above his handiwork, invisible, refined out of existence, indifferent, paring his fingernails' (219) (*215*). But this is a misunderstanding. If the godlike artist is *within* his handiwork he can hardly be said to be indifferent. The artist may show 'indifferent sympathy' to his characters, as Joyce said in a review written in 1903,[88] but sympathy none the less. What Joyce wanted to avoid by this paradoxical statement was didacticism or partisanship. He had admired Parnell and Ibsen for their 'impersonality', yet Parnell was as dedicated to the national cause as Ibsen was to exposing narrow ideals of life through his art. Impersonality implied greater objectivity, which is not the same as indifference, and was associated in Joyce's mind with heroism. Joyce could not have written his work in Ireland, and exile was therefore a weapon, as Stephen says, with which to continually assess his country. Through the eyes of Europe he would judge with greater insight than would have been possible if he had remained.

As Joyce challenged the social and political order of his country he trod on the verge of revolutionary ideas. The Celtic revivalists for their part had displayed a latent hostility towards him because, as Stanislaus Joyce remarked, he separated himself from the purely national movement by calling himself a 'socialist'.[89] In an entry from his diary dated 1903, Stanislaus provides the following information about his brother's activities: 'He is not an artist he says. He is interesting himself in politics – in which he says [he has] original ideas.'[90] Surprisingly, the fascination for politics came first. By 1904, however, Joyce modified this overriding concern somewhat by linking his radical ideas to his sense of being a 'modern' artist: 'Jim boasts – for he often boasts now – of being modern. He calls himself a socialist but attaches himself to no school of socialism.'[91] So Joyce did have a perspective, despite his 'silence' or veiled intentions. His response to these radical ideas, and the way that they influenced his views of later events in Irish history, are the politics I propose to examine here.

Chapter 2

Young Europe

1 Trieste

In whatever part of Europe he resided, Joyce, like Dante, carried with him a consciousness of the political situation of his city and of his country. Even casual remarks indicate the special interest Joyce took in the degree to which other countries mirrored or failed to mirror his own. Trieste was for him, as his friend Italo Svevo said,[1] a little Ireland, a city he could contemplate with more detachment than his own. When Joyce came to this sea-coast town in 1904 it was under Austro-Hungarian imperial rule, although its population was predominantly Italian. Italian claims to Istria and the Trentino dated back many centuries, and nationalists described those regions as 'terre irredente' ('unredeemed lands'). Joyce alluded to this fervid nationalist feeling in *Giacomo Joyce*: 'Trieste is waking rawly: raw sunlight over its huddled browntiled roofs, testudoform; a multitude of prostrate bugs await a national deliverance.'[2] The political situation in Trieste was complex. The Slavs developed their own nationalist movement which, although it remained a significant force, was not as widespread as irredentism. In Ireland the Unionists were opposed to independence, and in this aspect of two rival nationalisms Trieste differed from Dublin. But for Joyce there were striking political resemblances between the two cities. The theme of the occupied city was perfectly represented in them. Trieste had been ruled by the Austrians for almost as long as the British ruled Dublin, and both cities claimed a language different from that of their conquerors. Joyce expressed an abiding interest in Trieste's plight and he later purchased Giulio Caprin's *Trieste e l'Italia*,★ published in 1915, an overtly propagandistic pamphlet. Roberto Prezioso, editor

---

★ Stephen's comments in 'Proteus' on Kevin Egan (based on the Fenian Joseph Casey

of the city's major newspaper, *Il Piccolo della sera*, was quickly persuaded by Joyce of the similarity between irredentism and the Irish independence movement, since Ireland too awaited its 'redemption' from British rule. At his request Joyce wrote a series of articles on the Irish political situation in 1907, and on the delays in the passage of the Home Rule Bills in 1910 and 1912. The novelist Silvio Benco, who worked for the same paper and at Prezioso's request corrected Joyce's Italian, also held irredentist views and had been arrested and repeatedly questioned by the police from 1890 to 1896. Prezioso hoped to exploit the parallel and stir up political support for irredentism.

Joyce's own politics at this time were not limited to any purely nationalistic movements. In *Stephen Hero* (175) (*170*), Stephen believes that Father Artifoni tolerated the outbursts of his pupil because he supposed that they must have been the outcome of 'too fervid Irishism'. Stephen, however, rebukes his teacher for being unable 'to associate audacity of thought with any temper but that of the irredentist.' 'Redeeming' the homeland entailed a different perspective for Joyce as well as for Stephen. In his letters from 1904 to 1907 he debated strenuously with Stanislaus, who took a conservative position, on the question of socialism. 'It is a mistake for you to imagine that my political opinions are those of a universal lover: but they are those of a socialistic artist', Joyce insisted in 1905.[3] In declaring himself a socialist, Joyce was not being exceptional. For those who wished to revolutionise the established order, adherence to socialism, the *avant-garde* movement of the time, was common enough. In Ireland, moreover, Yeats, in his quarrels with extremists, had argued that every man should describe his Utopia before discussing national issues.[4] Joyce now undertook to give shape to his own Utopian views.

---

whom Joyce met in Paris – see *JJ*, pp. 129–30), are reminiscent of Caprin's discussion of the Triestine patriot Guglielmo Oberdan, who had been sentenced to death in 1882 for an assassination plot. Caprin complained that Italy had forgotten Oberdan: 'L'Italia nuova dimentica presto il martire e dimentica Trieste' ('The new Italy forgets quickly the martyr and forgets Trieste'). But Trieste, he maintained, though betrayed, loved Italy too dearly to betray it ('Ma ama troppo l'Italia per poterla tradire, essa la tradita') (*Trieste e l'Italia*: Milan, 1915, p. 11). On Sandymount Strand Stephen thinks of Kevin Egan ('unsought by any save by me') who had been involved in an abortive gunpowder plot to rescue Fenian leaders from Clerkenwell prison in 1867. Stephen too remarks how 'they have forgotten Kevin Egan, not he them' (*43; 54*).

In Trieste, with this purpose in mind, Joyce resolved to consider Italian thought, partly as expressed in creative work, but mostly in relation to issues of the day. He read widely, and acquainted himself principally with writings that impinged upon those political interests which had been fixed firmly in his mind before he left Dublin. He delved into movements for national liberation parallel to that of Ireland. The struggle of Catholic Poland had always drawn the sympathy of Irishmen, and in Dublin Joyce had noted how 'The tenor air in *The Bohemian Girl*, 'When the fair land of Poland', always brought down the house.'[5] In Italy, another example besides irredentism, was the *Risorgimento* ('resurrection'), the movement for the union and liberation of Italy which had gathered momentum in the middle of the nineteenth century. Joyce purchased the *Saggio su la rivoluzione* of the Neapolitan Carlo Pisacane, who believed that national revolution would pave the way for social revolution. In 1857 he had led a futile military expedition into Calabria against the Bourbons similar to Emmet's uprising against the British. Pisacene's central appeal for Italian republicans – like that of Emmet for Irish republicans – was the ardour of his self-immolation on the altar of *la patria*.★ In contemporary thought, Joyce read mainly in and around socialism. As Benedetto Croce wrote, on later looking back at this period in Italian political history, 'socialism conquered all, or almost all, the flower of the younger generation. . . . To remain uninfluenced by it, or to assume as some did, an attitude of unreasoning hostility toward it, was a sure sign of inferiority.'[6] Joyce, however, did not shrink from reading the works of those who were unsympathetic to socialism. He found that certain criticisms illuminated aspects of socialism with which he was not familiar. The conclusions he drew from his reading, at first tentative, became more and more decisive. As an exile Joyce felt that he could scarcely

---

★ The political testament which Pisacane wrote shortly before the insurrection, stressed the sacrificial nature of his action: 'Ogni mia recompensa io la troverò nel fondo della mia coscienza a nell'animo di questi cari e generosi amici che mi hanno recato il loro concorso e hanno diviso i battiti del mie cuore e le mio speranze: che se il nostro sacrifizio non apporta alcun bene all' Italia, sarà almeno una gloria per essa l'aver prodotto dei figli che vollero immolarsi al suo avvenire' (*Saggio su la rivoluzione*, ed. Giaime Pintor (Torino, 1956), p. 56). ('I will find my reward deep in my conscience and in the mind of these dear and generous friends who have given me their approval and who have shared my heartbeats and my hopes: if our sacrifice does not benefit Italy in any way, it will at least be her glory to have borne sons who wished to immolate themselves for her future.')

take an active role in European politics, but he remained fascinated none the less, and commented on the political scene.

One of his first interests was the work of Guglielmo Ferrero,* a native of Portici who was an historian, sociologist and journalist. Though today Ferrero's name is not often heard, in Joyce's day he was an international figure and had Theodore Roosevelt among his admirers. Ferrero was like Walter Lippmann in his philosophical approach to events. He had married the daughter of Cesare Lombroso, founder of the Italian school of penal law, and had collaborated with him in the publication of *La Donna delinquente, la prostituta e la donna normale* in 1893, a widely read work in the previously neglected field of female offenders. Joyce admired Ferrero enough to buy a picture postcard of him to send to Stanislaus, and described the bespectacled and 'delicate-looking' journalist amusingly as 'a terrified Y.M.C.A. man . . . the type you would expect to find in some quiet nook in the Coffee Palace nibbling a bun hastily and apologetically between the hours of half-past twelve and one'.[7]†

Joyce probably first started reading Ferrero in *Il Piccolo della sera* since in Rome he asked Stanislaus to send along any interesting articles by him appearing in the Triestine newspaper.[8] In 1905 and 1906 Joyce would certainly have read Ferrero's leaders on such topical subjects as the Russo-Japanese War. Ferrero shrewdly predicted that the war would disprove the nineteenth century belief that Russia was invulnerable.[9] Bloom echoes this appraisal of the war by asserting, 'The Russians [would] only be an eight o'clock breakfast for the Japanese' (*58; 70*). Ferrero also dealt in his columns with the possibility of a Russian Revolution based on the Austrian example of 1866,[10] and cautioned contemporary youth about the misguidance of public opinion as exemplified in the Dreyfus uproar.[11] That Ferrero was a Dreyfusard journalist stirred Joyce's imagination and, as we shall see, led him to inquire about Ferrero's views on anti-Semitism.

Ferrero's international reputation, however, was established by his five volume history, *Grandezza e decadenza di Roma*, published

---

* (1871–1942).
† The article by Susan L. Humphreys, 'Ferrero Etc.: James Joyce's Debt to Guglielmo Ferrero' in *James Joyce Quarterly* 16 (Spring 1979), pp. 239–51, appeared after I had sent my typescript to the publishers. Although we make similar points, our emphases are different.

between 1902 and 1907. In retrospect, it seems surprising that Ferrero, who in his columns attended exclusively to political and social dilemmas of contemporary interest, should suddenly produce a prodigious work on late Republican and early Imperial Rome. This contradiction is apparent only, however, for Ferrero approached Roman history with a modern perspective. He saw in the past the germ of those problems which afflicted the present. The notion of 'decadence', for example, was then in vogue, exemplified in the lifestyles of writers like D'Annunzio. Ferrero boldly asked whether the Italians were 'decadent' offspring of the Latin family of Imperial Rome. Nineteenth century historians, like Mommsen, had portrayed Caesar as a complete and perfect man, a 'saviour-tyrant'. Ferrero saw Caesar instead as a demagogue, and he aimed to alert his countrymen in time against the danger of demagogy and political adventurism. Abroad Ferrero's work outsold the historical works of Carlyle, Michelet, and Taine, and in Italy it stirred up a bitter controversy among classical scholars, historians, and philosophers, who criticised it as the work of a dilettante.[12] When a Bill creating a Chair in Philosophy of History at the University of Rome for Ferrero was later introduced in Parliament in 1910, the move was vociferously opposed, especially by Benedetto Croce. But the liberal wing of the irredentist party rallied to Ferrero's defence. *Il Piccolo della sera*, for example, claimed that his work showed profound and original insight, as indeed it did.[13]

Joyce was not as cantankerous about *Grandezza e decadenza di Roma* as Ferrero's compatriots were. In 1907, in 'Ireland, Island of Saints and Sages', he referred to Ferrero's work. He cited in particular Ferrero's criticism of the findings of German scholars. Joyce was probably alluding to Ferrero's dismissal of those conclusions about Caesar as a hero, and allowed that 'it may be so.' But as far as their contribution to European culture went, Joyce pointed out that it was those very Germans who first presented Shakespeare as a poet of world significance to his compatriots, and the only ones in Europe to concern themselves with Celtic language and history.[14] Joyce thought well enough of Ferrero to read the work, probably all of it. He refers to the chapter on Horace in the fourth volume, where Ferrero argued that the *Odes*, by relating the deterioration of the moral fibre of the people to the questionable political policies of Augustus, are a reflection of the Augustan age. Joyce's only remark is that, in that case, 'perhaps, poets should be let live.'[15] He probably realised for the first time that Horace's involvement with his age was in some way similar to his own task as a novelist in relation to Irish society.

Ferrero was a controversial figure in national politics as well. In his writings he disapproved of what he termed Italian parliamentary dictatorship and had repeatedly attacked the corrupt regime and pro–Austrian policies of Prime Minister Francesco Crispi.* Although Ferrero started off as a socialist, he now advocated instead British parliamentarianism. Joyce respected Ferrero's critical acumen but disagreed with his anglophilia. In his article for *Il Piccolo*, Joyce criticised the English Parliament for having delayed passage of the Home Rule Bill for twenty-one years. Rather, what pleased Joyce especially was Ferrero's willingness to include Ireland in his discussion of European affairs. Joyce reported to Stanislaus in a letter of November 1906 that Ferrero had included the Irish among his three great classes of emigrants. In a popular book of his early period Ferrero had categorised these groups as the '*plasmativa*':

> it means conquering, imposing their own language . . . the
> English: the adhesive (forming a little group with national
> traditions and sympathies) the Chinese and the Irish!!!!: the
> diffusive (entering into the new society and forming part of it) the
> Germans.[16]

This book, *L'Europa giovane* (1897), whose title echoed Mazzini's 'Young Europe' movement that was to link the various European nations together in a common crusade, was the one mentioned most by Joyce in his letters to Stanislaus. It exerted a great influence on the youth of the day and Ferrero attributed its success to the fact that it was a book of ideas 'written in an easily understood and lively style' and that it was the first of its kind by a journalist.[17] The substance of the book was an account of the author's travels to England, Germany, Russia, and Scandinavia and the observations he formed of these cultures. Ferrero's admiring description of the Scandinavian cities Abo, Stockholm, and Copenhagen impressed Joyce who now wrote to Stanislaus that he longed to visit Denmark.[18] Ferrero's lavish praise for England and Germany displeased his nationalistic compatriots however, who accused him of disparaging his country by attempting to replace Italian culture with an injection of foreign

---

* In *Finnegans Wake* (618.34) 'Crispianity' might ironically allude to Francesco Crispi (1819–1901), who died unreconciled to Christianity, and who was generally known as a free-thinker.

cultures.[19] In effect, Ferrero was doing for Italy what Joyce was hoping to do for Ireland.

L'Europa giovane was not, however, a collection of tourist impressions.★ The central argument of the book is that economic growth is the barometer of social progress, and that those nations with developing industries represent a superior culture. Ferrero emphasised that the changes the Industrial Revolution wrought in all constructive human activity heralded a new Europe. He took the homespun example of the manufacture of biscuits and cakes to indicate the substantial differences between Latin and Anglo-Saxon cultures. Cakes in London would not be found edible by an Italian, whereas he appreciated English biscuits as master works of art. The fact that biscuits were made by machines and cakes were individual creations of a worker explained this difference. The English surpassed the Italians in mechanical ability, Ferrero concluded, but the Italians excelled in craftsmanship.[20] Joyce was sufficiently stirred by this ludicrous point of comparison between English and Italian life to spend his last two lire on cakes so as to taste the veracity of Ferrero's statements.[21] Unfortunately, he never stated how his palate felt about the national characteristics of pastry.

Ferrero discussed Irish national traits too. He included Parnell as representative of his theory about 'great political men'. Ferrero described them as possessing in general a moral and intellectual character contrary to that of the people whom they govern. In Parnell's case, he possessed the English trai of 'calculating fanaticism' as opposed to the inflammable Irish temperament. Parnell's case, he possessed the English trait of 'calculating because there existed the 'schemer' in him who studied how to manipulate the people's passions for a definite purpose. If, on the other hand, Ferrero concluded, Parnell had been Irish, that is a 'romantic fanatic', his popularity would not have endured as long as it did.[22] Joyce would probably have agreed that Parnell was 'calculating', but he did not consider him a 'fanatic'. Later, in 'The Shade of Parnell', Joyce would describe Parnell's distinguishing feature as that of 'melancholy serenity'.[23] The views of Ferrero and Joyce converged, however, on the crucial issue of Parnell's

---

★ Joyce warned against the same interpretation of *Dubliners*. In September 1905 he wrote to William Heinemann about *Dubliners* and insisted the book was not 'a collection of tourist impressions but an attempt to represent certain aspects of the life of one of the European capitals' (II, p. 109).

downfall. Ferrero must have been the first, if not the only, well-known European Joyce discovered who had defended Parnell against his detractors in the divorce scandal.

Joyce was able to mould some of Ferrero's political ideas into fiction. In a letter to Stanislaus, Joyce explicitly states that Ferrero inspired his story 'Two Gallants'.[24] Moreover, when Joyce ran into the printer's objections for publication of this story, he recommended, in a letter to Grant Richards, that the printer read Ferrero in order to remove his prejudices:

> Is it the small gold coin in the . . . story or the code of honour
> which the two gallants live by which shocks him? I see nothing
> which would shock him in either of these things. His idea of
> gallantry has grown up in him (probably) during the reading of
> the novels of the elder Dumas and during the performance of
> romantic plays which presented to him cavaliers and ladies in full
> dress. I would strongly recommend to him the chapters wherein
> Ferrero examines the moral code of the soldier and (incidentally)
> of the gallant. But it would be useless for I am sure that in his heart
> of hearts he is a militarist.[25]

In *L'Europa giovane* the moral code of the soldier consists in arousing men's 'inert brutality'.[26] Ferrero associates this militaristic activity, which he considered typical of the Germanic races, with the art of gallantry. In Berlin, for example, a casual encounter between a youth and a girl in the street will, after engaging in a brief conversation, easily result in an affair the next day; the girl will be a mistress without even knowing her lover's name. Such 'brutal' encounters resemble the equally anonymous ones on the battlefield. The male lacks all patience regarding the art of 'gallantry' because not love but biological need impels him to seek women. Ferrero's point is that sexual relations are adjusted to the brutality of the male rather than to the gallantry which the female might desire.[27] It is this absence of gallantry which leads Joyce to entitle his story ironically 'Two Gallants'. Corley's account of his 'conquest' of the servant girl recalls Ferrero's description of the Berlin rendezvous:

> I was going along Dame Street and I spotted a fine tart under
> Waterhouse's clock and said good-night, you know. So we went
> for a walk round by the canal and she told me she was a slavey in a
> house in Baggot Street. I put my arm round her and squeezed her a
> bit that night. (53–4) (*50–1*)

The Irish servant girl, moreover, even after having made several similar appointments with Corley, is ignorant of his name.[28]

Joyce completes Ferrero's theme by exaggerating Corley's military bearing. He is, we are told, 'the son of an inspector of police' who 'had inherited his father's frame and gait.' Far from being a 'gay Lothario' he comports himself instead more like a robot, walking with 'his hands by his side, holding himself erect and swaying his head from side to side.' His head is 'large, globular and oily . . . and his large round hat . . . looked like a bulb which had grown out of another.' Soldier-like, he 'always stared straight before him as if he were on parade' and had to move his whole trunk 'when he wished to gaze after some one in the street' (54) (*51*). Joyce is here caricaturing Corley's repulsive traits in order to suggest Ferrero's point of view.

Joyce takes up Ferrero's point that the debasement of love is an index to the national temperament,★ and relates it to the socio-political situation of Ireland. Joyce indicates that the absence of gallantry in relations between male and female results in the exploitation of women. And this degradation of women in turn signals the degradation of Ireland. For example, the harp which 'heedless that her coverings had fallen about her knees, seemed weary alike of the eyes of strangers and of her master's hands' (58) (*54*), is clearly an analogue for the servant girl. The harp is traditionally a symbol for Ireland, and the slavey can be seen in the same light. The lovelessness that characterises the relationship between Corley and the slavey is part of Joyce's indictment of Irish society. Joyce, moreover, associates sexual cruelty – for Lenehan observes that Corley's 'bulk, his easy pace, and the solid sound of his boots had something of the conqueror in them' (59) (*55*) – with England's equally brutal conquest of Ireland. Corley plays a principal role in yoking together these two images of 'conquest', for

---

★ Corley displays the horror of this reduction of the sexual instinct to mere bestiality by cadging a gold coin from the servant girl. Joyce may have borrowed this epiphanic detail from Ferrero's discussion of the Scandinavian Siegfried sagas. Unlike the heroes of the *Iliad*, who were incited to war by Helen of Troy, a sexual motive, their Germanic counterparts battled among themselves not for women but either for personal prestige or for gold. The reward prized by the victors was not the kisses of a 'slave', as Ferrero puts it, but the possession of a treasure. The Scandinavian is, in effect, the 'father' of the modern Englishman who is indifferent to love, but whose passion for gold inspired him to undertake the most dangerous exploits in the world (*L'Europa giovane*, pp. 136, 139).

he not only misuses the servant girl, but dishonours Ireland as well. His relationship with the police, for he 'was often to be seen walking with policemen in plain clothes' (54–5) (*51*), suggests that he is a 'base betrayer'. In *Ulysses*, the womaniser is Blazes Boylan, while Buck Mulligan, who is prepared to fecundate any woman in the country free of charge, is Ireland's 'gay betrayer'. The story may not seem to be dealing explicitly with these issues. For Joyce, however, the brutalism of love and politics were interconnected. He strongly objected to militarism, and to whatever manner that militarism chose to express itself.

Ferrero argued that Latin societies, as opposed to the Germanic races, moved incessantly towards what he termed the 'agony of Caesarism'; that is, government by classes who do not represent productive labour. These classes, moreover, want to enjoy sensual pleasures, intellectual and artistic satisfaction, without making an effort to produce anything. They extort from the agricultural populace the expense of a civilisation of which it sees only two representatives: the policeman and the publican.[29] For Joyce Ireland too suffered the 'agony of Caesarism' since he considered his homeland to be an 'aristocratic country without an aristocracy'.[30]

What aroused Joyce's interest, in addition to the discussion on Latin and Germanic races, was what Ferrero had to say about the Jews. Before Joyce left Dublin, the problem of the Jew in the modern world (especially as evidenced in the Dreyfus case) had gained international prominence. In the middle months of 1904, moreover, a violent outburst of anti-Semitism, a boycott of Jewish tradesmen, occurred in Limerick.[31] On the continent Joyce now came to recognise the similarity of his own position to that of the Jews. He assembled a number of books on the Jews, and constantly attended to any details which could prove useful for his portrait of Bloom. In *L'Europa giovane*, Joyce read what he called the 'fine chapter on Antisemitism' and took interest in the fact that Georg Brandes, the eminent Danish critic and friend of Ibsen, and Cesare Lombroso were Jews.[32]* Ferrero's conclusions about anti-Semitism, however, may not have proved congenial to Joyce. Ferrero claimed that the

---

* Ferrero attributed to the Jew the genius of 'proselytism', and claimed that 'propaganda' was the greatest creation of Hebrew genius. This explains why the Jew, Ferrero argues, is proficient in journalism. Every Jewish genius, in fact, is a bit of a journalist (*L'Europa giovane*, pp. 368–72). Although Joyce disliked propaganda, he may have received a hint for Bloom's profession in these statements.

ancients had cause to be anti-Semitic because, in spite of all their vices and cruelties, they still represented a kind of rational equilibrium. The Jew, on the other hand, presented a 'barbaric passion' for the ideal of proselytism, the effect of which was bloodshed. Ferrero modifies these somewhat unenlightened views by asserting that contemporary anti-Semitism is unjust. The modern Jew, according to Ferrero, is an active force in his society. His 'Messianic conscience', his mysticism, his egoism and ethical spirit no longer corrupt social thought. But Ferrero maintains that this 'extraordinary race' has always obstinately believed that it possessed the secret for man's redemption. Their solution was first Messianic, then Christian, and either socialism or anarchism for contemporary times.[33]* Joyce could not agree with Ferrero's dismissal of socialism as a particularly 'Jewish' solution to man's salvation. An Irishman could accept the same solution for his own situation as an artist.

Ferrero's uncomplimentary comments about the political activity of the Jews and Richard Wagner's statements about their artistic incapacities in *Judaism in Music* (which Joyce had with him in Trieste), expressed some of the modern attitudes towards the Jews. In 'Cyclops', Joyce exposed a range of other attitudes that could be taken up. The first narrator, 'I', like the Citizen, expresses utter loathing for Bloom. He comments that Bloom is not an Irishman, but what he calls a 'Jerusalem cuckoo' (*335; 436*). J. J. O'Molloy displays a milder distaste for Bloom. When John Wyse Nolan asks, 'why can't a jew love his country like the next fellow?', O'Molloy quips, 'Why not? . . . when he's quite sure which country it is' (*337; 438*).† He also ridicules the notion that the Jews are still waiting for their Messiah (*337; 438*). Although Martin Cunningham is more charitable towards Bloom, he still describes him as a 'perverted Jew' (*337; 438*).‡ A counter-attack on these views appeared in the work of

---

* Otto Weininger later argued in a similar manner in *Sex and Character* (London, 1906), pp. 306–7, claiming that the Jew is at the opposite pole from the aristocrat by embracing anarchy and communism.

† This remark was originally used by Joyce in *Giacomo Joyce* (9) apropos of his Jewish pupil, Amalia Popper. On account of her irredentist views, she had expressed her approval of the expulsion of the music critic, Ettore Albini, from La Scala in Milan because he had failed to stand during the playing of the national anthem.

‡ Bloom confronts the hostility of the people around him by asserting, 'I belong to a race . . . that is hated and persecuted. Also now. This very moment. This very instant.' The Citizen asks if he is referring to the new Jerusalem, but Bloom indicates

an economist of the *Risorgimento*. This happened to be Carlo Cattaneo,* a Milanese intellectual of liberal-democratic persuasion, and a friend of Pisacane. Joyce read his *Ricerche economiche sulle interdizioni imposte dalla legge civile agli Israeliti* (1836), an essay inspired by a dispute between France and Switzerland concerning the right of French citizens of Jewish origin to own land in those parts of Switzerland where Jews were normally excluded from such tenure. Cattaneo explained how centuries of persecutions and legal restrictions had limited the economic activity of European Jews. He argued that this situation had been detrimental both to the Jewish communities and to the countries in which they lived. In his opinion, discrimination had alienated the Jews from the mainstream of European culture. By prohibiting the Jews from owning land, from attending institutions of higher learning, and barring them from many professions, several countries had failed to take advantage of the intellectual and economic resources of this unique group of people. In Cattaneo's view, such failure had retarded the progress of those countries. An example of Cattaneo's argument is a passage in which, after stressing the importance of education, he lists a number of Jews who had distinguished themselves in various fields:

> I legislatori che interessandosi alla morale publica ne hanno studiato le fonti, apersero ai giovani Israeliti i cancelli delle

---

that Zionism is not the issue at stake: 'I'm talking about injustice.' Though Bloom is not a Zionist, he is not entirely out of sympathy: 'Nothing doing. Still an idea behind it' (*60; 72*). On the other hand, he considers Dlugacz, the Jewish pork-butcher, an 'enthusiast' for his espousal of Zionism (*68; 83*). And later he dismisses all talk of the Jews as having a national mission: 'Dear, O dear! All that long business about that brought us out of the land of Egypt and into the house of bondage *alleluia*' (*122; 155*). (When Ottocaro Weiss broached this subject, Joyce wryly remarked, 'That's all very well, but believe me, a warship with a captain named Kanalgitter and his aide named Captain Afterduft would be the funniest thing the old Mediterranean has ever seen.' (*JJ*, p. 408)). Stephen's parable of the plums suggests that Ireland too is not a 'promised land', but sterile. (Bloom had thought of Palestine as a barren land (61; 73). In 'Ithaca' (*61; 73*), Bloom and Stephen state that one of the points of contact between the Irish and the Jews existed in 'the restoration . . . of Zion and the possibility of Irish political autonomy or devolution' (*689; 807*).

* Cattaneo (1801–1869) would, in fact, write on the Irish agricultural question at the request of the British Government in 1844. In 'Su lo Stato dell'Irlanda nell'anno 1844', Cattaneo warned that if Ireland continued to depend solely on the potato crop, a crop failure would have devastating consequences. He recommended as a solution a system of crop rotation which would increase the productivity of the land and reduce the danger of famine. British politics, however, rendered these sound proposals inapplicable and, unfortunately, his prediction came true.

università e delle accademie. Altri gli avviano artificiosamente alle arti meccaniche, all'agricoltura, alla vita militare. Mendelsohn, che scrisse egregiamente sull'immortalità dell'anima, era ebreo; Spinosa, che lasciò il suo nome al più audace volo dell'idealismo, era ebreo; l'incisore Jesi é un ebreo, il compositore Mayerbeer é un ebreo; Basevi, l'avvocato che a Mantova prese la difesa di Andrea Hofer, è un ebreo; Rubino Ventura, ebreo modenese, comanda l'esercito del possente sovrano di Lahore ch'egli addestrò nella tattica europea. L'arte usuraia non è un affare di sangue ma di educazione e di posizione; e gli ebrei sono capaci d'altri generi di bene e d'altri generi di male.

(Legislators concerned with public morals have studied the sources, have opened the gates of the universities and academies to young Israelites. Others artfully prepare them for mechanical skills, agriculture and military life. Mendelssohn, who wrote excellently on the immortality of the soul, was a Jew; Spinoza, who made his name in the boldest flights of idealism, was a Jew; the engraver Jesi is a Jew, the composer Meyerbeer is a Jew; Basevi, the lawyer who defended Andrea Hofer in Mantua, is a Jew; Rubino Ventura, a Jew from Modena, leads the army, which he trained in European tactics, of the powerful sovereign of Lahore. The art of usury is not a matter of blood, but one of education and rank; and the Jews are capable of other kinds of good and other kinds of evil.)[34]

Joyce, doubtless stimulated by Cattaneo's enlightening judgments, made Bloom continental in outlook (*646; 777*), and 'a cultured allroundman' (*235; 301–2*). He used Cattaneo's defence of the achievements of the Jews, moreover, as the basis for Bloom's repartee to the chauvinistic Citizen:

Mendelssohn was a jew and Karl Marx and Mercadante and Spinoza. And the Saviour was a jew and his father was a jew . . . Your God was a jew. Christ was a jew like me. (*342; 444–5*)

The composer Meyerbeer also lingers on Bloom's mind throughout the day. His list has its humorous touches, but the spirit in which it is delivered is Cattaneo's. The irony at work here is only partial, not pervasive. That Bloom is misinformed (Mercadante, for instance, was not a Jew) evokes amusement, yet he is not made the butt of satire. Although he is not speaking as Joyce, Bloom registers genuine emotion despite its imperfect expression. His view is not discredited, nor its value diminished. Joyce withdraws a little from his hero in order not to appear patronising or sentimental. But he does not abandon Bloom. Bloom indicates that prejudice, in the form of anti-Semitism, exists alongside the demand for political freedom. Joyce's point, too, is that anti-Semitism is the touchstone for bigotry.* By exposing this underlying discrepancy in Irish nationalism, he maintains that 'indifferent sympathy' towards his hero of which he spoke in his early critical writing.

Joyce was especially alive to discussions of exile, since it was here that he felt his position to be closest to that of the Jews. In *L'Europa giovane*, Ferrero called German geniuses of Hebrew origin, like Karl Marx, Heine, and Max Nordau, 'esuli volontari' because although they published their books in Germany, they lived elsewhere. Joyce had described his own situation in Trieste to Stanislaus as being that of a 'voluntary exile'.[35] Ferrero argued that in their exile from the mother country – although the Jews felt themselves to be aliens – the profound differences between the mother and her children were subdued.[36] Joyce took a different view. In *Exiles* he distinguished between an 'economic' and a 'spiritual' exile. In the former category are those who left Ireland 'to seek the bread by which men live.' The others, 'her most favoured children', left her 'to seek in other lands that food of the spirit by which a nation of human beings is sustained in life' (129) (*99*). Exile did not mean losing interest in the mother country; Joyce took Ireland into exile with him wherever he went. While he played up those differences which compelled him to leave in the first place, for Joyce exile was, nevertheless, a means by which to keep continual contact with the homeland.

Joyce noted, moreover, Ferrero's comparison of Jesus and Marx:

> He says that Karl Marx has the apocalyptic imagination and makes Armageddon a war between capital and labour. The most arrogant statement made by Israel so far, he says, not excluding the gospel of Jesus is Marx's proclamation that socialism is the fulfillment of a natural law.[37]

Joyce agreed that Messianic notions make up part of the Jewish temperament. In *Ulysses* there are constant references to the end of the world. At times such references signify simply destruction, especially that of fire and brimstone, as evoked by the phrase, 'Elijah is coming', which announces the forthcoming visit to Dublin of the

---

* See pp. 131 ff.

evangelist, J. Alexander Dowie. In 'Circe', Bloom displays a milder version of the 'apocalyptic imagination'. His Messianic goals and his plans for social reform are combined and mocked in his promise of the new Bloomusalem in the Nova Hibernia of the future (*484; 606*).

Ferrero argued that socialism exhibits many of the characteristic elements of religious creations, such as Christianity, on a social basis. In *Ulysses*, we are told that Bloom upset Molly by saying that Christ was the 'first socialist' (*742–3; 878*). Ferrero protested that Jesus launched a programme of moral reform, not one of political revolution. Though the intellectual contents of Christianity and socialism are dissimilar, Ferrero indicated that the conclusion is the same. Both strive for the general 'redemption' of humanity. In the latter case it is not for the advent of God's reign but for the advent of socialism in the government of the people and a 'transfiguration' of the world in a final apotheosis of universal love.[38] To speak of Christianity and socialism as having the common aim of 'redemption' reminded Joyce that his art shared this purpose too. He cast himself in the role of a literary Messiah and at times said so explicitly, as in a letter of 1912 to Nora Barnacle: 'I hope that the day may come when I shall be able to give you the fame of being beside me when I have entered into my kingdom.'[39]* Joyce probably recognised in Ferrero's comments that his fascination for the Christlike qualities of the artist could be made consonant with his socialistic views. This was a perspective he would develop in *Stephen Hero*.†

Ferrero's writings acted as a kind of whetstone for Joyce's maturing political views. As an exile, Joyce had resolved to enter into the spirit of the new Europe, and he had hoped to discover hints of this spirit in *L'Europa giovane*. Joyce admired Ferrero's effort to escape parochialism, and Ferrero's continental perspective resembled his own. Ferrero's conclusions, however, proved to be somewhat generalised for Joyce's purposes. For an analysis of the Irish political scene Joyce relied on his own perceptions. Ferrero's commentary on socialism was likewise acute, but Joyce did not consider him sympathetic enough to the movement. Joyce had considerable sympathy for progressive movements, and it was with these that he now wanted to be most closely associated.

---

* In his review of 'Ibsen's New Drama' in 1900 (*CW*, p. 63), Joyce said of Ibsen, 'Many years more, however, must pass before he will enter into his kingdom in jubilation, although, as he stands to-day, all has been done on his part to ensure his own worthiness to enter therein.'

† See below, p. 76.

2 Rome

When someone in a wineshop in Rome asked, 'è socialista il Signor
Giacomo?',* the proprietor, a friend of Joyce, answered amusingly,
'É un po' di tutto.'† Joyce had, in fact, just made some comment
about the struggle between the various factions at the socialist party
congress being held there in 1906.[40] What impressed Joyce was, as
Herbert Gorman noted, 'the spectacle of the delegates representing
the various types of socialism plunging into endless internecine
warfare concerning conflicting theories of dogma and action,
arguing, orating, denouncing, and expounding'.[41] When the
socialist party assembled on 7–10 October under the presidency of
the venerable Andrea Costa, there existed four rival factions. The
reformists asserted their freedom to enter into alliances with parties
of the left in parliament in order to secure favourable labour and
social legislation. The integralists, headed by Enrico Ferri and his
henchman Oddino Morgari, accepted all the various forms of action
advocated by the different socialist schools of thought. Arturo
Labriola's syndicalists, while remaining within the party, excluded
parliamentary activity from their platform, favouring the direct
action method of the general strike. Finally, the intransigents, by
repudiating all forms of co-operation with other parties, including
the syndicalists, represented the extreme left. In correspondence
with his brother, Joyce dwelt on the split between Ferri and Labriola.
Labriola, Joyce wrote, was a person who interested him very
much.[42]

Arturo Labriola was, like Joyce's other favourites, Ferrero,
Bruno, and Vico, a Neapolitan. He was a Professor of Economics at
the University of Naples, and became known for his adroit polemics
as a journalist for the Neapolitan socialist newspaper, *La Propaganda*,
and also for *Avanti!*, the party's national newspaper, in Rome.‡ Ferri
edited *Avanti!* from April 1903 until January 1908, and was Professor

---

* 'Is Mr James a socialist?'
† 'He's a little of everything.'
‡ Arturo Labriola (1873–1959) is not to be confused with Antonio Labriola
(1843–1904), Italy's major Marxist theorist of the time. This famous historian-
philosopher in fact rebaptised Arturo 'il Labriolino' and accused him of exploiting
their homonymous surnames. (Gaetano Arfè, *Storia del socialismo italiano* (Torino,
1965), p. 111). A torrential, persuasive orator, Arturo Labriola became leader of the
syndicalists at the Rome congress of 1900. After the congress of Imola in 1902 he
moved to Milan and there revived the weekly journal, *Avanguardia Socialista*.

of Penal Law at Rome. An eminent disciple of Cesare Lombroso along with Ferrero, Ferri was one of the founders of the school of 'Positive Criminology'.* From a socialist perspective he argued that criminality was determined by economic conditions and hereditary factors associated with them (in the same way that Gerhart Hauptmann in his dramas had employed heredity as a socialistic theme). Labriola's principal significance as a socialist was his formidable opposition to the kind of parliamentary socialism known as 'reformism' advocated by such men as Filippo Turati. So, when Labriola, along with the more revolutionary syndicalists, was expelled from the party at the 1908 congress in Florence, the reformists gained a decisive victory. Ferri's initial sympathies lay with the left-wing factions of the party. His views changed considerably, however, as he passed first to the right, and then finally left the party in 1911.

Joyce followed the dispute carefully, and argued against his brother's assessment of Labriola:

> You are wrong . . . in supposing that the intellectuals taught Labriola socialism. Intellectualism, instead, is a partial develop-ment, an alloy of sociological liberalism, of the original socialism which was really nothing but the manifesto of a class. Ferri, for example, seems a more intellectual and capable person than Labriola. But the latter contends that interest in psychiatry and criminology and literature and religion are beside the question. He wishes to hasten *directly* the emergence of the proletariat. And to do this he would include in his ranks Catholics and Jews, liberals and conservatives.[43]

Labriola, in fact, attributed his conversion to socialism to his contact with the scientific philosophy of positivism, and this influence accounted for his leaving the Church and made him a secularist and anti-clericalist.[44] Being well-versed in economics, Labriola's articles for the highly intellectual *Avanguardia Socialista* included subtle analyses of Marx's *Das Kapital*. And he eventually wrote a book on Marx as economist and theorist of socialism. Labriola was, in effect,

---

* Enrico Ferri (1856–1929) exercised a wide influence on criminological theory in Italy. In his best known work, *Socialism and Positive Science* (1894), Ferri maintained that Marxism was the social counterpart to the evolutionary theories of Darwin and Spencer. He joined the Italian socialist party, or PSI, at its second congress at Reggio Emilia in 1893 which followed the initial conference held at Genoa in 1892. See below, pp. 81–2 for a discussion of Lombroso's theory in relation to *Stephen Hero*.

the most important of the Italian syndicalist writers.[45] Joyce described Labriola's views accurately, but was mistaken, therefore, in regarding Ferri as a more intellectual person than Labriola.

Ferri, on the other hand, distinguished himself as a criminological theorist, but as a socialist he was much less important than Labriola. His flirtation with the various factions of the socialist party did not establish him as an exponent of any one aspect of socialist theory. He was more of a pragmatist and devoted his efforts mainly in trying to keep the party together, preferably under his own leadership. In this respect, Joyce was justified in maintaining that Ferri was a more 'capable' person than Labriola.

The proceedings of the socialist congress held in 1906 can be clarified by reference to the prevalent attitudes in the conferences immediately preceding it. At the Imola congress of 1902, Turati's reformism gained a large majority over the left wing led by Ferri. The congress approved the motion put forward by this parliamentary group in support of the government of Prime Minister Giolitti. But when the socialist party met again at Bologna in 1904, the results were reversed. Ferri's left wing 'intransigent' group, which rejected all electoral transactions with non-socialist elements, and Labriola's syndicalists took control of the party.

In another letter to Stanislaus, Joyce took issue with the syndicalists on one aspect of socialist theory:

> If, as all classes of socialists agree, a general European war, an international war, has become an impossibility I do not see how a general international strike or even a general national strike is a possibility. The Italian army is not directed against the Austrian army so much as against the Italian people.* Of course, the sindacalists are anti-militarists but I don't see how that saves them from the logical conclusion of revolution in a conscriptive country like this. It is strange that Italian socialism in its latest stage should approach so closely the English variety.[46]

These remarks demonstrate that Joyce's socialism was indeed, as he told Stanislaus, 'unsteady and ill-informed'.[47] Socialists were in principle opposed to war, but to argue that war was an impossibility was, in retrospect, to take an incredibly utopian view of the international situation. Italian revolutionary syndicalism was heavily influenced not by the English variety, but by the analogous

---

* This statement is similar to those made by the anarchists. See below, p. 108.

French experience, especially by George Sorel's *Avenir socialiste des syndicats*, published in 1898. Sorel differed from Marx in holding that the revolution should be accomplished not by workers as informal groups, but by organised trade unions. The revolution, moreover, was to be carried out by the 'direct action' method of a general strike. Sorel also taught that these workers' syndicates should engage in violent class warfare against the bourgeois state. Sorel's views formed the basis of those that Labriola advocated at the national congress of 1904. By September of that year the first successful general national strike in the world had already taken place. In retaliation against a series of massacres carried out by the authorities of striking workers in various parts of Italy, the trade unions declared a general strike. For four days Italy seemed to be under syndicalist control. The leaders finally called off the demonstration, satisfied that they had proved to the masses, in Labriola's famous remark, that 'five minutes of direct action were worth as many years of parliamentary chatter.'[48] So the social revolution Joyce claimed was the 'logical conclusion' of syndicalist policy had already begun.

The immediate effect of the general strike on national politics, however, was a noticeable swing to the right. In subsequent elections the number of socialist parliamentary representatives was cut by half through the withholding of the customary support from the small bourgeoisie, which had been hurt most by the situation.[49] The election results also induced the tactful Ferri to eventually adopt the middle course policy which attempted to 'integrate' the right and left wings of the party (hence the name 'integralism') heading into the 1906 congress.

Joyce followed the socialist congress in the columns of *Avanti!*, the paper Mussolini would eventually edit from 1912 to 1914.[50]* The socialist party started *Avanti!* (Forward!), with a name borrowed from the German socialist paper *Vorwärts*, in 1896. It served a unifying purpose by promoting an exchange of view-points between socialists from disparate regions of the north and south, and also enabled Italians (as well as Joyce) to keep abreast with

---

* At this time Joyce was also reading the satirical socialist weekly published in Rome, *L'Asino* ('The Ass'), whose anti-clericalism and anti-Vaticanism he shared (II, pp. 151, 157). He must have been particularly delighted with the issue wholly dedicated to Giordano Bruno on 17 February 1907 in commemoration of his death. *L'Asino* claimed that in being itself accused of pornography by the Church, it had an illustrious predecessor. Socialists also esteemed Bruno as an heroic exponent of free thought against whom they termed 'Jesuit reactionaries'.

international socialist movements. At the time of the 1906 congress, Ferri was editor.

Joyce approved of the syndicalists' objection to parliamentarianism and summarised their policies in a letter to Stanislaus:

> They are trades-unionists or rather trade-unionists with a definite anti-social programme. Their weapons are unions and strikes. They decline to interfere in politics or religion or legal questions. They do not desire the conquest of public powers which, they say, only serve in the end to support the middle class government. They assert they are the true socialists because they wish the future social order to proceed equally from the overthrow of the entire present social organisation and from the automatic emergence of the proletariat in trades-unions and guilds and the like.[51]

Joyce seems to have absorbed syndicalist thought in a more perceptive manner than Ferri, who accused Labriola's group of being nebulous as to whether it approved of parliamentary action.[52] Ferri, moreover, argued that one of the fundamental theoretical errors of syndicalism was that a syndicate should be composed of manual labourers, irrespective of their political opinions. He claimed that a lack of political formation led to a spirit of class egoism. To avoid this pitfall one must elevate the conscience of the workers towards a positive comprehension of the relationship between man and the external world, the individual, the class structure, the national and international community. The only way to accomplish this end was by giving them a 'socialist' conscience.[53] Joyce, however, preferred Labriola's policy of including within the socialist ranks people of different creeds and political beliefs as a more effective means of achieving the emergence of the proletariat.

Syndicalism proclaimed the necessity of transferring the centre of proletarian revolutionary activity from the party to the workers' syndicates, understood as politically neutral units. For it was feared that political differences among workers not organised in trade unions would prevent collective action, whereas their membership would give the workers a sense of solidarity. This policy did not mean adhering to any political party as such, but being 'socialist' in sharing the revolutionary end of overthrowing capitalist society, although by different means. Labriola argued that conceiving of socialism as a 'legislative process' meant involving the socialist movement with that of capitalist society and minimising the struggle that existed between both.[54]

Labriola offered a more elaborate defence of syndicalism on the second day the congress assembled when he spoke, as Joyce reported, 'with extraordinarily rapid eloquence for two hours and a half'.[55] He responded, in the first place, to an attack by Oddino Morgari, author of the famous phrase, 'Integralism is a mood rather than a concept', by which Morgari meant that integralism was an expedient, rather than a set of co-ordinated doctrines, to unify the various factions of the socialist party. Labriola said that Morgari's integralism was as eclectic and as equivocal as was Ferri's, who had, the day before, announced the equally confusing slogan, 'We are for reforms against reformism and for syndicates against syndicalism.' Labriola then repudiated what Morgari referred to as 'anarchist degeneracy' in three aspects of syndicalist thought. He countered the first accusation (the inordinate use of the general strike) by referring to the successful 1904 strike and the less successful one in 1905 as being the only instances of such action. To the criticism of his policy of making the trade unions a kind of 'antistate', Labriola responded that syndicalism was an internal movement affirming its autonomy against all external authorities, political and economic. To the charge of corporate degeneracy, he enunciated that the general strike was a symbol of the overthrow of capitalism, and an effective means of fostering the revolutionary spirit among proletariats. It ensured that socialism was a working class, economic and revolutionary phenomenon. The general strike was not a manifestation of ordinary politics, but an abbreviated formula of social revolution.

Labriola then proceeded to tackle the question of the 'intellectuals'. Joyce wrote that he 'attacked' them.[56] Labriola, in fact, attacked the intellectuals as such, but maintained that there existed a place for the socialist intellectual in the proletarian movement. What distinguished the intellectual from the socialist intellectual, Labriola explained, consisted merely in co-ordinating the intellectual's activity towards that of the proletariat. Socialism could not accommodate intellectuals as such. Working class society could not accept parasites, nor could it welcome unproductiveness. The intellectual could only exist in working class society by renouncing his parasitism and making his every thought an instrument for proletarian interests.[57] Joyce had misinterpreted Labriola's ban on non-socialist intellectuals as a general indictment of the group.*

Despite Labriola's brilliant defence, the integralist motion,

* 'A Painful Case' mirrors this divergence in interests between the socialist intellectual and the socialist worker. Mr Duffy claims he left the meetings of an Irish

supported by the reformists, proved victorious in the ballot. The party as a whole preferred to steer a middle course between the policies of the reformists and those of the syndicalists. In the end, the congress adopted four major resolutions. In the first place, the socialist party agreed to use legal means to carry out their revolutionary aims, and to hold in abeyance the use of violence for those circumstances when the ruling classes thwarted legal action. Better conditions for workers would be achieved through social legislation and, if necessary, through the general strike. The socialists reaffirmed their anti-militarism and called for the eventual abolition of the army. Finally, as to parliamentary tactics, it was agreed that a socialist party should not, in principle, support the policies of a bourgeois government, but that if an exceptional situation arose, the parliamentary group should act in accordance with the decision of the majority of party delegates.[58] This policy of the centre, which contained something for everyone, did not solve the issues raised during the debate, but provided instead a working compromise. The same issues would re-emerge at the next party congress in 1908.

Joyce did not express his reaction to the congressional results. He did inform his brother, however, that

As a result of the socialist congress the two sub-editors of the *Avanti!* resigned. Ferri replaced them by Cicotti, formerly editor of the *Lavoratore* of Trieste and – Labriola, who is to be German correspondent of the paper. The funny part is that the two who resigned are members of the party of which L is the head.[59]

These two members were Paolo Orano★ and Virgilio Panella.[60] Ferri's appointment of Labriola was another example of his political tact, for he did not wish to alienate syndicalists completely from the party.

Syndicalism arose in part as a protest against the encroachments of

---

Socialist Party because 'The workmen's discussions were too timorous; the interest they took in the question of wages was inordinate. He felt that they were hard-featured realists and that they resented an exactitude which was the product of a leisure not within their reach' (123) (*111*).

★ When the *Fiera Letteraria* invited Joyce, as a representative of Ireland, in 1928 to give a lecture in Florence, Joyce wrote to Paolo Orano, who had become an ardent Fascist by this time, that James Stephens should take his place (III. 177). There may be a disguised reference to Orano under the name of Paul Horan in *Finnegans Wake* (49.15).

the State. Trade-unionists rejected social-democratic theories of the primacy of political action, substituting it with the measure of the general strike, or what they called the 'general lock-out of the capitalist class'. This aspect of syndicalist theory which advocated 'antistatism' took its origins from the anarchism represented by Bakunin and Proudhon. The syndicalists, like the anarchists, opposed the creation of a Workers' State to replace that run by capitalists. They considered the state to be a tool of capitalist oppression and that as such it should be abolished along with the capitalist order. The syndicalists aimed to establish in its place a social order based on the organisation of workers in production units. The great majority of Italian socialists, like Ferri, resisted syndicalism however, because their policy proved to be a political liability. Anarchists were mainly looked upon as terrorists on account of the recent wave of assassinations between 1890 and 1901, such as those of King Humbert II in Italy and of President McKinley in the United States. The Italian socialists, therefore, did not want to be associated in any way with the anarchists or their doctrine,★ because they feared the adverse political effects such an alliance would incur. Joyce followed closely the activities of the violent left wing. He informed Stanislaus from Rome,

> I hear a report that there was a third bomb thrown today in the Piazza di Spagna. I hardly think these can be the work of the anarchists. They are very clumsily made and do no damage. It may be a trick of the police to justify them in making arrests on suspicion as the King of Greece is to be here in a few days. I hope to Jesus he won't pass by this building during his visit as there might be a serious explosion.[61]

He repudiated the violent tactics of the anarchists, which were similar to the dynamite outrages of the Fenians, outright. At the same time he was not blind to the supralegal manoeuvres that were adopted to thwart them.

The importance of the Italian socialist congress in Joyce's political development is usually underestimated,[62] or altogether overlooked. Joyce's conclusions about socialism determined how he viewed the political situation in Ireland to a greater extent than has been

---

★ Ferri was fond of quoting Sorel's statement that the syndicalists were anarchists because they encouraged the proletariat not to participate in bourgeois politics (*Avanti!*, 2 September 1906).

generally acknowledged. In the first place, the anti-parliamentarianism of the syndicalists led Joyce to comment that Labriola 'reminds me somewhat of Griffith.'[63] Griffith's Sinn Féin movement was not a party as such, but a loose organisation which, like the syndicalists, denounced parliamentary activity as ineffectual. Joyce's choice of Labriola over Ferri indicated his impatience with gradualism, whether in Irish or in Italian politics. Griffith's movement did not come to grips with the social question,* however, and for Joyce this was the most pressing issue. He was drawn to syndicalism because Labriola planned to hasten the automatic emergence of the proletariat. Joyce considered this principle to be the key one, and he exhorted Stanislaus to see his point:

> You have often shown opposition to my socialistic tendencies. But can you not see plainly . . . that a deferment of the emancipation of the proletariat, a reaction to clericalism or aristocracy or bourgeoisism would mean a revulsion to tyrannies of all kinds.[64]

The nationalists limited themselves to combating only one form of tyranny – that of the foreign conqueror. Joyce saw instead 'tyrannies of all kinds' holding Ireland captive, and it was precisely these tyrannies that he determined to oppose in his works.

---

* See below, pp. 127–8.

Chapter 3

Perspectives: Socialism and Anarchism

1 'A Portrait of the Artist'

In *A Portrait of the Artist as a Young Man*, as has become clear, Stephen rejects spiritual and secular authorities in order to discover and achieve his own identity. His rebellion is associated with the principle of individual freedom. In the first version of 'A Portrait of the Artist',[1] Joyce had asserted this principle in a tone which is at once more radical and more openly defiant than in the final text. Joyce proclaimed that, after annihilating and rebuilding experience out of his life, the artist emerges with a single purpose – to reunite 'the children of the spirit' against 'fraud and principality'. His task is not that of abnegation alone, since 'a thousand eternities were to be reaffirmed' against Church and State. Poets are the voice of liberty, as Walt Whitman declared in his Preface to the *Leaves of Grass*, and their aim is 'to cheer up slaves and horrify despots.'[2] The unnamed hero of Joyce's piece rebukes his contemporaries for hazarding 'the extremes of heterodoxy' only where 'the social monster' permitted. The 'social monster' may allude to Hobbes's 'Leviathan', or sovereign civil power, but it is clear from the context that Joyce also means the Church. The artist's revenge consisted in railing at the 'emancipates' – that is, the pseudo-liberated – and in isolating himself from them. 'Reculer pour mieux sauter': he withdraws in order to prepare a new onslaught.

Joyce indicates that this forthright manner characterised his early rebelliousness, especially against the Church: 'His Nego . . . was written amid a chorus of peddling Jews' gibberish and Gentile clamour, was drawn up valiantly while true believers prophesied fried atheism and was hurled against the obscene hells of Our Holy Mother.'* This 'Nego', which anticipates Stephen's 'non serviam',

* The Catholic Church.

is the artist's battle-cry in much the same way that Zola's 'J'accuse' had alerted the public against injustice in the Dreyfus case. The artist no longer relies on such outspokenness, however, to achieve his ends: 'but, that outburst over, it was urbanity in warfare', or what Richard Ellmann has termed 'obliquity'.[3] As Stephen put it in *Stephen Hero* (151) (*146*), 'The attitude which was constitutional with him was a silent self-occupied, contemptuous manner and his intelligence, moreover, persuaded him that the tomahawk, as an effective instrument of warfare, had become obsolete.' Indirectness was part of 'the enigma of a manner' which he set himself upon to shield his heroism: 'His reluctance to debate scandal, to seem curious of others, aided him in his real indictment and was not without a satisfactory flavour of the heroic.' Urbanity would eradicate 'old tyranny' in favour of a 'mature civilization', which Joyce describes in the peroration:

> Already the messages of citizens were flashed along the wires of the world, already the generous idea had emerged from a thirty years' war in Germany and was directing the councils of the Latins. To those multitudes, not as yet in the wombs of humanity but surely engenderable there, he would give the word: Man and woman, out of you comes the nation that is to come, the lightening of your masses in travail; the competitive order is employed against itself, the aristocracies are supplanted; and amid the general paralysis of an insane society, the confederate will issues in action.

This vision might be understood as a democratic one, like that described by Walt Whitman in his poem, 'Years of the Modern':

> I see not America only, not only Liberty's nation but other
>   nations preparing,
> I see tremendous entrances and exits, new combinations,
>   the solidarity of races,
> I see that force advancing with irresistible power on the
>   world's stage, . . .
> I see Freedom, completely arm'd and victorious and very
>   haughty, with Law on one side and Peace on the other,
> A stupendous trio all issuing forth against the idea of caste;

What historic denouements are these we so rapidly
   approach?
I see men marching and countermarching by swift millions,
I see the frontiers and boundaries of the old aristocracies
   broken,
I see the landmarks of European kings removed,
I see this day the People beginning their landmarks.[4]

In *Democratic Vistas*, which Joyce had in his library, Whitman
declared the purpose of democracy to be that of 'supplanting old
belief in the necessary absoluteness of established dynastic rulership,
temporal, ecclesiastical, and scholastic.'[5] The 'generous idea',
however, is not democracy but socialism. Joyce disclosed the kind of
socialism he was referring to on the last pages of this same first draft
in the following memorandum: 'Our vanguard of politicians put up
the banners of anarchy and communism; our artists seek the simplest
liberation of rhythms.'
   Joyce alludes to the peculiar way in which the notion of 'liberation'
coincides in art and in politics. For instance, Whitman's preoccupation with liberating verse from its conventional metrical patterns
in order to create 'free verse', corresponded to his political aim of
opening up democratic vistas. Joyce, however, understood his art to
have shared the revolutionary aim of emancipating the masses with
the *avant-garde* movements in politics. This alliance of political and
artistic radicalism, as representative of advanced opinion in the two
spheres of artistic and social thought, can be traced back to the 1870s
in France. The symbolist revolution in literature, ushered in by
Rimbaud, divided poetry into the formal or conventional and the
experimental or *avant-garde*. Rimbaud linked his aesthetic ideas with
his revolutionary political views, since he joined the insurrection
against Prussian occupation troops in 1871 which set up the short-
lived Paris Commune. The vanguard in art, as Renato Poggioli has
pointed out, originally remained subordinate to the ideals of political
radicalism.[6] Joyce, however, did not countenance the view that art
should hold second place to politics. To alter the minds of men
required the utmost delicacy in yoking together effectively the
materials that constitute art: 'For the artist the rhythms of phrase and
period, the symbols of word and allusion, were paramount things.'
Well-thought-out political opinions must tally with deftness in
artistic execution. Both ingredients are crucial, since it is the nuance

of his phrasing that will determine the success or failure of the artist's enterprise.

In his conclusion to this first draft, Joyce envisages a utopian future of socialistic enlightenment. If by the 'thirty years' war in Germany' is meant the period from 1875,[7] when factional rivalry was ended by the fusion of the Eisenach and Lassallean parties at the Gotha Congress, then Joyce is pointing to the outgrowth of the socialist movement into anarchy and communism. Marx, for example, released a pungent *Critique of the Gotha Programme* (1875), from which Joyce seems to have borrowed more than a turn of phrase.* In speaking of 'those multitudes, not as yet in the wombs of humanity but surely engenderable there', and of the 'masses in travail', Joyce is adapting Marx's description of a future communist society

> not as it has *developed* in its own foundations, but, on the contrary, just as it *emerges* from capitalist society; which is thus in every respect, economically, morally and intellectually, still stamped with the birth marks of the old society from whose womb it emerges.

The 'competitive order' which is arrayed against itself, then, is capitalist society.†

The socialism directing the 'councils of the Latins' was not entirely Marxist though. The First International Workingmen's Association, founded in 1864, was a loose federation of independent workers' organisations from various countries. Its members adhered mainly to the trends of socialism represented by Marx and by Bakunin. Marx wanted the workers to be organised politically with a view to conquering the state. Bakunin opposed this strategy of replacing contemporary political systems with centralised socialism, claiming that Marx wanted to impose a more rigid authoritarianism than that which he intended to supplant. Bakunin, as well as anarchists generally, characterised politics as involving either the exercise or restraint of power. The anarchists distinguished between 'society' and the 'state'. They argued that the state produced an authoritarian and bureaucratic society which stifled individual initiative and

---

* See below, p. 127 for Joyce's view of *Das Kapital*.

† Inequalities are inevitable in the new order, Marx maintained, since it 'has just emerged after prolonged birth pangs from capitalist society' (*Critique of the Gotha Programme* (Peking, 1972), pp. 15–7).

spontaneity. Man's natural social tendencies were best expressed in voluntary associations. For the anarchists 'social man' takes precedence of 'political man'. Marx apparently took Bakunin's charges into account later in his *Critique of the Gotha Programme*, since he tried to make it clear in this document for the first time that he did not accept the state in itself, and that he also advocated voluntary associations as the best way of achieving ultimate freedom.[8] Bakunin, however, was not content to witness the gradual withering-away of the proletarian State promised by Marx, and proposed instead that such an instrument of bourgeois oppression be annihilated at once. This conflict in principle led to a power struggle between Marx and Bakunin which reached a climax at the Hague Congress of the First International held in September 1872. Bakunin had the support of most of the Latin countries, but Marx controlled the directorate of the International, known as the General Council. Although the majority at the congress supported the stand of the General Council led by Marx, and expelled Bakunin, the growing anti-Marxist element was a force to be reckoned with. France and Switzerland were divided in their loyalty to Marx, while Italy and Spain represented Bakuninist strongholds. Marx's astonishing proposal that the General Council should be transferred from London to New York was accepted with the result that the International quickly died from inactivity. Anarchism, however, continued as a formidable influence, especially in the Latin countries.

The anarchists, like Bakunin, fascinated Joyce because, whereas Marx dictated an impersonal class warfare, they sought to liberate the individual from those forces that smothered human potentialities. This point of view coincided with Joyce's aim of liberating 'from the personalised lumps of matter that which is their individuating rhythm',* and of supplanting the aristocracies through his art. The artist's 'word', then, is not only tinged with Marxist ideology, but it is also delivered in the anarchist spirit by subordinating immediate political success to the fashioning of a 'new man' in the womb of the old society.[9] It contains a Joycean nuance too, since it calls for a new man *and* woman; it is not only a manifesto, but, in the language of *Finnegans Wake*,† a 'mamafesta' as

---

* Or, in the words of *A Portrait* (174) (*170*), 'he would create proudly out of the freedom and power of his soul, as the great artificer whose name he bore, a living thing, new and soaring and beautiful, impalpable, imperishable.'

† Joyce plays with the various interpretations, including the Freudian and the

well. In the completed *A Portrait of the Artist as a Young Man* (80) (78), Stephen links his art with the writings of these revolutionaries: 'All the leisure which his school life left him was passed in the company of subversive writers whose gibes and violence of speech set up a ferment in his brain before they passed out of it into his crude writings.' Joyce never loses sight of a conspiratorial element in the art he proposes to achieve.

2   Stephen Hero

Joyce's knowledge of anarchist literature was extensive and Herbert Gorman noted that 'among the many whose works he had read may be mentioned Most, Malatesta, Stirner, Bakunin, Kropotkin, Elisée Reclus, Spencer and Benjamin Tucker'.[10] Joyce's library in Trieste indicates that he also read Proudhon, the first to declare himself openly to be an anarchist. In addition he had with him Paul Eltzbacher's *Anarchism* (published by Benjamin Tucker) in translation, a pioneer survey of the various trends of anarchist thought which included chapters on William Godwin and Tolstoy.

The popular image of the anarchist, cultivated by such works as Conrad's *The Secret Agent*, is that of a cruel, bearded, wild-eyed, bomb-throwing revolutionary. And indeed the anarchists engaged in 'propaganda by the deed', the use of assassination as a political weapon, and other criminal activities at the turn of the century. Dostoevsky, in *The Possessed*, described the desperate attempts by the Russian terrorist Nechayev (who had fascinated Bakunin) to make a clean sweep of the whole social order; and Turgenev used Bakunin himself as a model for *Rudin*, his first novel. Not all classes of anarchists, however, advocated the policy of propaganda by the deed. Tolstoy, Proudhon and Benjamin Tucker deprecated its use and espoused pacifism instead. Tucker proposed passive resistance as a more suitable tactic, and Tolstoy related non-resistance to evil by violence to Christian ethics. Violence can be overcome only by a moral revolution; that is, by the triumph of the Christian conscience in mutual co-operation and in loving each other. Tolstoy also declared that such a commitment implied the renunciation of State authority: 'A man who conditionally promises in advance to submit to laws which are made and will be made by men, by this very

Marxist, of Anna Livia's untitled mamafesta in *Finnegans Wake* (114–16).

promise renounces Christianity.'[11] In this way, the improbable combination of anarchism and pacifism was realised.

Anarchism exerted an important doctrinal influence on the socialist movement, as well as on liberal philosophies. As a political philosophy it refuted all social forms which rest on the basis of coercive authority. In particular, the anarchists maintained that the State, with its countless burdens and restraints, thwarted personal liberty. Like anarchism, liberalism expressed a similar concern for the value of individual freedom. Joyce showed an interest in liberalism too, and possessed a copy of John Stuart Mill's *On Liberty*, published in 1859, a classic attack on 'tyrannical majorities' in democracies. Mill argued that the activities of the State and the function of government should be reduced to a minimum:

> A government cannot have too much of the kind of activity which does not impede, but aids and stimulates, individual exertion and development. The mischief begins when, instead of calling forth the activity and powers of individuals and bodies, it substitutes its own activity for theirs; when, instead of informing, advising, and upon occasion, denouncing, it makes them work in fetters, or bids them stand aside and does their work instead for them. The worth of a State, in the long run, is the worth of individuals composing it; and a State which postpones the interest of *their* mental expansion and elevation to a little more of administrative skill, or of that semblance of it which practice gives in the details of business; a State which dwarfs its men, in order that they may be more docile instruments in its hands even for beneficial purposes – will find that with small men no great thing can really be accomplished; and that the perfection of machinery to which it has sacrificed everything will in the end avail it nothing, for want of the vital power which, in order that the machine might work more smoothly, it has preferred to banish.[12]

Anarchists, on the other hand, believed that liberty without social and economic equality was impossible: 'liberty without socialism is privilege, injustice; and socialism without liberty is slavery and brutality.' Liberty could be achieved only by abolishing economic monopolies and political institutions.[13]

In its positive sense of an ideal, anarchism did not denote political chaos or 'anarchy' in its commonly accepted sense, but called for a new society unimpeded by coercive elements, those represented by political, economic or religious authorities. Anarchists agreed substantially on these ultimate general aims, but proposed various tactics to ensure their success. Proudhon's mutualism was an attempt to reform society peacefully by the spreading of workers' associations devoted primarily to mutual credit between producers. The anarcho-syndicalists, like Sorel and Labriola, promoted the general strike as the weapon with which to liquidate the State and hasten the direct association of the wage-earning class. As we have seen, collectivists, like Bakunin, the geographer Reclus, and Kropotkin, did not want to place common ownership of the means of production under the control of the democratic State, as the Marxists did, but in the hands of the people through autonomous, voluntary associations. In this way they claimed the individual could realise himself more fully. The anarchist-communists, led by Errico Malatesta, while conceding the need for communal ownership, cast suspicion on mutual co-operation and free association and rejected the anti-Marxism of the collectivists. Malatesta pressed instead for the abolition not only of the State, but of governmental rule at all levels (local, regional, or national). Max Stirner and Benjamin Tucker represented the individualistic part of the anarchist movement which believed that all forms of communal organisations inevitably became authoritarian systems, and upheld the indissoluble right of the individual to resist majority decisions made without his consent.

Joyce learned from all these radicals, but his principal political authority was Benjamin Tucker, chief American exponent of individualist anarchism.[14] Joyce is reported to have said of him, 'Oh! he was the great political thinker!'[15] Tucker depicted Church and State as a 'double-headed monster' which sustained itself by keeping people 'drugged with the superstitious reverence for the fiction of authority'.[16] In his *Instead of a Book By a Man Too Busy to Write One* (1897), a title which could not have failed to please Joyce, he analysed the regimentation of society, and particularly of Irish society in 1881:

> IRELAND'S chief danger: the liability of her people – besotted with superstition; trampled on by tyranny; ground into the dust beneath the weight of two despotisms, one religious, the other political; victims, on the one hand, of as cruel a Church and, on the other, of as heartless a State as have ever blackened with ignorance or reddened with blood the records of civilized nations – to forget the wise advice of their cooler leaders, give full vent to the passions

which their oppressors are aiming to foment, and rush headlong
and blindly into riotous and ruinous revolution.[17]

Joyce found these terms applicable to Irish society in 1904 as well. He
mounted his attack on these institutions, as we have seen, in both the
first draft version and the completed *A Portrait of the Artist*.

Tucker's statements reflected Bakunin's *God and the State* (1882),
which had as keynote the repudiation of all forms of coercive
authority. Bakunin was perhaps the most eloquent as well as the
most thoroughgoing of the anarchists. In a fiery passage he
denounced 'all the tormentors, all the oppressors, and all the
exploiters of humanity – priests, monarchs, statesmen, soldiers,
public and private financiers, officials of all sorts, policemen,
gendarmes, jailers and executioners, monopolists, economists,
politicians of all shades, down to the smallest vendor of sweetmeats'.[18] But he accuses the Church and the State ('my two *bêtes
noires*', he calls them) of being the fundamental institutions of man's
enslavement. Every State has been the implement by which the few
trample on the majority. And every Church has joined forces with
the State in the subjugation of mankind.

In a youthful essay on 'Force', Joyce maintained that subjugation
of men by force is futile, and expressed a hatred of violence which
proved to be lifelong.[19] He preferred to find subjugation 'better used
than for the vain shedding of blood'. He mentioned in particular
instances where mind is pitted against force, as when the sailor
outwits the elements in order to steer his vessel safely to port. Later,
in a discussion with Frank Budgen in Zürich, Joyce spoke about
force in the political sphere. He maintained that 'government is in
the last resort the use of force.'[20] This statement recalls the attitude of
anarchists, like Tucker who claimed, 'Aggression is simply another
name for government. Aggression, invasion, and government are
incontrovertible terms. The essence of government is control, or the
attempt to control.'[21] 'The artist's method', on the other hand, 'is
persuasion', Joyce said. He argued that governments employ force,
whereas the artist relies on the efficacy of the written word.

Joyce recognised that the Church considered anarchism to be the
most pernicious threat to both the natural and supernatural orders as
ordained by its teaching. In *Stephen Hero*, which he had been writing
intermittently from 1904 to 1907, Joyce demonstrated how such a
social and political philosophy as anarchism can influence the
conception of a hero and his audience and shape artistic endeavour as

well. Stephen is described as a 'fiery-hearted revolutionary' who, in a discussion with Cranly, proclaims:

> All modern political and religious criticism* dispenses with presumptive States, presumptive Redeemers and Churches. It examines the entire community in action and reconstructs the spectacle of redemption. If you were an esthetic philosopher you would take note of all my vagaries because here you have the spectacle of the esthetic instinct in action. (191) (*186*)

The modern political criticism which dismisses both Church and State is anarchism. Deprived of legitimacy, political and religious authority is reduced to nothing more than the exercise of coercion. Stephen explains that this modern criticism 'examines and reconstructs the spectacle of redemption', a point of view put forward by Ferrero in *L'Europa giovane*, where he spoke of the similarities between Christianity and socialism. Underlying this radical perspective, Stephen stresses, is 'the spectacle of the esthetic instinct in action'. In other words, the artist as literary Messiah reconstructs the spectacle of redemption and legitimises his role of redeemer in his works by affirming that which presumptive States and presumptive Churches negate. He declares all social conventions to be incompatible with individuality:

> He wished to express his nature freely and fully for the benefit of a society which he would enrich and also for his own benefit, seeing that it was part of his life to do so. It was not part of his life to undertake an extensive alteration of society but he felt the need to express himself such an urgent need, such a real need, that he was determined no conventions of a society, however plausibly mingling pity with its tyranny, should be allowed to stand in his way, and though a taste for elegance and detail unfitted him for the part of demagogue, from his general attitude he might have been

---

* The modern religious criticism Stephen refers to may include 'modernism', a movement in Roman Catholic thought in the early 1900s until it was finally condemned by Pope Pius X in 1907. Modernists took their cue from the kind of Christology and Biblical exegesis undertaken in Germany by Frederich Strauss and in France by Ernest Renan. In his *Life of Jesus*, published in 1835, Strauss argued essentially that the Gospels were not historical documents, but only myths. The keynote of Renan's *Vie de Jésus*, published in 1863, was his rejection of the supernatural. Joyce read both of these books (II. p. 76). Similarly the modernists attempted to explain religion in terms of an immanent rather than a transcendent principle.

supposed not unjustly an ally of collectivist politicans, who are
often very seriously upbraided by opponents who believe in
Jehovahs, and decalogues and judgments with sacrificing the
reality to an abstraction. (151–2) (*146–7*)

The artist and the collectivist, then, work in tandem against all
institutions impeding the liberty of the individual.

Joyce is in league not only with the collectivists, however, but also
with the individualists who understood freedom to be essentially
self-liberation. Stirner, for example, sought the absolute independence of the person, and rejected society as well as the State. The true
'egoist', he claimed, cherishes his 'exclusiveness', and the only social
interaction he allows himself is with other 'egoists'. Although
Stephen is not a solipsist, an essential part of his temperament is the
'ineradicable egoism' which he calls 'redeemer' (39) (*34*). He
perceives that 'egoism' is intertwined with his literary task of
liberation, as well as with his urge for self-expression. His startling
declaration in *Ulysses* (*645; 748*), that 'Ireland must be important
because it belongs to me', is matched by the one made here: 'My own
mind is more interesting to me than the entire country' (249) (*248*).
His boldness recalls Stirner's sweeping assertion, 'Nothing is more
to me than myself!' We are also told that Lynch ponders 'Stephen's
unapologetic egoism, his remorseless lack of sentiment for himself
no less than for others' (156) (*151*). Stephen seems to display what
Stirner calls the indispensable quality of 'ataraxy' – of imperturb-
ability, of almost stoical indifference.[22]

This attitude might be considered merely egoistic, and indeed
Stephen is described as a 'wholehearted young egoist' (130) (*125*).
Joyce called Ibsen an egoarch,[23] and earlier had written of his 'inward
heroism'.[24] He asked Stanislaus, 'Do you not think the search for
heroics damn vulgar – and yet how are we to describe Ibsen?' He
then stated his conviction that 'the whole structure of heroism is, and
always was, a damned lie and there cannot be any substitute for the
individual passion as motive power for everything – art and
philosophy included.'[25] Tucker, who accepted Stirner's doctrine,
claimed that the anarchists were egoists 'in the farthest and fullest
sense!'[26] By this statement Tucker meant that what we usually
regard as moral obligations are in reality mere social conventions.
For this reason, anarchists

> look upon all obligations, not as moral, but as social, and even
> then not really as obligations except as these have been consciously

and voluntarily assumed. If a man makes an agreement with men, the latter may combine to hold him to his agreement; but, in the absence of such agreement, no man, as far as the Anarchists are aware, has made any agreement with God or with any other power or any other order whatsoever.[27]

Stirner had defined egoism as enlightened self-interest and Tucker, like Joyce, interpreted it to be the only motivating force in human conduct: 'As far as motive is concerned, altruism is out of the question.'[28] In other words, both Tucker and Joyce believed that the individual should not sacrifice himself for the community.

In *The Ego and His Own*, published in 1845, Stirner's amoral egoist does not seek a 'revolution' which physically eliminates the established order. Rather by his self-assertive 'insurrection' he leaves it in order to elevate himself above it:

> Revolution and insurrection must not be looked upon as synonymous. The former consists in an overturning of conditions, of the established condition or *status*, the State or society, and is accordingly a *political* or *social* act; the latter has indeed for its unavoidable consequence a transformation of circumstances, yet does not start from it but from men's discontent with themselves, is not an armed rising, but a rising of individuals, a getting up, without regard to the arrangements that spring from it. The Revolution aimed at new *arrangements*; insurrection leads us no longer to *let* ourselves be arranged, but to arrange ourselves, and sets no glittering hope on 'institutions'. It is not a fight against the established since, if it prospers, the established collapses of itself; it is only a working forth of me out of the established. If I leave the established, it is dead and passes into decay. Now, as my object is not the overthrow of an established order but my elevation above it, my purpose and deed are not a political or social but (as directed toward myself and my ownness alone) an *egoistic* purpose and deed.
>
> The revolution commands one to make *arrangements*, the insurrection demands that he *rise* or *exalt himself*.[29]

Stephen, similarly, will not overthrow those authorities which encroach upon his individual liberty, or subjugate the ego. Institutions exist because of voluntary servitude and, as he tells Lynch, 'A Church is not a fixture like Gibraltar: no more is an institution. Subtract its human members from it and its solidity becomes less evident. I, at least, will subtract myself' (239) (*233*). Stephen's individual rebellion is a working forth of himself out of the established. Stirner interpreted God's cause to be an egoistic one as well: 'Should God take up the cause of truth if he were not himself truth?'[30] Consequently, God devotes himself, according to Stirner, only to himself. The egoist in Stirner's sense is godlike just as the artist in *A Portrait* is godlike. Their aim, apparently, is not a committed political or social act. Stirner calls his purpose egoistic, Stephen esthetic, but both have far-reaching political implications.

Mr Duffy in 'A Painful Case' also embodies this principle of egoism, for he had 'neither companions nor friends, church nor creed. He lived his spiritual life without any communion with others' (121) (*109*). He suffers from the 'soul's incurable loneliness': 'We cannot give ourselves, it said: we are our own' (124) (*111*). Joyce indicates that egoism, when it becomes solipsistic, is harmful, a deprivation of life. In *Ulysses* Stephen asks himself 'Who helps to believe? *Egomen*' (*214; 275*). In other words, he who helps me believe is 'I, myself' (Joyce probably means *egomet*). It is conceivable that Joyce also had Stirner in mind when he described Shem as 'self exiled in upon his ego' (184), as opposed to the banishment of egoism and the sacrifice of self for the community advocated in Campanella's *Città del sole*, which appears as 'Heliotropolis' in *Finnegans Wake* (594). Like Shem, the artist in *Stephen Hero* is estranged from the world in which he moves and (as with Lermontov's *A Hero of Our Time*) there is considerable irony implicit in the title of the work.

Stephen proceeds to devise a revolutionary aesthetic corresponding to modern political theory. He terms his unpopular manifesto 'the first of my explosives' (86) (*81*), since it comes as a bombshell to those of his classmates like Moynihan who, in his first inaugural address before the college debating society, maintained that 'the true way to better the lot of the working classes was not by teaching them to disbelieve in a spiritual and material order, working together in harmony' but by taking refuge in Christ and the Church (177) (*172*). Other speakers 'praised the work done by the Jesuits in training the youth of Ireland for the higher walks of life.' Stephen, on the other hand, despises the Jesuits for being

> in the habit of attaching to their order the souls of thousands of the insecurely respectable middle-class by offering them a refined asylum, an interested, a considerate confessional, a particular

amiableness of manners which their spiritual adventures in no way entitled them. (125) (*119–20*)

He also refuses to subscribe to the programme of the patriots, as we have seen, and this refusal resulted in a theory of art that was at once 'severe and liberal' (81) (*77*). Art is a subtle tool and, alluding to Shelley, Stephen argues that 'society is itself . . . the complex body in which certain laws are involved and overwrapped and he therefore proclaimed as the realm of the poet the realm of these unalterable laws' (82–3) (*78*). In other words, the poet concerns himself with the universal and permanent forms of value. If these laws at work in society remain constant, the circumstances in which they operate, however, do change. The poet must search for new modes of art to reflect this change since the old forms are played out, consigned by their conventions to the past. The value of art cannot be judged by its fidelity to conventions. Rather, the poet is the intense centre of the life of his age by breaking away from tradition, from regular forms. Such an artistic creed might have led Stephen to accept a 'spiritual anarchy' in literature, but he insists paradoxically on a 'classical' style.★ By classical Stephen does not allude to the art of Athens and Rome, the Italian Renaissance or any other particular age. He declares that 'Classicism is not the manner of any fixed age or of any fixed country: it is a constant state of the artistic mind. It is a temper of security and satisfaction and patience' (83) (*78*). The classical temper, in opposition to the romantic,† which produces unsubstantial images, focuses on the local and the concrete only to go

---

★ Stephen's statement appears paradoxical because 'neo-classicism' in the modern period tends to be associated with conservatism. Writers like Pound and Eliot are described as 'neo-classicists' even though they revived older linguistic norms in order to write 'new' poetry. Their technical innovations and experiments with theories of language and form can scarcely be called traditional. Joyce, therefore, was not in an exceptional situation. He faced the common problem of the modern artist in trying to reconcile the old and the new. In any case, the stress on 'classical' order and discipline in literature led Yeats, Pound, Lewis and Eliot to demand the same in politics. They rejected the ideals of democracy in favour of fascism. Joyce's artistic theory implied a political orientation different from that of his contemporaries. He challenged, as I will try to show, the 'paternalistic' society in Ireland presided over by British and Catholic authorities. He had no sympathy for fascism either (see pp. 227 ff.).

† Joyce did not adhere strictly to the characteristic divergences between classicism and romanticism. Stephen, for instance, will not conform to established social norms – a 'classical' trait – but instead rebels against them, in a typical 'romantic' attitude. It is apparent from the paper he reads before the college society that the qualities of both 'tempers' are necessarily present in every work of art. What Stephen seems to be

beyond them. The secret of artistic success consists in disentangling 'the subtle soul of the image from its mesh of defining circumstances most exactly and re-embody it in artistic circumstances chosen as the most exact for it in its new office' (82) (77). Classicism, then, becomes a controlling principle, a method of selecting images, of giving order and form to ordinary experience.

Stephen takes up his position all the more ardently since he imagines that it had been put 'under ban' (39) (*34*). What sets the 'modern' artist apart from his predecessors, who also deciphered these 'unalterable laws', is his reluctance 'to give pledges' (209) (*204*), and his reluctance to make or accept 'absolute statements' (210) (*205*). The modern spirit is characterised by its speculative approach, by its ruthless examination of social and political phenomena. This tendency to anatomise phenomena leads Stephen to apply the epithet 'vivisective' to the modern spirit in order to distinguish it from the ancient or 'category-burdened' spirit (209) (*204*):

> The modern spirit is vivisective. Vivisection itself is the most modern process one can conceive. The ancient spirit accepted phenomena with a bad grace. The ancient method investigated law with the lantern of justice, morality with the lantern of revelation, art with the lantern of tradition. But all these lanterns have magical properties: they transform and disfigure. The modern method examines its territory by the light of day. Italy has added a science to civilisation by putting out the lantern of justice and considering the criminal in production and in action. (190–1) (*186*)

In adhering to this modern principle, Stephen alludes to Cesare Lombroso, whose positivistic theories, by their reliance on the scientific observation of social phenomena, opposed any kind of metaphysical explanation for criminal behaviour. Lombroso believed instead that criminal behaviour depended on tendencies determined by the physical constitution of the delinquent. The structures of this constitution would be analysed by the science of criminal anthropology, which minimised the moral responsibility of the offender and concentrated on the effect produced on him by his environment. Lombroso emphasised society's duty to reform the criminal rather than to protect itself against him. His writings

---

calling for is a fusion of classical vigour and patience to the intense romantic imagination (see also *CW*, pp. 73–83).

exerted a great influence on many of the notable advocates of Italian socialism. And Joyce also found himself defending Lombroso's criminological theories in a 'socialistic outburst' against one of the clerks with whom he worked in Rome.[31]

This vivisective spirit arising out of socialism, according to Joyce, marks the uprooting of feudal principles.[32] As a literary artist, Stephen professes a fierce 'scorn for the rabblement' and 'contempt for authority' (127) (*122–3*), in contrast to his docile companions who 'respected spiritual and temporal authorities, the spiritual authorities of Catholicism and of patriotism, and the temporal authorities of the hierarchy and the government' (178) (*172–3*). He upbraids his contemporaries for still clinging to medieval ideas of political and social structure. To Aquinas, for example, the State consisted of a 'corpus politicum et morale', a body politic with moral ends. The 'corpus mysticum' or Mystical Body of the Church, on the other hand, represented its supernatural counterpart. The feudalism embraced by Dublin society can also be explained in terms of what John of Salisbury called the 'Christian commonwealth', a body, 'endowed with life by the benefit of divine favour' with the prince as its head, and the priesthood as its soul.[33] Stephen expands the feudal idea by including patriotism with Catholicism. In *A Portrait of the Artist*, Stephen detects this feudal attitude in Davin, whose

> nurse had taught him Irish and shaped his rude imagination by the broken lights of Irish myth. He stood towards this myth upon which no individual mind had ever drawn out a line of beauty and to its unwieldy tales that divided themselves as they moved down the cycles in the same attitude as towards the Roman catholic religion, the attitude of a dull-witted loyal serf. Whatsoever of thought or of feeling came to him from England or by way of English culture his mind stood armed against in obedience to a password. (184) (*181*)

Stephen is determined to launch single-handedly an anarchistic attack on these 'spiritual' authorities, as well as, if he can, to smash the feudal machinery installed by the English and perpetuated by the Catholic Church.

In wanting to subvert the feudal order in Ireland, Joyce followed the precedent of Michael Davitt in *The Fall of Feudalism in Ireland* (1904), a book Joyce had with him in Trieste. Davitt took over Richard Cobden's characterisation of Ireland as the only nation where feudalism 'with its twin monopolies, landed and ecclesiastical' was still in power. Davitt described the plight of the Irish peasantry as a battle waged against internal and external forces of what he termed the 'feudal garrison'.[34] In *Ulysses* we are told that Bloom had supported the agrarian policy of Davitt. In particular,

> When the evicted tenants' question, then at its first inception, bulked largely in people's minds though, it goes without saying, not contributing a copper or pinning his faith absolutely to its dictums, some of which wouldn't exactly hold water, he at the outset in principle, at all events, was in thorough sympathy with peasant possession, as voicing the trend of modern opinion, a partiality, however, which, realising his mistake, he was subsequently partly cured of, and even was twitted with going a step further than Michael Davitt in the striking views he at one time inculcated as a backtothelander. (*656–7; 764*)

One of the reasons why Bloom resented 'the innuendo put upon him' by the pugnacious, supposedly patriotic Citizen was because of these radical views he once held. Davitt's plans were, as George Moore's *Parnell and His Ireland* makes clear,[35] a form of agrarian socialism.

By allegedly going a step further as a 'backtothelander', Bloom must have advocated a more extreme policy than Davitt's. The formidable example of Tolstoy who, though an upper-class landowner, dressed as a peasant for most of his life in order not to lose touch with his native soil and traditions, was much in Joyce's mind at this time. Joyce may have been prompted to impart such views to his own hero by Levin in *Anna Karenina* (a book he immensely admired) who shares Bloom's sympathy for the peasantry. Levin, moreover, while deriving his strength from contact with the soil also develops his own theories of agricultural management.

Benjamin Tucker, writing in 1881, at the height of the land agitation movement, discounted violent revolution as the solution to Ireland's fight against the twin despotisms of Church and State. He claimed that Ireland's true order was the Land League,

> the nearest approach, on a large scale, to perfect Anarchistic organization that the world has yet seen. An immense number of local groups, scattered over large sections of two continents separated by three thousand miles of ocean; each group

autonomous, each free; each composed of varying numbers of individuals of all ages, sexes, races, equally autonomous and free; each inspired by a common, central, purpose; each supported entirely by voluntary contributions; each obeying its own judgment; each guided in the formation of its judgment and the choice of its conduct by the advice of a central council of picked men, having no power to enforce its orders except that inherent in the convincing logic of the reasons on which the orders are based; all coordinated and federated, with a minimum of machinery and without sacrifice of spontaneity, into a vast working unit, whose unparallelled power makes tyrants tremble and armies of no avail.[36]

Tucker's description of the Land League as a non-violent anarchistic oganisation must have fascinated Joyce. Tucker's understanding of the movement transcended Davitt's vision, just as Bloom's views apparently did. Joyce may have had Tucker's anarchistic version of the Land League in mind as a more extreme policy than Davitt's agrarian socialism.*

Although Davitt is overshadowed by Parnell in his work, Joyce may have based some of his political opinions on *The Fall of Feudalism in Ireland*. For example, Davitt provides a background to Joyce's anarchist attack upon ecclesiastical and imperial powers when he places responsibility for the Great Famine on the 'political and spiritual governors of the people': 'Both authorities preached law and order – one by coercion, soldiers, police and evictions; the other in homilies, sermons and denunciation.'[37] He believed, as Joyce did, that the success of the national cause depended on the overthrow of the secular power of the Catholic hierarchy.[38]

Davitt, like Joyce, also claimed that England and the Vatican connived against Irish interests. The famous incident of the Parnell tribute Davitt saw as a prime instance in which Rome was made a 'cat's paw' by England. England's 'traditional conduct' towards Ireland was always to use the 'Catholicity of the country . . . as a

---

* Tucker's explanation for the failure of the Land League did not prove as congenial. He claimed the peasants were acting blindly in obedience to 'leaders who betrayed them at the critical moment': 'Had the people realized the power they were exercising and understood the economic situation, they would not have resumed the payment of rent at Parnell's bidding, and today they might have been free' (*Instead of a Book*, pp. 412, 416). Joyce always claimed to the contrary that the Irish people had betrayed their leaders, especially in Parnell's case.

handmaid to coercion'.[39]* Davitt blamed Pope Adrian IV's Bull, *Laudabiliter*, as the cause of Ireland's problems, a view put forward by Joyce in 'Ireland, Island of Saints and Sages'. In this attitude Davitt may have inspired Joyce with his remarks on Ireland as a 'semi-temporal fief to the holy see':

> The greatest of all Ireland's evils and misfortunes were due to the action of one of the popes, who commissioned King Henry II of England to invade and subdue the country. 'The honour and glory of God' was, probably, the pretext of this commission. The results, unfortunately, would lead to the conclusion that the enemy of mankind's salvation, rather than the glory of our Redeemer, was more served in the acts of conquest and aggression which drew their justification from the bull of Pope Nicholas Brakespeare. Be that as it may, the secular or political effects of Roman intervention in our struggles to regain the right of nationhood of which we were thus despoiled, have generally been selfish, short-sighted, or unfair . . . no pope has ever lent direct aid, in wine or in weapons, or indirect encouragement of any kind, to the cause of an independent Irish nation.[40]

In effect, Davitt and Joyce agree that Ireland's anathema is Roman dictation.

In *Stephen Hero*, Stephen rebels against the social as well as the political norms inculcated by the Church. His rebellion leads him to cultivate 'an independence of the soul which could brook very few subjections' (116) (*111*). He denounces the bourgeois family in the form of his 'father's presumptions as the most deadly part of a tyranny, internal and external, which he determined to fight with might and main' (214) (*209*). As Stanislaus says, John Joyce represented 'feudalism' too for his artistic son.[41] Stephen finds in his godfather, Mr Fulham, the same aristocratic notions, respect for feudal distinctions and 'natural submission to what he regarded as the dispenser of these distinctions' (250) (*249*) as displayed by his father. Stephen discovers the weak point in his godfather's armour to be the fact that, like most of his countrymen, Mr Fulham was 'a

---

* The glorious exception to this rule, Davitt says, was Archbishop Croke, known as the 'Land League archbishop', whose fellow bishops described him to Pope Leo as 'a kind of Irish Garibaldi against law and authority' (*The Fall of Feudalism in Ireland*, p. 400). Bloom, it may be remembered, is ludicrously referred to as the 'Irish-Caruso Garibaldi' in 'Cyclops' (*317; 411*).

persuaded politician' (242) (*240*) who saw in 'the pride of the church the only refuge of men against a threatening democracy' (243) (*240*). Mr Fulham, moreover, had affection for 'the feudal machinery and desired nothing better than it should crush him – a common wish of the human adorer whether he cast himself under Juggernaut or pray God with tears of affection to mortify him or swoon under the hand of his mistress' (250) (*250*). Stephen detests these attitudes he regards as symptomatic of 'the pride of the burgher'. The feudal aristocracy has given way to a rural burgher class which he finds equally obnoxious.

In a discussion with Lynch (206) (*201*), Stephen also attacks the Catholic notion of marriage as being unacceptable, and he ridicules middle-class notions of sexual normality and morality exemplified by Emma's 'burgher cowardice' in flatly rejecting his straight-forward proposition (215) (*210*). Stephen also despises what he calls her 'middle-class affectations' (72) (*67*). After convincing himself that he could not locate a 'spiritual principle' or 'soul' in Emma (161) (*156*), Stephen insists that a woman should give herself freely, without his resorting to the 'simoniacal' practice of having to bargain for her body. When Lynch likens a woman's prerogative to the artist's intention of selling his verses to a public he despises, Stephen defends his position by making an unusual political statement:

> I do not want to sell my poetical mind to the public. I expect reward from the public for my verses because I believe my verses are to be numbered among the spiritual assets of the State. That is not a simoniacal exchange. I do not sell what Glynn calls the divine afflatus: I do not swear to love, honour and obey the public until my dying day – do I? A woman's body is a corporal asset of the State: if she traffic with it she must sell it either as a harlot or as a married woman or as a working celibate or as a mistress. But a woman is (incidentally) a human being and a human being's love and freedom is not a spiritual asset of the State. Can the State buy and sell electricity? It is not possible. Simony is monstrous because it revolts our notion of what is humanly possible. A human being can exert freedom to produce or accept or love to procreate or to satisfy. Love gives and freedom takes. The woman in the black straw hat gave something before she sold her body to the State; Emma will sell herself to the State but give nothing. (207) (*202–3*)

Stephen recognises the absurd side of his argument, however, for he was not 'sufficiently doctrinaire to wish to have his theory put to the test by a general revolution of society'. Still, he believed his theory not to be 'utterly impracticable' (208) (*203*).

On the national front, Stephen considers Cranly's companions as representing the rabblement 'in a stage of partial fermentation', and expresses what he objects to most in his fellow-students in addition to their heteronomy:

> They admired Gladstone . . . and they believed in the adjustment of Catholic teaching to everyday needs, in the Church diplomatic. Without displaying an English desire for an aristocracy of substance they held violent measures to be unseemly and in their relations among themselves and towards their superiors they displayed a nervous and (whenever there was question of authority) a very English liberalism . . . The memory of Terence MacManus was not less revered by them than the memory of Cardinal Cullen. (177–8) (*172–3*)

Joyce detested Gladstone, the 'moral' assassin of Parnell, and he regarded his brand of liberalism along with Vaticanism to be 'the most powerful weapons that England can use against Ireland'.[42] Nevertheless, as Stephen said earlier (57–8) (*53*), 'The watchcry was Faith and Fatherland, a sacred word in that world of cleverly inflammable enthusiasms.' Stephen believes that the Church had always betrayed the nationalist cause, and he indicates this by ironically linking the name of Terence Bellew MacManus, an Irish patriot who had taken part in the insurrection of 1848, with that of Cardinal Cullen, a fierce opponent of Fenianism. When MacManus died in San Francisco in 1861, his body was transported to Ireland by the Fenians for a patriot's burial. Cullen, who was now Archbishop of Dublin, refused to allow the funeral ceremony to be held in his diocese. In *A Portrait* (39) (*38*), John Casey refers to this incident: 'And didn't they [the bishops] dishonour the ashes of Terence Bellew MacManus?' In *Stephen Hero*, Stephen reacts to the beliefs of his fellow-students by casting himself in the image of the deer that Joyce applied to Parnell, and he 'flung them disdain from flashing antlers' (39) (*35*).

In a conversation with Madden, the 'spokesman of the patriotic party' Sinn Féin (44) (*39*), of that 'compact body of national revivalists' (43) (*38–9*), Stephen assails the British State by maintaining that there is no distinction between 'administering English Law and administering English bullets: there is the same oath of allegiance for both professions' (68) (*63*). When Madden separates the Church from the police, condemning the latter as 'aliens, traitors, oppressors of the people,' Stephen puts them in the same Bakuninist category:

> The old peasant down the country . . . says 'I'll put the priest on Tom an' I'll put the polisman on Mickey' . . . he balances the priest against the polisman and a very nice balance it is for they are both of good girth. A compensative system! (69) (*64*)

In *A Portrait of the Artist* (225) (*221*) Stephen also rails at the figure of Irish womanhood, 'a priested peasant with a brother a policeman'. Moreover, on contemplating his sister's death, Stephen finds that

> The entire apparatus of the State seemed to him at fault from its first to its last operation. No young man can contemplate the fact of death with extreme satisfaction and no young man, specialised by fate or her step-sister chance for an organ of sensitiveness and intellectiveness, can contemplate the network of falsities and trivialities which make up the funeral of a dead burgher without extreme disgust. (173) (*168*)

Joyce did not advocate complete impartiality or political indifference in *Stephen Hero*. Stephen displays a militant spirit against institutions. The social criticism is scathing and the moral judgment ponderous throughout. In this passage, for example, the funeral itself does not seem to warrant Stephen's violent reaction to it. Yet part of the 'network of falsities and trivialities' for Stephen is the formality of receiving sympathy for the death of his sister. He complains that phrases such as, 'It's a great trial for your poor mother', were always being uttered in 'the same listless monotone'. Stephen adduces the simple funeral service as another rigid function of the State as well as of the Church. The artificiality, or what Stephen later calls the 'hopeless pretence' and 'unredeemable servility' (223) (*218*) of the lives of those around him forms part of his indictment of the 'burgher' class as a whole. This socialist hatred of the middle-class is mixed with the anarchist rejection of the State.

Stephen also combats the 'burgher' notion of art as 'the poet Byron in undress pouring out verses just as a city fountain pours out water' (37) (*33*). 'He persuaded himself', on the contrary, 'that it is necessary for an artist to labour incessantly at his art if he wishes to express completely even the simplest conception and he believed that every moment of inspiration must be paid for in advance' (37) (*32–3*). The objections to this kind of art are then recorded:

> The young men in the college regarded art as a continental vice and they said in effect, 'If we must have art are there not enough subjects in Holy Writ?' – for an artist with them was a man who painted pictures. It was a bad sign for a young man to show interest in anything but his examinations or his prospective 'job'. It was all very well to be able to talk about it but really art was all 'rot': besides it was probably immoral; they knew (or, at least, they had heard) about studios. They didn't want that kind of thing in their country. Talk about beauty, talk about rhythms, talk about esthetic – they knew what all the fine talk covered. (38) (*34*)

Stephen's revolt against the parochialism of his country sounds the 'modern' note in art. André Malraux, in a different context, observed that modern art originated with the artist's repudiation of bourgeois culture.[43] Of equal importance for Stephen, in addition to the antinomy between the bourgeois and artistic spirit, is that between his aspirations and those of the Church: 'He declared for himself the life of an artist. Well! And he feared that the Church would obstruct his desire' (209) (*204–5*).

More than English liberalism, the British Government, or patriotism, therefore, the Catholic Church, upholder of an archaic faith, represents the prime obstacle to individual liberty 'for everyone knows that the Pope cannot govern Italy as he governs Ireland' (152) (*147*). The artist must generate enough force 'to propel himself out of so strong and intricate a tyranny . . . to place him beyond the region of reattraction' in order to avoid the fate of the islanders who 'entrust their wills and minds to others that they may ensure for themselves a life of spiritual paralysis' (151) (*146*). The result of Roman supremacy is

> an island in which all the power and riches are in keeping of those whose kingdom is not of this world, an island in which Caesar confesses Christ and Christ confesses Caesar that together they may wax fat upon a starveling rabblement which is bidden ironically to take to itself this consolation in hardship 'The Kingdom of God is within you'. (151) (*146*)

Stephen's allegations are twofold. He incriminates the Church for preaching that its 'kingdom is not of this world', while in actuality Ireland's temporal power and riches are in its custody. Spiritual and temporal powers, Catholic Church and British State, work in collusion, moreover, at the expense of the native inhabitants, or 'starveling rabblement'. Stephen describes Catholicism as a 'plague':

> He seemed to see the vermin begotten in the catacombs in an age of sickness and cruelty issuing forth upon the plains and mountains of Europe. Like the plague of locusts described in Callista they seemed to choke the rivers and fill the valleys up. They obscured the sun. Contempt of human nature, weakness, nervous tremblings, fear of day and joy, distrust of man and life, hemiplegia of the will, beset the body burdened and disaffected in its members by its black tyrannous lice. (198–9) (*194*)

Joyce called the Jesuits 'black lice' in a letter to Stanislaus.[44] Stephen refers as well to Cardinal Newman's novel, *Callista*, published in 1856, which is about the clash between Christianity and paganism in a third century Roman provincial town in North Africa. In a discussion at a dinner party held by Jucundus, a trinket dealer, for two intimate friends, Cornelius, a government official, expresses his fears about the spread of Christianity. Aristo, a young Greek artist, tries to quell these fears:

> 'Why in the world should you have this frantic dread of these poor scarecrows of Christians,' said Aristo, 'all because they hold an opinion? Why are you not afraid of the bats and the moles? It's an opinion: there have been other opinions before them, and there will be other opinions after. Let them alone, and they'd die away; make a hubbub, about them, and they'll spread.' 'Spread?' cried Jucundus, who was under the two-fold excitement of personal feeling and of wine, 'spread, they'll spread? Yes, they'll spread. Yes, grow, like scorpions, twenty at a birth. The country already swarms with them; they are as many as frogs or grasshoppers; they start up everywhere under one's nose, when one least expects them. The air breeds them like plague-flies; the wind drifts them like locusts. No one's safe; anyone may be a Christian; it's an epidemic. Great Jove! I may be a Christian before I know where I am. Heaven and earth! is it not monstrous?' . . .
> 'I can't deny that in Italy they *have* grown,' said Cornelius; 'they *have* grown in numbers and in wealth, and they intermarry with us. Thus the upper class becomes to a certain extent infected. We may find it necessary to repress them; but, as you would repress vermin, without fearing them.'[45]

In 'Oxen of the Sun', Stephen casts Ireland, after the coming of the English, in a somewhat similar image of sterility: 'Look forth now, my people, upon the land of beheast . . . from Pisgah . . . unto a land flowing with milk and money. But thou hast suckled me with a bitter milk: my moon and my sun thou hast quenched forever. And thou hast left me alone for ever in the dark ways of my bitterness' (*393; 514*). Defiantly, Stephen asserts the sovereignty of the individual over his own body and mind.

To offset these execrable reflections 'the Church sent an embassy of nimble pleaders into his ears' (208) (*203*). These ambassadors propose a compromise, 'to make one with us, on equal terms' (211) (*206*). They recognise that Stephen is 'the greatest sceptic concerning the perfervid enthusiasms of the patriots' because as an artist 'he had nothing but contempt for a work which had arisen out of any but the most stable mood of the mind' (209) (*204*). And these envoys also understand his artistic creed which called the modern spirit 'vivisective' (209) (*204*). But since it is a mark of the modern spirit to be shy in the presence of all absolute statements, they argue, it is conceivable that Stephen, wearing the 'thorny crown of the heretic' (209) (*205*), will not always hold these convictions. Furthermore,

> You believe in an aristocracy: believe also in the eminence of the aristocratic class and in the order of society which secures that eminence. Do you imagine that manners will become less ignoble, intellectual and artistic endeavour less conditioned, if the ignorant, enthusiastic, spiritual slovens whom we have subjected subject us? Not one of those slovens understands your aims as an artist or wants your sympathy: we, on the contrary, understand your aims and often are in sympathy with them and we solicit your support and consider your comradeship an honour. You are fond of saying that the Absolute is dead. If that be so it is possible that we are all wrong and if once you accept that as a possibility what remains for you but an intellectual disdain. With us you can exercise your contemptuous faculties when you are recognised as one of the patrician order and you will not even be obliged to grant a truce to the very doctrines, the success of which has secured you your patricianship. Make one with us. Your life will be insured from grosser troubles, your art will be safeguarded against the intrusion of revolutionary notions which no artist of whom history tells us has ever made himself champion. (210–11) (*205–6*)

The indomitable spirit of this 'acute sympathetic alien', however, refuses to submit to the 'martial mind of the Irish Church' (77) (*73*). Earlier, Stephen's fellow-students had maintained that the Church's 'exercise of authority might be sometimes questionable, its intention, never' (198) (*193*). Stephen, however, finds it impossible 'that a soul should decree servitude for its portion over which the image of beauty had fallen as a mantle' (198) (*193–4*). As an artist, he conceives himself as a being apart in every order.* He rebuffs Cranly, 'You want me . . . to toe the line with those sycophants and hypocrites in the college. I will never do so' (146) (*141*). It will be his distinction as an artist to embrace those revolutionary notions which his predecessors had feared to 'champion'. He realises that his position will make him an outlaw in the existing social and political order: still, 'The life of an errant seemed to him far less ignoble than the life of one who had accepted the tyranny of the mediocre because the cost of being exceptional was too high' (184) (*179*).

The revolution Stephen desires is not to be 'brought about by violence but gradually' (211) (*206*). Joyce stresses yet again his opposition to physical violence. Through the medium of art, the revolution will be a bloodless one; but his art will be no less trenchant for that. Stephen will try to subvert the patrician order he is pleaded to join, a goal envisaged by Joyce at the end of his early 'Portrait'. Stephen indicts the patricians of Ireland for leading lives of automatons:

> 'The toy life which the Jesuits permit these docile young men to live is what I call a stationary march. The marionette life which the Jesuit himself lives as a dispenser of illumination and rectitude is another variety of the stationary march', he tells Cranly. (191) (*187*)

Stephen impresses upon Cranly that his art will proceed from a free and noble source: 'It is too troublesome for me to adopt the manner of these slaves. I refuse to be terrorised into stupidity' (189) (*184*). And he describes how he will salvage his life from the pestilence of Catholicism:

> Exultation of the mind before joyful beauty, exultation of the body in free and confederate labours, every natural impulse towards health and wisdom and happiness had been corroded by

---

* Cf. *A Portrait* (164) (*161*): 'What had come of the pride of his spirit which had always made him conceive himself as a being apart in every order?'

the pest of these vermin. The spectacle of the world in thrall filled him with the fire of courage. He, at least, though living at the farthest remove from the centre of European culture, marooned on an island in the ocean, though inheriting a will broken by doubt and a soul the steadfastness of whose hate became as weak as water in siren arms, would live his own life according to what he recognised as the voice of a new humanity, active, unafraid and unashamed. (199) (*194*)

Stephen's fellow-students submit their bodies as well as their intellects to Catholic precepts. McCann's insistence on the necessity of living the virtue of chastity, for example, Stephen finds 'unjust and unnatural' (56) (*52*). Accordingly, he despises the company of what he calls 'those foolish and grotesque virginities' (198) (*193*). The nationalists too have surrendered themselves to this tyranny. For this reason, Stephen avows, 'The so-desired community for the realizing of which Madden sought to engage his personal force seemed to him anything but ideal and the liberation which would have satisfied Madden would by no means have satisfied him' (57) (*53*). As he tells Mr Heffernan in a later scene, 'I care nothing for these principles of nationalism. . . . I have enough bodily liberty' (249) (*247*). Through that ineradicable egoism he calls redeemer he will liberate the patricians from their intellectual and bodily slavery. The modern mind of the artist seeks to demolish this feudal machinery of vassalage, and combats its corrosive effects. Stephen comments that 'If the call to a larger and nobler life ever came to visit them they heard it with secret gladness but always they decided to defer their lives until a favourable moment because they felt unready' (178) (*173*). Stephen hopes his art will prove to be that propitious moment: 'I wish to bring to the world the spiritual renewal which the poet brings to it,' (197) (*192*) he confides to Lynch. By encompassing within his art all of life's possibilities (that is, 'To walk nobly on the surface of the earth, to express oneself without pretence, to acknowledge one's own humanity' (147) (*142*)), the artist affirms the spirit of man. Stephen, like Joyce, finds the source of this life-giving and life-sustaining force in Europe: 'he was aware of some movement already proceeding out of Europe. Of this last phrase he was fond for it seemed to him to unroll the measurable world before the feet of the islanders' (39) (*35*). His theory of art would expand the insular mentality and represented a signal, a 'trumpet-call', enkindling those around him towards liberty (53) (*49*).

In both *A Portrait* and *Stephen Hero*, Joyce registers his conviction that Ireland, dominated by the despotisms of Church and State and by the enthusiasms of patriotism, was deprived of freedom. In both these books Joyce implies that the artist's perspective will emancipate a future generation from these excesses, so that the children conceived by the daughters of the nation will no longer be imprisoned. The revolutionary ideas on which Joyce's are based are more pronounced in *Stephen Hero*. Though in a less assertive manner, these radical ideas will re-emerge in both *Dubliners* and *Ulysses*.

3 Dubliners

In *A Portrait of the Artist*, Joyce had represented the growth of a human being from infancy to young manhood. In *Dubliners*, written between 1904 and 1907, he conceived of the city itself as a human being in four stages of life: those of childhood, adolescence, maturity, and public life.[46] In contrast to the principle of freedom which governs individual growth in *A Portrait*, Dublin is depicted as an imprisoned city and person. The treatment of Irish life under all its aspects which is offered, is at once expressly political and other times only implicitly so. Joyce presents people in their relation to both nationalism and love; for him there is no discontinuity between individual and communal life. What is evinced in a situation describing love becomes a paradigm for the Irish political scene. Eveline's inability to leave Ireland in order to seek happiness and love, for instance, parallels the aggrieved inertness of parliamentary politics in 'Ivy Day in the Committee Room'. For Joyce any pattern of human relationships that involves to some extent authority, assumes a political character.

In adhering to this perspective, Joyce learned from Tolstoy, who considered the pattern of authority and submission to be a basic one in human existence. Joyce wrote to his daughter that he greatly admired Tolstoy's 'Masters and Servants' 'in spite of a little propaganda in it'.[47] Joyce surmised its message in a passage he marked out from an essay on child education by Tolstoy:

People are divided into two classes – masters and slaves; and

however much we may talk to him [the child] in words about
equality and the brotherhood of man, all conditions of his life,
from his getting up to his evening meal, show him the contrary.[48]

'Masters and Servants' (one of those 'tall stories' Anna Livia alludes
to in her monologue (427)), contrasts the greed for wealth of the
merchant Vassili and the selfless toil and service of his peasant
servant Nikita, whom Vassili continually cheats out of his wages. In
order to anticipate competitors in a sale, the master bids his servant
to drive him to a distant town in spite of a blizzard. When they
become hopelessly lost in the storm, Vassili decides to leave Nikita
behind and makes his way alone by horse. However, the heavy
snowfall reduces visibility considerably, and Vassili finds that he has
travelled in a circle back to the sleigh. Nikita, by this time slowly
freezing to death, asks his master to give the money due to him either
to his son or to his wife. At this request, Vassili experiences an
interior, spiritual conversion. He wraps his huge fur coat about them
both, and discovers for the first time the feeling of brotherly love.
Joyce probably considered the ethical view at work in Tolstoy's
story to be an admirable one, but, at the same time, it was delivered
sentimentally. The story, moreover, is written as a parable; Joyce
was determined that his stories would not be didactic. Still,
Tolstoy's message was a simple one, and it was for a similar quality
that Joyce praised another Russian writer, Vladimir Korolenko.[49]
His *Makár's Dream*, for example, presents a man who refuses to obey
the sentence passed on his life by God because of its injustice. The
simplicity of its demand for basic justice and universal tolerance
appealed to Joyce's sense of how art should work.

Joyce's message was a simple one too, but his mind moved
circuitously, and his art proceeded in the same manner. He informed
Frank Budgen, 'I want the reader to understand always through
suggestion rather than direct statement.'[50] This indirect approach
was one which Joyce shared with Turgenev. In a letter to Stanislaus,
Joyce said that after reading *Lear of the Steppes* he found Turgenev
'useful technically'.[51] He was probably referring to the dexterity
with which Turgenev discovered in local settings classical characters
like Hamlet and King Lear. Turgenev's handling of these themes
may have encouraged Joyce, who was then embarking on a similar
experiment with an Irish Ulysses, Hamlet and other figures. When
Stanislaus remarked that some of his brother's stories displayed a
Russian ability, Joyce answered, 'You probably mean a scrupulous

brute force'.[52] By this curious reply Joyce probably meant that although his method was tangential, his treatment of Ireland would, paradoxically, not be indulgent, but trenchant.* Joyce found his own point of view corroborated by some of Turgenev's writings. He singled out the *Sportsman's Notebook* to Arthur Power, remarking 'how local it was – and yet out of that germ he became a great international writer'.[53] (Turgenev declared, like Joyce, that he was a European; his 'Westernist' views clashed with the Slavophils in much the same way as Joyce opposed those who extolled an Irish Ireland.) Turgenev's book seemed an innocuous, lyrical account of wanderings in the Russian countryside. He did not sentimentalise the peasantry, but showed them at work and in their dealings with their masters. Yet by condemning nothing outright, combining compassion with reserve, Turgenev undermined the Russian social system, which he considered debasing to both masters and peasants alike. Czar Alexander II admitted that after reading the stories he never lost sight of the necessity for emancipating the serfs.† In *Dubliners*, although withholding comment, Joyce is at pains to show the citizens of Dublin as prisoners of a social system he considered ignoble. Secular and spiritual authorities are unobtrusive, but their presence none the less encloses and disables the lives of Dubliners. Joyce observed in Turgenev how a writer could be critical of prevailing structures, even subversive, without being tendentious.

In 'A Portrait of the Artist' Joyce indicated that the confederate will would have to contend with 'the general paralysis of an insane society', as manifested in the 'toy life' of docile Irishmen in *Stephen Hero*. Congruent with the surrender of the will to the Church, is the 'selling' of a woman's body to the State, the married woman and working celibate included. As Stephen tells Bloom in 'Eumaeus' (*633; 731*), their countrymen sell much more than the harlot and do 'a roaring trade': 'Fear not them that sell the body but have not power to buy the soul.' It is this trading in bodies and souls which accounts for how the city as a person in *Dubliners* can be metaphorically stricken with hemiplegia or general paralysis. The

---

* This is not to say that he would only deal with Dublin's negative aspects. In 'The Dead' Joyce underlines its positive qualities too.

† Joyce wrote to George V 'begging' the King to inform him whether he considered the reference to Edward VII in 'Ivy Day in the Committee Room' offensive to the memory of his father. The King's private secretary replied by letter that it was inconsistent 'with rule for His Majesty to express his opinion in such cases' (II, p. 292). King George V was not as forthcoming as Czar Alexander II.

word 'paralysis', therefore, becomes the key to *Dubliners* – a key both moral and political.

Gentle Maria in 'Clay' is unwittingly a servant of Church and State. As a working celibate she is a corporal asset of the State, and her frustrated longings for love and married life represent a spiritual paralysis. Mr Duffy in 'A Painful Case' is also an 'outcast from life's feast', and the joylessness of Irish life is part of Joyce's indictment. In 'Araby', Church control prohibits the young girl, identified only as 'Mangan's sister', from going to the bazaar because 'there would be a retreat that week in her convent.' This spirituality, always demanding a higher love at the expense of a mortal one, leads the young boy to evoke her name 'in strange prayers and praises', and to watch her with 'confused adoration'. The pervert in 'An Encounter' represents another form of diseased love, and the homosexual temper stood to Joyce as an example of the consequence of English public-school education.[54]* The brutality of the rigid social system in which Dubliners live is another reason why the desire for happiness remains unfulfilled. Farrington, whose wife 'bullied her husband when he was sober and was bullied by him when he was drunk', is an unknowing victim of this environment.† In 'A Boarding House', the abject submission of Bob Doran, who had once boasted of his 'free-thinking and denied the existence of God to his companions', in agreeing to a shotgun wedding on account of social pressures brings into focus a more subtle form of brutality. Bob Doran is trapped by the falsity of the so-called 'moral' environment. Eveline and Little Chandler both recognise the need to escape from this cramped atmosphere but feel powerless to propel themselves out of what Stephen called its 'intricate tyranny'. 'Paralysis', then, becomes a subtle way of expressing what in *Stephen Hero* is described crudely as the 'plague of Catholicism'.

The claims of nationality are as equally constrictive as those of religion. 'Ivy Day in the Committee Room' exposes the subservience of Irish parliamentarians to the British State which Parnell challenged. Their stagnation as a political force indicates their

---

* For example, in 1909 Joyce wrote that Oscar Wilde, 'far from being a perverted monster who sprang in some inexplicable way from the civilization of modern England, is the logical and inescapable product of the Anglo-Saxon college and university system, with its secrecy and restrictions' (*CW*, p. 204).

† In a letter to Stanislaus (II, p. 192), Joyce avowed, 'I am no friend of tyranny, as you know, but if many husbands are brutal the atmosphere in which they live (vide Counterparts) is brutal and few wives and homes can satisfy the desire for happiness.'

inability to secure legislation for Irish independence. In 'A Mother', where Mrs Kearney attempts to exploit the Irishness of the name of her daughter Kathleen for a better salary for her musical performance, Joyce exposes the affectedness of the new national forces associated with the Gaelic Revival. Mrs Kearney's demand for payment links her with the self-seeking politicians in 'Ivy Day'. Jimmy Doyle's father in 'After the Race' began as 'an advanced Nationalist' too but had to modify his views early on. His prosperity in business, it appears, can be attributed to his ability in securing police contracts. (Corley's brutality is complemented by his suspicious association with the police.) Mr Duffy's unwillingness 'to submit himself to the criticisms of an obtuse middle class which entrusted its morality to policemen and its fine art to impresarios', however, is similar to Stephen's outbursts against the burgher class in *Stephen Hero*. And the parallel between the police force and the priesthood is underlined in 'Grace',[55] where both practise their professions in a non-spiritual, perfunctory manner, subsisting on the contributions of tax-paying and churchgoing Dubliners. The priest and policeman, upholders of Church and State, combine physical and moral coercion to manacle body and soul alike.

General paralysis, therefore, stifles individual self-realisation and national aspirations. The priest who loses grip of his vocation in 'The Sisters', and the priest presented as a black sheep in 'Ivy Day', attest to the degeneration of spiritual and political life. Joyce believed that his art would counteract this spiritual and political paralysis. He interpreted his role in *Dubliners* to be once again that of redeemer. By exposing the unpromising and infelicitous lives of his countrymen, Joyce aimed to bring them to an awareness of the hemiplegic condition of the individual and of the city engendered by spiritual and secular autarchy. And he believed that the composition of *Dubliners* constituted 'the first step towards the spiritual liberation of my country'.[57]

4 Ulysses

Joyce's hopes for the spiritual liberation of his country culminated in *Ulysses*. Bloom and Stephen are not 'superfluous men', like Turgenev's estranged heroes, indulging in negative illusions, or engaging in pointless combat. Nor are they like the anarchists who opposed Church and State in their writings with vitriolic ridicule and in their lives with violence. Joyce, through the remarks of his characters, goes underground a little. In order to reform men's minds Bloom and Stephen resort not to propaganda by the deed, nor to any form of propaganda but to urbanity in warfare. The artist as revolutionary employs the 'cold steelpen' (7; 6), in Stephen's terms, not the gun. He tells Private Carr, representative of the British State, as the latter is about to punch him, 'Personally, I detest action' (589; 687). As an artist he believes in the supremacy of the word over force.

Bloom also disapproves of violent action, as exemplified in the Phoenix Park murders, and he reveals his pacifist views to Stephen: 'I resent violence or intolerance in any shape or form. It never reaches anything or stops anything. A revolution must come on the due instalments plan' (643; 745). Bloom clearly demonstrated the superiority of the word over 'force, hatred, history all that', when he defended his race against the chauvinistic Citizen. Bloom's opposition to violence also prevents him from 'slaying the suitors' in 'Ithaca'. In his discussion with Stephen, the name of Ferdinand Lassalle '(reformer, duellist)' (687; 805) was mentioned. Lassalle, a German socialist of Jewish origin immortalised in George Meredith's *The Tragic Comedians*, was killed in a duel over a love affair.* Bloom, 'the world's greatest reformer' (481; 604), dismisses 'duel by combat' (733; 866) as a means of retribution for Molly's adultery.

The Irish political situation in 1904 consisted in the conflict, as Joyce said in his lecture on Mangan, 'between my native land and the foreign powers – Anglo Saxon and Roman.'[58] In the opening chapter of *Ulysses* Stephen challenges Jesus' statement that 'A man cannot be the slave of two masters at once' (Matthew 6: 24). 'I am the servant of two masters,' he declares firmly to the Sassenach Haines, 'an English and an Italian . . . The imperial British State . . . and the holy Roman Catholic apostolic church' (20; 24). In actuality, Stephen, 'a server of a servant' (11; 12), has another master, Ireland, who wants him for odd jobs. Similarly, Joyce wrote with resentment in his essay on 'Fenianism' that Ireland 'has fulfilled what has hitherto been considered an impossible task – serving both God and Mammon, letting herself by milked by England and yet increasing Peter's pence'.[59] In a review of Lady Gregory's *Poets and Dreamers* he reiterated this view: 'Out of the material and spiritual

---

* For Joyce on Lassalle, see below, p. 127.

battle which has gone so hardly with her Ireland has emerged with many memories of beliefs, and with one belief – a belief in the incurable ignobility of the forces that have overcome her.'[60] Joyce's covert patriotism consisted in overthrowing this dual tyranny through the unrehearsed alliance between Bloom and Stephen.

The tirades against God in *God and the State* provided the springboard for Joyce's two-pronged attack. In Bakunin's view, the essence of religion is the debasement of humanity for the greater glory of God. 'God being everything,' he writes, 'the real world and men are nothing; God being truth, justice, goodness, beauty, power, and life, man is falsehood, iniquity, evil, ugliness, impotence and death. God being master, man is the slave.'[61] Even the relationship between God and man is reduced to that of master and slave, and religion signifies the negation of freedom and equality. To achieve freedom, Bakunin argues, man must put to use the two 'most precious qualities' with which he is endowed: the power to think and the desire to rebel. Human history began by an act of thought and rebellion. If Adam and Eve had remained loyal to God, humanity would have been condemned to perpetual submission. But Satan – 'the eternal rebel, the first freethinker and the emancipator of worlds' – urged them to disobey and eat of the fruit of knowledge and liberty.[62]

Stephen's 'non serviam' in *A Portrait* is political as well as spiritual. When he tells Cranly, 'I will not serve that in which I no longer believe whether it calls itself my home, my fatherland or my church' (251) (246–7), he is acting not only as Lucifer, but also as anarchist rebel. His statement leads Stephen to an anarchistic stance which regards 'all institutions and parties based on the idea of regulating social change of governmental action and man-made laws as counter-revolutionary'.[63] His demand for absolute freedom to realise his artistic aims implies anarchistic or libertarian thought. In *Ulysses*, the Church, in the form of his mother's ghost, besieges Stephen continually. Richard Rowan also recounted how 'I fought against her spirit while she lived to the bitter end. [*He presses his hand to his forehead*] It fights against me still – in here' (24) (23). Stephen, however, heroically asserts 'No, mother. Let me be and let me live' (10; 11). In a dramatic sequence at Bella Cohen's, Stephen's mother preys on the mind of her son and exhorts him to repent, but Stephen defiantly exclaims, '*Non serviam* . . . Break my spirit all of you if you can! I'll bring you all to heel!' (582; 683) For Stephen the essence of the artist as creative individual is the struggle of the imagination against subservience to external authority.

One of the anarchists who attacked the Church and the notion of God and whom Joyce mentions along with Photius and pseudo-malachi as the 'brood of mockers' (*197; 253*), was Johann Most. Most had headed a small anarchist opposition in South Germany to the fusion of the socialist parties under the Gotha Programme. In 1882 he emigrated to the USA, where he was later imprisoned for having incited the assassination of President McKinley, and quickly become the foremost exponent of conspiratorial anarchism. He advocated terrorist action against Church and State by the individual, as he made painfully clear in his pamphlet of 1885 entitled *Science of Revolutionary Warfare. Manual for instruction in the use and preparation of nitro-glycerine and dynamite, gun cotton, fulminating mercury, bombs, fuse, poisons, etc., etc.* in which he called for the extermination of the 'miserable brood', the 'reptile brood', the 'race of parasites'. His subversive activities made world news and prompted Henry James to use him as a model for the revolutionary Hoffendahl in *The Princess Cassamassima*.[64]

Most's diatribes against religion were aimed against a society in which evangelists, of the Alexander Dowie type in *Ulysses*, often commanded more newspaper space than politicians. In *The Beast of Property*, which dealt with man's voracity for wealth, he claimed that the 'priests of pulpit, press, and party' seek to destroy the intellect of the people,[65] a point taken up by Joyce in 'Aeolus'. Robert Adams argues that the German anarchist can scarcely be thought of as a mocker of the Church.[66] Joyce, however, in the passage directly beneath the sentence, 'Brood of mockers: Photius, pseudomalachi, Johann Most', paraphrases Most's satire of Christian theology in a pamphlet entitled *The Deistic Pestilence*:

That is the God of the Jewish-Christian ideology – an allwise botch, who created man perfect, without enabling him to retain that perfection – who created the devil, but still could not keep him under control. An Almighty, who damned millions of innocents for the faults of a few – who caused the deluge to destroy mankind excepting a very few with whom to start a new generation, no better than the preceding who created a Heaven for the fools who believe in the 'gospel' and a hell for the enlightened who repudiate it. A Godly Charlatan *who created himself through the Holy Ghost, and then sent himself as mediator between himself and*

*others, and who held in contempt and derided by his enemies, was nailed to
a cross, like a bat on a barndoor; who was buried – arose from the dead –
descended to hell – ascended to Heaven, and since then for eighteen
hundred years has been sitting at his own right hand to judge the living –
and the dead when the living have ceased to exist.* ★ A terrible despot!
whose history should be written in letters of blood, for it is one of
terror.[67]

He Who Himself begot, middler of the Holy Ghost, and Himself
sent himself, Agenbuyer, between Himself and others, who, put
upon His friends, stripped and whipped, was nailed like bat to
barndoor, starved on crosstree, Who let him bury, stood up,
harrowed hell, fared into heaven and there these nineteen hundred
years sitteth on the right hand of His Own Self but yet shall come
in the latter day to doom the quick and dead when all the quick
shall be dead already. (197–8; 253)

Another passage reminiscent of the irrelevant style of Most is the
parody of the Apostles' Creed in 'Cyclops' (329; 427). That Most's
radical paper, *Die Freiheit*, welcomed the Phoenix Park murders, and
the fact that Tucker engaged in a continuous debate with Most,[68]
might have also prompted Joyce to call him a 'mocker'.

Most claimed that divine history is founded on blood and terror.
Bakunin had previously argued in a similar manner about religion:

God . . . always greedy for victims of blood, sent into the world,
as an expiatory victim, his only son, that he might be killed by
men. . . . All religions are cruel, all founded on blood; for all rest
principally on the idea of sacrifice – that is, on the perpetual
immolation of humanity to the insatiable vengeance of divinity. In
this bloody mystery man is always the victim, and the priest – a
man also, but a man privileged by grace – is the divine
executioner. That explains why the priests of all religions . . .
almost always have at the bottom of their hearts . . . something
cruel and sanguinary.[69]

When Bloom sees an advertisement announcing the arrival of the
fanatical evangelist, Dr John Alexander Dowie, he is reminded of the
blood-thirstiness of God:[70]

★ My italics.

Blood of the Lamb.

. . . Are you saved? All are washed in the blood of the lamb. God wants blood victim. Birth, hymen, martyr, war, foundation of a building, sacrifice, kidney burnt-offering, druid's altars. (*151; 190*)

Bloom sees 'Religions. Christmas turkeys and geese. Slaughter of innocents' (*172; 218*) as interrelated. His thoughts on the Holy Eucharist reveal a hidden connection between that sacrament and cannibalism:

Corpus. Body. Corpse. Good idea the Latin. Stupefies them first. Hospice for the dying. They don't seem to chew it; only swallow it down. Rum idea: eating bits of a corpse why cannibals cotton to it. (*80; 99*)

Similarly, Stephen characterises God as a 'Ghoul! Chewer of corpses!' (*10; 11*) When his mother's ghost terrorises him, he exclaims 'The corpsechewer! Raw head and bloody bones!' (*581; 682*)

The concept of God as divine executioner of His Only Son is expressed as 'dio boia, hangman god' (*213; 274*) in the discussion on Shakespeare in 'Scylla and Charybdis'.* Bakunin declared, 'Until now all human history has been only a perpetual and bloody immolation of millions of poor human beings in honor of some pitiless abstraction – God, country, power of State.' He claimed that the masses were being prodded to continual self-sacrifice to one of those 'devouring abstractions, the vampires of history, ever nourished upon human blood'.[71] Joyce also feared those big words which make us so unhappy. In 'Proteus' (*47–8; 60*), the hangman god is transformed in Stephen's mind into the 'pale vampire', death, who comes like the Flying Dutchman in a phantom ship with 'his bat sails bloodying the sea, mouth to her mouth's kiss' to drain his mother's lifeblood on her 'bridebed, childbed, bed of death, ghostcandled'. This train of thought resembles that of Bloom's on blood victims, and the notion of the crucified God, hanger and

---

* John Vickery claims that 'dio boia' may owe something to Sir James Frazer's concept of the 'dying god' in *The Golden Bough* (see *The Literary Impact of The Golden Bough* (Princeton, 1973), p. 375). The pungency of Joyce's imagery derives not, I think, from the ordinary ritualistic treatment of the 'hanged god' which Frazer describes with such equanimity, but rather from the belligerency of the political criticism of the anarchists.

hanged, relates to Most's image of his being nailed like a bat on a barndoor.

Joyce calls God 'Bawd and Butcher' (*242; 311*). He referred to God in a similar fashion in a passage from *Giacomo Joyce* (11) where he comments after Amalia Popper's operation, 'The surgeon's knife has probed in her entrails and withdrawn, leaving the raw jagged gash of its passage on her belly . . . O cruel wound! Libidinous God!' In 'Oxen of the Sun' (*390; 509*) Stephen discusses conception by 'potency of vampires mouth to mouth' and reiterates the image of God as an 'omnivorous being' who chews the corpses of 'cancerous females emaciated by parturition, corpulent professional gentlemen' (*420; 550*), and the like. Both Bloom and Stephen, then, view God as the ogre depicted by Bakunin.

Joyce likewise arraigned the State, another 'vampire of history', as a 'monster fed with our blood' that 'must be starved' in the note-sheets for *Ulysses* in the British Museum.[72] The hangman god's accomplice is Sir Horace Rumbold, representative of the British State. He is introduced as the 'worldrenowned headsman' about to execute an Irish revolutionary (*308; 398–9*), later threatens to hang Bloom (*471; 595–6*), and inflicts capital punishment on the patriotic Croppy Boy in the name of King Edward VII (*593; 691*). The Croppy Boy desperately grunts his confession that he forgot to pray for his mother's rest in the mutilated words 'Horhot ho hray ho rhother's rest.' As a result, Rumbold would put Stephen symbolically to death, since he too had forgotten (wilfully) to pray at his mother's deathbed. Stephen sees the British State along with the Church as impediments to his mind and art, and, tapping his forehead, declares mental warfare on them: 'But in here it is I must kill the priest and king' (*589; 688*). When Old Grummy Granny, symbol of Ireland, urges Stephen to resist the British soldiers and thrusts a dagger towards his hand (*600; 696*), he refuses to be martyred, recognising in the 'old sow that eats her farrow' (*595; 692*) his country's blood-thirstiness and cannibalism as well.

Stephen moreover, refutes the British State in particular by disavowing the existence of a king and his own vengeful country by reversing the maxim of Caiaphas, the high priest who presided over the trial of Jesus, that 'it is right that a man should die for his country':

I have no king myself at the moment. . . . But this is the point. You die for your country, suppose. (*He places his arm on Private*

Carr's sleeve). Not that I wish it for you. But I say: Let my country die for me. Up to the present it has done so. I don't want it to die. Damn death. Long live life! *(591; 689)*★

What Stephen is implying is that the State has no right to demand the service of the citizen's mind and body for its own devious ends. The well-being and continued existence of the individual and the body politic is certainly a nobler aim than that of making sacrificial victims of both. In arguing this way, Stephen upholds Proudhon's position in *What is Property?*:

> The State occupies the same position today toward the bondholders that the city of Calais did, when besieged by Edward III, toward its notables. The English conqueror consented to spare its inhabitants, provided it would surrender to him its most distinguished citizens to do with as he pleased. Eustache and several others offered themselves; it was noble in them, and our ministers should recommend their example to the bond-holders. But had the city the right to surrender them? Assuredly not. The right to security is absolute; the country can require no one to sacrifice himself. The soldier standing guard within the enemy's range is no exception to this rule. Wherever a citizen stands guard, the country stands guard with him; to-day it is the turn of one, to-morrow of the other. When danger and devotion are common, flight is parricide. No one has the right to flee from danger; no one can serve as a scapegoat. The maxim of Caiaphas – *it is right that a man should die for his nation* – is that of the populace and of tyrants: the two extremes of social degradation.[73]

Stephen's remarks as well as Proudhon's are based on the belief that individual liberty is inviolable.

Bloom similarly renounces the State by pungently describing His Majesty the King 'sitting on his throne, sucking red jujubes white' *(151; 190)*. This description was inspired by 'a sugarsticky girl shovelling scoopfuls of creams for a christian brother.' The Christian brothers, representative of God, and the King, seem on the surface to be inoffensive, lenient rulers. In the minds of Bloom and Stephen, however, these authorities feed on blood rather than on sweetmeats. The predatory collusion of Church and State is highlighted in 'Circe' *(591; 689)*, where King Edward VII watches

---

★ For a discussion of this passage in connection with Easter 1916, see below, p. 163.

the executions performed by Sir Horace Rumbold '*with the halo of Joking Jesus, a white jujube in his phosphorescent face*'.

Joyce not only opposed the tyrannies of priests and kings, but also the so-called more liberal 'democracies'. In his note-sheets in the British Museum he defined the democratic institution of election as '20 fools to elect 1 genius.'[74] Joyce's statement paraphrases Malatesta's views on democratic government in his pamphlet on *Anarchy*:

> Will it be . . . a government elected by universal suffrage, and thus the more or less sincere expression of the wishes of the majority? But if you consider these worthy electors as unable to look after their own interests themselves, how is it that they will know how to choose for themselves the shepherds who must guide them? And how will they be able to solve this problem of social alchemy, of producing the election of a genius from the votes of a mass of fools? And what will happen to the minorities which are still the most intelligent, most active and radical part of a society?[75]

Joyce shared Malatesta's view of democracy, but he could not agree with the call for a violent revolution.

Joyce's attack on the State assumes another form in the continual presence of policemen. Bakunin listed them as a group oppressing mankind. Joyce points out how one form of authority sustains another. When the vice-regal cavalcade passes through Dublin, it is 'greeted by obsequious policemen, out of Parkgate' (*239; 306*). These policemen also know on which side their bread is buttered:

> Foodheated faces, sweating helmets, patting their truncheons. After their feed with a good load of fat soup under their belts. Policeman's lot is oft a happy one. (*162; 205*)

The constables are later described as 'sweating Irish stew into their shirts' (*166; 210*). If they are obsequious, so are Dublin's citizens. A prime example is the unnamed speaker in 'Cyclops', who begins: 'I was just passing the time of day with old Troy of the D.M.P.' (*292; 376*), the Dublin Metropolitan Police. Joyce draws our attention to his sycophancy before authority when he has him say at the end of the episode that the Citizen, had he hit Bloom with the biscuit tin, would have been lagged for assault and battery, and Joe Hynes for aiding and abetting him (*345; 448*). Bloom, on the other hand, regards any connection with the police to be unsavoury. He censures their spies, like Corny Kelleher, for 'Egging raw youths on to get in the know' while 'drawing secret service pay from the castle' (*163; 206–7*). This motive explains why 'those plain clothes men are always courting slaveys' in the manner of Corley. As upholders of the State, they are only too eager to repress civilians. Benjamin Tucker, representative of anarchist feeling on this subject, opposed the necessity of a police force:

> Even the simple police function of protecting person and property they [the Anarchists] deny to governments supported by compulsory taxation. Protection they look upon as a thing to be secured, as long as it is necessary, by voluntary association and co-operation for self-defence, or as a commodity to be purchased, like any other commodity, of those who offer the best article at the lowest price. In their view it is in itself an invasion of the individual to compel him to pay for or suffer a protection against invasion that he has not asked for and does not desire.[76]

Tucker argues that protection is a commodity to be asked for by the individual, not something to be imposed on him. Bloom adopts a somewhat similar attitude in 'Eumaeus' when he tells Stephen,

> A lot of those policemen, whom he cordially disliked, were admittedly unscrupulous in their service of the Crown. Never on the spot when wanted but in quiet parts of the city, Pembroke Road, for example, the guardians of the law were well in evidence, the obvious reason being they were paid to protect the upper classes. (*615; 707*)

Joyce does not allow Bloom's criticism of the police to be as severe as that of the anarchists. (He indicates this by Bloom's amusing and paradoxical 'cordial' dislike.) Bloom's remarks may be delivered in an offhand manner, but his indictment is to the point: the police do not extend their service to the whole of society but only to an elitist segment.

Bloom's objection to the police is complemented by his remarks on the British Army: 'Another thing he commented on was equipping soldiers with firearms or sidearms of any description, which was tantamount to inciting them against civilians should by any chance they fall out over anything' (*615; 707*). Stephen alludes to an event in Mitchelstown in 1887 when the police opened fire on the people, killing one and wounding several others: 'Khaki Hamlets don't hesitate to shoot' (*187; 239–40*). 'Don't hesitate to shoot' became the rallying cry of the Irish against the British policy of 'coercion' in the 1880s. The attitudes of Bloom and Stephen on military and police authority dovetail with those of the anarchists, like Tolstoy, who stated bluntly that 'governments need armies particularly to protect them against their oppressed and enslaved subjects.'[77] Joyce adhered to the same view for in a letter referred to earlier on Italian syndicalist theory he argued that 'The Italian army is not directed against the Austrian army so much as against the Italian people.' In 'Ireland at the Bar' Joyce maintained that the only violent deaths in Ireland in 1907 were at the hands of British troops in Belfast, 'where the soldiers fired without warning on an unarmed crowd and killed a man and a woman'.[78] In his notes for 'Cyclops', Joyce included the following entry: 'State: 12 soldiers shoot, none is bloodguilty.'[79] Uppermost in Joyce's mind once again are the ironical assertions of anarchists like Tucker who claimed that 'Murder by the State is laudable' whereas 'murder by an individual is criminal.'[80] The skirmish with the British soldiers, Privates Carr and Compton, which ends with Stephen getting bashed in the jaw, indicates Joyce's view of the coercive nature of government.

In 'Ireland, Island of Saints and Sages', Joyce reinforced his view that such regimentation of Irish society resulted in individual and national paralysis:

> The soul of the country is weakened by centuries of useless
> struggle and broken treaties, and individual initiative is paralysed
> by the influence and admonitions of the church, while its body is
> manacled by the police, the tax office, and the garrison.[81]

At the same time, Joyce recalls Tucker's view of governments as 'invasive', denying the liberty of individuals. His notes for 'Cyclops' indicate that Joyce adopted the anarchist view of the police and army: 'police provoke crimes or disappear, armies war.'[82] Like the anarchists too he repudiated the idea of government: 'why add govt to moral & material forces existing.'[83]

In 'Oxen of the Sun', Stephen, like Tucker and Bakunin, discloses the complicity between 'moral' and 'material' forces. While in the lying-in hospital in Holles Street with his cronies, Stephen toasts the sovereign pontiff and 'he gave them for a pledge the vicar of Christ which also as he said is vicar of Bray' (*391; 510*). In alluding to a song about a priest who changed his theology with the ruling political power of the time.[84] Stephen emphasises the connivance between papal and secular authorities. This argument is bolstered by a historical precedent when the conversation shifts to the papal bull,

Laudabiliter (399–401; 522–4). In 'Wandering Rocks', both Bloom and Stephen indicate their refusal to serve God or King by tactfully ignoring Father Conmee and the British viceregal procession.

Joyce's opposition to British rule is underlined by MacHugh's remark in 'Aeolus'. MacHugh, a classics teacher at the University, dispraises the materialistic aspect of the British Empire: 'I speak the tongue of a race the acme of whose mentality is the maxim: time is money. Material domination. *Dominus!* Lord! Where is the spirituality? Lord Jesus! Lord Salisbury!' *(133; 169)*. This statement deflates Mr Deasy's proclamation that an Englishman's proudest boast was 'I paid my way!' *(30; 37)*, but the irony is double-edged since it was the *Greek* philosopher Theophrastus who is said to have coined the expression, 'Time is money'. MacHugh, nevertheless, makes his point, that spiritual and temporal 'masters' earn the same title, by referring to Lord Salisbury, an opponent of Home Rule. MacHugh goes on to say that he ought to profess Greek, the language of the mind, and declares 'The closetmaker and the cloacamaker will never be lords of our spirit' *(133; 169)*. Joyce too believed that the Anglo-Saxon civilisation was 'almost entirely a materialistic' one.[85] In his lecture on *Daniel Defoe* in Trieste, he cast Robinson Crusoe and Friday in the roles of conquering and conquered race:

> The true symbol of the British conquest is Robinson Crusoe, cast away on a desert island, in his pocket a knife and a pipe, becomes an architect, a carpenter, a knife-grinder, an astronomer, a baker, a shipwright, a potter, a saddler, a farmer, a tailor, an umbrella-maker, and a clergyman. He is the true prototype of the British colonist, as Friday (the trusty savage who arrives on an unlucky day) is the symbol of the subject races. The whole Anglo-Saxon spirit is in Crusoe.[86]

Joyce condemned Britain's economic and the Pope's spiritual domination over Ireland since the former hindered political independence and the latter artistic independence. That is why for Stephen Irish art is 'the cracked lookinglass of a servant' *(7; 6)*.

MacHugh's remarks also reveal an opposition to the idea of imperial despotism, Roman or British. Stephen is of the same mind. In 'Nestor' he thought of the oppression of the Irish under Caesarism, and he later refers to the present foreign rulers as 'the brutish empire' *(594; 692)*, or the 'usurper' of the first episode. The similarity between Rome and Britain is constantly alluded to throughout *Ulysses*. Joyce was prompted by Bakunin's argument in *God and the State* in MacHugh's preference for the Greek over Latin civilisation:

> Human emancipation, that is the name of the Greek civilization. And the name of the Roman civilization? Conquest, with all its brutal consequences. And its last word? The omnipotence of the Caesars. Which means the degradation and enslavement of nations and men.
>
> To-day even, what is it that kills, what is it that crushes brutally, materially, in all European countries, liberty and humanity? It is the triumph of Caesarism or Roman principle.[87]

Human emancipation was in accordance with Joyce's plan to 'Hellenize' Ireland, in Buck Mulligan's words.

In addition to Bakunin, Tucker and the other radicals, Joyce relied on Kropotkin to deepen the anarchist strain of *Ulysses*. In 'Aeolus' MacHugh says that Stephen and O'Madden Burke 'look like communards' (*134; 170*). J. J. O'Molloy adds, 'Like fellows who had blown up the Bastille.' Joyce had in his library an Italian version of Kropotkin's *The Great French Revolution*, and his article on 'The Commune of Paris' of 1871. In Kropotkin's view, the essence of the Commune of Paris of 1871 was its revolt against centralised authority, especially the political State.[88] In 1789 the destruction of the Bastille, 'the emblem and support of the royal power' according to Kropotkin,[89] represented the destruction of the State, and marked the beginning of the French Revolution. J. J. O'Molloy further implicates Stephen and O'Madden Burke as revolutionaries when he adds, 'Or was it you shot the lord lieutenant of Finland between you? You look as though you had done the deed.' Stephen denies that he shot General Bobrikoff – who was assassinated on 16 June 1904 – but, as an artist opposed to the use of force, he responds cryptically and ironically. 'We were only thinking about it' (*135; 171*). Similarly, Bloom is branded as an 'Anarchist' and 'dynamitard' in 'Circe' (*470; 595*),* but, as has become clear, he also advocates a non-violent revolution.

Bloom's social schemes throughout the day are delivered in utopian fantasy in his answer to the political question of Home Rule in 'Circe':

---

* Arnold Kramer too is branded as an 'anarchist' in Act III of *Michael Kramer* before being hounded and committing suicide.

I stand for the reform of municipal morals and the plain ten
commandments. New worlds for old. Union of all, jew, moslem
and gentile. Three acres and a cow for all children of nature.
Saloon motor hearses. Compulsory manual labour for all. All
parks open to the public day and night. Electric dish-scrubbers.
Tuberculosis, lunacy, war and mendicancy must now cease.
General amnesty, weekly carnival, with masked licence, bonuses
for all, esperanto the universal brotherhood. No more patriotism
of bar-spongers and dropsical impostors. (*489–90; 610*)

His speech is a mixture of freemasonry and of some of the Utopian
Socialist visionary programmes at the turn of the century, with
peculiar Bloomite twists. Political independence is not at all Bloom's
prime concern, but radical social reform. 'New Worlds for Old' is an
unknowingly anachronistic allusion to the title of H. G. Wells's
book, not published until 1908, in which he set out to define and
present the socialist position as a practical policy in solving
contemporary social conditions. Bloom's pronouncements also
recall the underlying theme of Kropotkin's *The Conquest of Bread*,
which Joyce read in an Italian translation. Kropotkin was convinced
that anarchist communism was manifesting itself everywhere in the
western world and moving towards the day when all private
property would eventually become common property:

> The bridges, for the use of which a toll was levied in the old days,
> have become public property and are free to all; so are the high
> roads, except in the East, where a toll is exacted from the traveller
> for every mile of his journey. Museums, free libraries, free
> schools, free meals, for children; parks and gardens open to all;
> streets paved and lighted, free to all; water supplied to every house
> without measure or stint – all such arrangements are founded on
> the principle 'Take what you need.'[90]

The anarchist-communist principle of needs ('from each according
to his means, to each according to his needs') opposed the wage
system. On this point anarchist communism differed from
collectivism. Bakunin, who believed in the radically different
maxim, 'From each according to his deeds', advocated the idea of
remuneration according to hours of labour.[91] Kropotkin, on the
other hand, envisaged communal storehouses from which each
person could take what he wanted, whether or not he contributed a
share of the labour. (This idea was first put forward by Sir Thomas

More in *Utopia*.) Kropotkin, moreover, assumed that in such a system men would work of their own accord, without any compulsion. Bloom seems to favour Bakunin's position by insisting on 'compulsory manual labour for all'. In 'Eumaeus', however, Bloom gets it marvellously confused so as to subsume the essence of both theories when he says, 'Everyone according to his needs, and everyone according to his deeds' (*619; 713*).

Bloom's statement echoes in part Marx's slogan in *The Critique of the Gotha Programme* too, 'From each according to his ability, to each according to his needs!'; that is, that each work according to his capacity and receive according to his wants. Marx held that in a higher phase of communist society labour would not only become a means of living but life's prime want.[92] These future societies envisaged by Marx and Kropotkin, however, proposed to strip the individual of capital entirely. What Bloom had in mind, apparently, was, as Joyce noted, 'Property could be collective, wages individual (according to needs? deeds?).'[93] Tucker, like Bloom, maintained against the Communists that labour should be paid: 'Not to abolish wages, but to make *every* man dependent upon wages and secure to every man his *whole* wages is the aim of Anarchistic Socialism.'[94] Joyce's borrowing is muddled, therefore, mixing bits of collectivist, Marxist, and individualist anarchist theory.

The reference to 'electric dishscrubbers' in Bloom's speech may owe its inclusion to a passage in which Kropotkin argues that woman also claims her share in the emancipation of humanity. Kropotkin, unlike the English socialist William Morris, upheld Godwin's belief that mechanisation would relieve men of unnecessary exertion and monotony. He was therefore delighted when a Mrs Cochrane in Illinois invented a dishwashing machine which would ease the burden of domestic labour:

> Her machine washes twelve dozen plates or dishes, wipes them and dries them, in less than three minutes. A factory in Illinois manufactures these machines and sells them at a price within reach of the average middle-class purse.[95]

In Kropotkin's view, modern technology would hasten the distribution of interesting work for all.

Kropotkin's influence on Bloom's utopian thinking is also evident in his proclamation to Stephen of an earthly paradise 'where you can live well . . . if you work':

I mean, of course . . . work in the widest possible sense. Also literary labour, not merely for the kudos of the thing. Writing for the newspapers which is the readiest channel nowadays. That's work too. Important work. . . . You have every bit as much right to live by your pen in pursuit of your philosophy as the peasant has. What? You both belong to Ireland, the brain and the brawn. Each is equally important! (*644–5; 747–8*)

Bloom now elucidates somewhat his garbled views on labour which he had delivered in 'Circe'. Encompassed in his statements is Kropotkin's ideal of living by a combination of manual and mental work, in a harmony which recognises both sides of human nature. In 'Circe', Bloom, dressed in workman's corduroy overalls, had denounced the capitalist system, the 'hideous hobgoblins produced by a horde of capitalistic lusts upon our prostituted labour' (*479; 602*). Now he tells Stephen, 'It's all very fine to boast of mutual superiority but what about mutual equality?' (*643; 745*). The competitive aspects of existing society would, in effect, be fatal to a co-operative society. Bloom's hatred of capitalism, however, is not based on Marx's conception of the class struggle. As Joyce noted,[96] Bloom 'hates class hate'. Like Kropotkin, he believed instead in the natural solidarity of men, on their mutual aid or co-operation. The description of Bloom Cottage, Flowerville, in 'Ithaca', moreover, and Bloom's plan of life on that estate reveals a penchant for 'industry combined with agriculture and brain work with manual work', to quote the subtitle of *Fields, Factories and Workshops*,[97] a book also in Joyce's library.

Aristotle wrote that man by nature is a political animal, that it is incumbent upon him to live in the State. Bloom, the modern Ulysses, embraces his own notions of statecraft. He, along with Stephen, abhors the coercive nature of the State, and its ally the Church, and their imposition of innumerable restraints which smother individual freedom and initiative. Through their unsuspected mutual support, Bloom and Stephen offer to their fellow Dubliners a vision of a classless, humanitarian, pacifist and co-operative society, devoid of all forms of hatred and sentimentality. As Joyce told Padraic Colum, violence in the physical life, and sentimentality in the emotional life, were equally distressing.[98] In Bloom and Stephen the claims of general human solidarity and the demands – equally urgent – of the individual who seeks absolute freedom are reconciled. Joyce's espousal of radical social ideals is

Chapter 4

The National Scene

1 Ourselves, oursouls alone

Exile has its disadvantages. A writer runs the risk of being denounced as a renegade. Dostoevsky, for instance, told Turgenev to procure a telescope so as to see Russia a little better.[1] Joyce's political vision did not suffer from any such myopia; in fact, he levelled this charge at his own compatriots. Like Turgenev, he viewed the homeland with irony and scepticism, but he never lost sight of the complexities that came with its political situation.

At the height of his political interest in Rome, Joyce remarked to Stanislaus how university friends like Thomas Kettle, Sheehy-Skeffington, and even Oliver Gogarty were all 'in the public eye and favour'. Their writings and lives, however, nauseated Joyce 'to the point of vomiting'. But frustration at not having *Dubliners* published provoked this outburst.[2] For Joyce still followed their political activity with passionate attention.

Joyce valued Thomas Kettle's opinions mainly because 'his Catholicism was an intellectual conviction, not just a phase of nationalism'.[3] Kettle, a member of Parliament, once summed up the difference between the English parties in the epigram, 'When in office, the Liberals forget their principles and the Tories remember their friends.'[4] Although he is not a model for any of Joyce's characters, some of his remarks suggested in part the wording of Robert Hand's article on the return of Richard Rowan to Ireland in *Exiles*.[5] Kettle counselled Ireland that 'in order to become deeply Irish, she must become European', a conviction shared by Joyce,[6] who feared that Ireland would become an 'afterthought of Europe'.[7] Joyce may have judged Kettle's preoccupation with the national question as 'too demonstrative' to be truly cosmopolitan, but he misunderstood the politician's role. His task is by definition to give a political character to the affairs of men, and the propagation of his views is the logical outcome of being 'demonstrative'. Kettle, moreover, stressed equally the cultural as well as the political aspect of Europeanisation:

> Ireland, a small nation, is, none the less, large enough to contain all the complexities of the twentieth century. There is no ecstasy and no agony of the modern soul remote from her experience; there is none of all the difficulties which beset men, eager to build at last a wise and stable society, that she has not encountered. In some of them she has even been the fore-runner of the world. If this generation has, for its first task, the recovery of the old Ireland, it has, for its second, the discovery of the new Europe. Ireland awaits her Goethe – but in Ireland he must not be a pagan – who will one day arise to teach her that while a strong people has its own self for centre, it has the universe for circumference. All cultures belong to a nation that has once taken sure hold of its own culture. A national literature that seeks to found itself in isolation from the general life of humanity can only produce the pale and waxen growths of a plant isolated from the sunlight. In gaining her own soul Ireland will gain the whole world.[8]

As a young man Joyce answered this call by making it his first priority to discover the new Europe and also invited the literary movement to look abroad for its models. Years later he insisted that all great writers 'were national first and it was the intensity of their own nationalism which made them international in the end'.[9] His perspective on this subject finally merged with Kettle's own. He had made it *his* task to forge Ireland's soul.

Although he respected Kettle's intellectual convictions, Joyce could not agree with his espousal of Catholicism. In his introduction to *The Day's Burden* (1910), Kettle laid down as his programme for Ireland Home Rule and the Ten Commandments, 'in equal parts'. In 'Circe' Bloom's platform contains Home Rule and the 'plain ten commandments' too, but also the incompatible provision of 'free love'. Joyce maintained that the Church had no right to meddle in politics and feared that its re-establishment as a political force in Europe would herald a new Inquisition.[10]

In his university days Joyce had debated with Arthur Chanel Clery, another fellow student, on the educational value of the theatre.[11] Clery too was now in the public eye, attracting considerable attention through his work as a free-lance journalist. He was an ardent Home Ruler at this time, but took no active part in politics. The Gaelic revival and Douglas Hyde's programme for 'de-Anglicisation' commanded the largest measure of his support. He contributed a weekly column for the *Leader*, whose Ireland for the Irish slogan was then sweeping over the country. As 'Chanel', the same *nom de plume* he adopted in *St Stephen's*, he was read all over the country.

Although furtively hostile to the *Leader's* policies, Joyce remained grateful to Clery for his favourable review of *Chamber Music* in its columns.[12] Clery perceptively noted that Joyce's verse lacked the purely Gaelic inspiration of Douglas Hyde's *Love Songs of Connacht* but was 'entirely earthly' and bore classical affinities instead.[13] That the poems did not arise from an Irish-Ireland was emphasised by Arthur Symons too, who introduced Joyce as 'a young Irishman who is in no Irish movement, literary or national, and has not even anything obviously in the Celtic manner.'[14] So even *Chamber Music*, in its own way, represented a gentle rebuke to the nationalistic clamour.

Disagreement, however, did not deter Joyce from using Clery's articles as sources for his work. Between 1902 and 1907 there appeared in the *Leader* a series of essays dealing with the topic of 'Irish Nationality'.[15] The idea of a 'nation' was very much in the air at this time, with journalists as different as D. P. Moran and Arthur Griffith defining their understanding of the term. Clery alone perceived the humorous possibilities of the sometimes heated discussion. In a column entitled 'On Tram-Car's Top', he presented the following conversation between an Englishman and a Gaelic Leaguer on the Boer War:

A 'Nationality's all b–humbug.'
B 'I suppose then you'd think it very foolish for an Englishman to volunteer and get killed in the war.'
A 'Oh! fighting for your country's different.'
B 'What do you mean by "your country" then?'
A 'What's the "–" use of asking silly questions. The place where you're born of course.'
B 'Your father was born in India, wasn't he? I suppose he sided with his Hindu fellow-countrymen in the mutiny.'
A 'Not d–likely. Of course your country's the same even out there.'

B 'Then it isn't the place you're born in that matters.'
A 'Well, of course, it's as if you were born in England, you
   know.'
B 'England and India being the same place?'
A 'Oh! well, it's the English Empire out there just the same. I
   suppose I was wrong in talking about "place".'[16]

Clery wrote another article entitled 'The Theory of Nationhood',
which explored the argument in a similar fashion.[17] Joyce may have
had Clery's treatment of the theme in mind when he has Bloom
being asked the same question in 'Cyclops' and with similar results.
Joyce, however, reverses the situation by questioning the idea of
Irish not English nationhood. Joyce's insertion of this seemingly
innocuous question of nationhood, therefore, indicates that he was
acquainted with topical political issues.

As an exile, Joyce believed he had freed himself from those 'mean
influences' he had accused the Irish Literary Theatre of succumbing
to in *The Day of the Rabblement*. As a consequence, he now reassessed
the Irish national scene. Of all the newspapers competing for the
nation's allegiance, he singled out the *United Irishman* for particular
attention. He claimed that it was 'the only newspaper of any
pretensions in Ireland' and believed that its policy alone would prove
beneficial to Ireland.[18] According to Stanislaus, Joyce read it 'every
week until a priest took an action for libel against the meagrely
financed paper and killed it' in 1906.[19] Joyce still found the *United
Irishman* 'hopelessly deaf' on account of its provincialism,[20] but he
was quick to note its importance for future developments in Irish
history. He saw it as a radical alternative to the daily press, such as
the *Freeman's Journal*, which concentrated on the establishment
politics of the Irish Party. (In 'Calypso' (*57; 68*) Bloom remembers
Griffith's mockery of the 'headpiece over the *Freeman* leader' which
depicted 'a Home Rule sun rising from behind the Bank of Ireland'.
In other words, an establishment version.) Griffith was putting
forward concrete proposals for economic self-sufficiency and
political independence as opposed to ineffectual parliamentary
chatter.

Griffith had founded the Cumann na nGaedheal (or 'Confeder-
ation of the Gaels') in 1900 in order to advance the cause of Irish
independence by 'cultivating a fraternal spirit amongst Irishmen'.
The more tangible objectives included support of Irish industries,
the study and teaching of Irish history, literature, language, music

and art, the cultivation of Irish national games, the discountenancing of everything tending towards the anglicisation of Ireland, the nationalisation of public boards, and a projected foreign policy.[21] Griffith announced his platform at the annual convention of Cumann na nGaedheal in 1902. Generally known as the 'Hungarian Policy', it appeared in the *United Irishman* between January and July 1904, and was later published as a pamphlet entitled *The Resurrection of Hungary*. The basic idea was that Hungary had won her independence from Austria through passive resistance. She had refused to recognise the abolition of her constitution of 1848 and, under the leadership of Francis Deak, had recalled her representatives from Vienna and had set up her own Diet in Budapest. Emperor Francis Joseph eventually submitted to Deak's pressure, and the Austro-Hungarian dual monarchy was established with the *Ausgleich* of 1867. In a similar vein, Griffith held that the Act of Union of 1800 was illegal because it abolished Henry Grattan's Constitution of 1782. He concluded that the Irish representatives, by sitting at Westminster, were helping to perpetuate an injustice. They also should withdraw from the Imperial Parliament and set up their own government at home, with the crown as the only link between Ireland and England.

Griffith's policy stirred considerable debate. John O'Leary thought the policy asked too much of the Irish people, while John MacBride maintained that it had come a hundred years too late. D. P. Moran, Griffith's nemesis, christened its supporters 'the green Hungarian band',[22] and parliamentarians as a whole found the Hungarian parallel unconvincing as well. Some, however, like Davitt, registered their approval. Thomas Kettle, who thought it a bit impractical, still called it 'the largest idea contributed to Irish politics for a generation'.[23] The spirit of Kettle's article in the *New Ireland Review* pleased Griffith. He acknowledged the justice of Kettle's demand for a more 'exhaustive plan' than he had proposed in his pamphlet, and promised to draw one up. 'We trust', he concluded, 'the other Parliamentarians will discuss it in the same spirit as Mr Kettle – looking only to the interests of Ireland.'[24]

Kettle noted the excellence of Griffith's literary style, and wrote that it read 'like a fairy tale, or, rather like an epic, spacious and rapid'.[25] Joyce also noted its literary quality, and he kept *The Resurrection of Hungary* in mind when writing the 'Circe' episode of *Ulysses*. Robert Tracy has demonstrated the extent of Joyce's borrowing from Griffith's pamphlet.[26] The climax of Griffith's narrative, for example, occurs at the moment Emperor Francis Joseph is invested with the 'iron crown' of St Stephen, dons the green mantle of St Stephen, and pledges to safeguard the Hungarian constitution. Bloom's dreams of glory are capped when he is proclaimed King of Ireland, 'Leopold the First', with 'saint Stephen's crown' (*480; 603*).[27] When Bloom shows all 'that he is wearing green socks' (*483; 606*), he imitates Francis Joseph's putting on the green mantle which, Tracy points out, should in fact be mulberry-coloured. Francis Joseph is greeted by 'Fifty-two workingmen from all counties of Hungary', and 'Thirty-two workmen . . . from all the counties of Ireland' attend Bloom's ceremony (*484; 606*). Finally, the Hungarian language is used during the coronation scene in Griffith, while Bloom speaks Hebrew (*487; 609*). The latter, I think, is a subtle indication of Joyce's position on the Irish language question. Griffith emphasised the nationalistic use of language, whereas Bloom as King of Ireland speaks, ironically, in Hebrew instead of in Gaelic.

Joyce, on the whole, deemed the Hungarian parallel for Ireland to be a political absurdity. In *Stephen Hero*, Stephen realises that

> many political absurdities arose from the lack of a just sense of comparison in public men. The orators of this patriotic party were not ashamed to cite the precedents of Switzerland and France. The intelligent centres of the movement were so scantily supplied that the analogies they gave out as exact and potent were really analogies built haphazard upon very inexact knowledge. The cry of a solitary Frenchman (A bas l'Angleterre!) at a Celtic re-union in Paris would be made by these enthusiasts the subject of a leading article in which would be shown the imminence of aid for Ireland from the French Government. A glowing example was to be found for Ireland in the case of Hungary, an example, as these patriots imagined, of a long-suffering minority, entitled by every right of race and justice to a separate freedom, finally emancipating itself. In emulation of that achievement bodies of young Gaels conflicted murderously in the Phoenix Park with whacking hurley-sticks, thrice armed in their just quarrel since their revolution had been blessed for them by the Anointed, and the same bodies were set aflame with indignation by the unwelcome presence of any young sceptic who was aware of the capable aggression of the Magyars upon the Latin and Slav and Teutonic populations, greater than themselves in number, which

are politically allied to them, and of the potency of a single
regiment of infantry to hold in check a town of twenty thousand
inhabitants. (66–7) (*62*)

The first part of his objections is peculiar to Stephen, but the end of
his argument is an adaptation of those put forward by some of
Griffith's opponents within his own movement. These were the
advocates of violence who claimed that Griffith had ignored the
complexities of the Magyar situation. The Magyar landed aristocracy, although a racial minority, had succeeded in subjecting the
Slavs and Rumanians after their victory in 1867. They then
proceeded to deny these races their cultural and linguistic rights. By
subtly manipulating the foreign policy of the Austro-Hungarian
Empire, the Magyars exerted an influence in central Europe
disproportionate to their numbers.[28]

In 'Cyclops' (*335; 436*) John Wyse Nolan tells the Citizen that
'Bloom gave the idea for Sinn Fein to Griffith', and Martin
Cunningham corroborates this information, adding 'he drew up all
the plans according to the Hungarian system' (*337; 438*). These
statements have caused as much controversy among critics as
Griffith's pamphlets once did. Robert Adams assumes that Joyce is
asking too much of the reader to accept the inference that Bloom
knew Griffith,[29] while Bernard Benstock promptly dismisses the
Griffith connection as a myth and a 'far-fetched rumor'. He
maintains that the 'hard-headed Citizen remains unimpressed with
the Nolan-Cunningham fabrication, and so should the perceptive
reader'.[30] It may be so, but Joyce indicates that one should also be
suspicious of the Citizen. Bloom himself does not claim to have had
any such influence on Griffith. If he did give Griffith a hint about the
Hungarian system it would probably have been as a point of
information rather than as a policy to be advocated. But Bloom
could have known Griffith since Griffith was not hard to meet. On
this basis one would also have to deny that Bloom had met Parnell
and that 'as a matter of strict history' he returned the Chief's hat after
the fracas over *United Ireland* (*654; 761*). While recognising all the
difficulties associated with the Nolan-Cunningham statements, I
think Joyce wants at least a possibility that Bloom gives a tip to
Griffith, thereby paving the way for the parody of *The Resurrection of
Hungary* in 'Circe'.

When Griffith was asked by some of his readers to become the
Irish Deak, he replied that he himself opposed any connection

between England and Ireland and that therefore he was a follower of the republican Kossuth. (At first a physical force leader, Kossuth advocated passive resistance after the abortive revolt of 1848–9.) But since the majority of Irishmen held moderate views, Griffith added, they could count on the co-operation of Irish separatists.[31] Apparently paradoxical, his policy was intended 'to convert by irresistible logic both parliamentarian and unionist'.[32] Deak is never mentioned in *Ulysses*, but one of Bloom's transformations is Kossuth (*495; 615*). Bloom, like Stephen, probably recognised the inadequacy of the Hungarian Policy as a political analogy, and he could only endorse its non-violent tactic.

Although Joyce preferred Griffith's movement to the Irish Party, he still followed the activities of the parliamentarians with equal attention.* He read the newspaper Kettle was editing, the *Nationist*, which was founded by 'certain ladies of patriotic and pious instincts' in September 1905.[33] They originally wanted Arthur Clery as editor, but he declined in favour of Kettle. The latter laid down as his political ideal 'complete independence' from England. Although he did not dismiss the Hungarian Policy outright, Kettle still believed his objective could best be accomplished by the Parliamentary Party. The paper also supported the Language Movement and opposed the Unionists.[34]

The Unionists in turn attacked the *Nationist*. The *Irish Times* derided the strange title chosen by Kettle as a travesty, since the invention of a new substantive necessarily called into being a new verb 'to nationise'; that is, 'to develop into a nation'. This terminology seemed to be at variance with the claim that Ireland *was*, in fact, a distinct nation.[35] Kettle replied that the coinage was called for since the term 'nationalist' had been 'narrowed and cheapened down almost to blank nothing'. The whole philosophy of Irish history was contained in the idea of nationhood. The neologism did not escape Joyce's notice. In *Finnegans Wake*, Shaun tells Shem not only that 'your birthwrong was' to 'do a certain office . . . in a certain holy office' but insists that 'our nationals should' and that 'all nationists must' follow suit (190).

---

* Later, in 1912, Joyce wrote a sub-editorial entitled 'Politics and Cattle Disease' in the *Freeman's Journal* on the foot and mouth disease which was then prevalent in Ireland. Joyce opposed a prolonged embargo on Irish cattle, and supported the Irish Party and its leader, John Dillon, in demanding that the English reopen their ports to healthy Irish stock (see *CW*, pp. 238–41).

Skeffington also worked for a while on the *Nationist*. He contributed a series of articles entitled 'Dialogues of the Day', which attempted to present the widest possible spectrum of opinions on social and political questions of contemporary interest. When publication of Kettle's journal ceased in April 1906, Skeffington started his own paper in July with the title *Dialogues of the Day*.

Joyce preferred the 'deafness' of the *United Irishman* to the 'alertness' of *Dialogues of the Day*.[36] He wrote Stanislaus that he would send him a copy of Skeffington's latest effort, and described it derisively as very 'brilliant':

> Three pages of puff by F.S.S.* at the end: full of thick-typed catch phrases such as 'this novelty in Irish journalism' 'order at once' 'absolutely unique'. An advt appears for some booklet by (very big letters) Thomas Kettle, M.P.[37]

The book by Kettle was *The Philosophy of Politics*, and part of the dialogue of that issue concentrated on his candidacy in the upcoming elections.

Joyce sent Stanislaus Griffith's parody of Skeffington's weekly commentary.[38] Griffith alludes to Kettle's victory, but ridicules the policy of the Irish Party in substituting 'devolution' for Home Rule: 'I don't like Devolution' said the Provost. 'The Irish ought always to be kept as they are.' Griffith then parodied the position of the Irish Party at Westminster by having the Provost proclaim his thesis 'to show the right of England to govern the Irish which has never been refuted'.[39] Skeffington commented that the take-off would please those critics who objected to his giving fair treatment to all political options, since Griffith made it perfectly clear on which side his sympathies were.[40] *Dialogues of the Day* eventually shared the same fate as the *Nationist*, and by September 1906 it too was defunct.

Griffith's paper, meanwhile, came under attack. A libel action against the *United Irishman* in May 1906 resulted in a decree for £500. Practically penniless, Griffith decided nevertheless to rechristen his paper *Sinn Féin*. It was not the first journal to bear that name since the *United Irishman* had greeted a monthly review entitled *Sinn Féin* published in Oldcastle in 1902 as 'another sign of how the intellectual life of the country has been quickened'.[41] The name, meaning simply 'Ourselves' or 'Ourselves alone', was in fact first suggested to Griffith by one of his supporters, Mary Butler, at the end of 1904.

---

* Francis Sheehy-Skeffington.

The words, moreover, were remarkably apposite in expressing the central principle of national self-reliance which Griffith expounded accordingly as the 'Sinn Féin Policy' at the 1905 convention of the National Council.

Griffith's programme consisted of an economic nationalism based on the protectionist theories of the German Friedrich List. He proposed to develop native industry as well as agriculture. Concentrating solely on agriculture, as the Redmondites had done, left Ireland insecure in the face of world competition. A national banking system would, if created, pump the necessary capital, previously invested in British enterprises, into home ventures. The establishment of an Irish consular service in Europe would help publicise Irish goods, while an Irish mercantile marine would open up foreign markets. At the 1906 convention Griffith also proposed a partial boycott of certain goods from which Britain derived her excise revenue.[42] Finally, Griffith moved for the introduction of an educational system more in accordance with national principles. Joyce commented on these resolutions in a letter to Stanislaus:

> A great deal of his programme perhaps is absurd but at least it tries to inaugurate some commercial life for Ireland and to tell you the truth once or twice in Trieste I felt myself humiliated when I heard the little Galatti girl sneering at my impoverished country.[43]

Joyce added that he too had aided Irish commerce when he 'took some steps' to secure an agency for Foxford tweeds in Trieste. Similarly, when *Sinn Féin* later advertised Irish gowns, Joyce offered to buy the patterns if 'Nora liked the style.'[44] Griffith's economic policies, Joyce maintained, justified the existence of his paper, and he endorsed the 'Sinn Féin Policy' as a more effective instrument than parliamentary agitation.[45]

When Stanislaus twitted Griffith for being afraid of the priests, Joyce agreed and added, probably with the Parnell affair in mind, 'he has every reason to be so'. 'But,' Joyce concluded, 'possibly, they are a little afraid of him too.'[46] Joyce's remarks were penetrating for, by his brother's own admission, Griffith's paper was unpopular with the students and teachers of University College because 'it was suspected of lukewarm Catholicism, of disrespect for priests'. The clergy took the side of Moran's *Leader* instead.[47] Griffith, in riposte, chided the hierarchy in his weekly columns whenever its actions hampered the growth of a self-reliant community. The priests were reprimanded for not taking effective steps to halt emigration, and he claimed that

> they 'next to the British Government' were 'responsible for the depopulation of the country': that they failed to encourage Irish trade and manufacturers: that the priests 'made life dull and unendurable for the people': that the Hierarchy had backed the Parliamentary Party against the Nationalists of '48 and '67: that they were apathetic on the question of the language. It was asserted that the priesthood with their exaggerated caution with regard to the natural relations of the sexes had 'brought a Calvinistic gloom and horror into Ireland': 'To-day the land is dotted with religious edifices but the men and women whose money built them are fleeing to America to seek for bread.'[48]

The Church opposed Griffith, according to Joyce, because he was 'holding out some secular liberty to the people', and Joyce concluded from this that the Church remained, as in the time of Adrian IV, Ireland's chief enemy. He added, 'but, I think, her time is almost up', for he stated prophetically, 'either *Sinn Féin* or Imperialism will conquer the present Ireland.'[49]

But why did Joyce, like Griffith, rule out parliamentarianism in the battle for Ireland? When Redmond emerged as the new leader of the Irish Party one of the charges held against him was a speech he delivered in Cambridge in 1895 where he said, 'the separation of Ireland from England was undesirable and impossible.'[50] Sinn Féiners were forced, as a result, to view Home Rule as a self-defeating objective. They described Home Rulers as 'Federal Imperialists' and refused to distinguish between the Home Ruler and the Irish Unionist, for both relied on a foreign power to direct their destinies.[51] The conjunction was unfair, but no matter. Home Rule and independent nationhood were not, then, synonymous terms according to Sinn Féiners. Independent nationhood meant establishing unilaterally the Irish people as sovereign rulers in their own country. Griffith claimed in his final article on *The Resurrection of Hungary* that the policy of parliamentarianism had been 'materially and morally disastrous to the country'. He also argued that no measure of any benefit had been passed at Westminster as a result of the speeches and actions of the Irish delegation. The measures generally considered to be of a profitable nature, including the Land Act of 1881, were passed, according to Griffith, 'as a result of the *unconscious carrying out by the people of the Hungarian policy* – the policy of Passive Resistance – with occasional excursions into the domain of active resistance at strategic points'.[52] Griffith's policy reminded Joyce of a variety of political ideals embraced by political writers whom he admired. He had already compared Labriola to Griffith, and their condemnation of the futility of parliamentary action. Now the non-violent boycott tactic of the Land League advocated by Parnell and Davitt, and Tolstoy's passive resistance also formed part of Griffith's policy.

Joyce's support of Sinn Féin's abstentionist policy might seem paradoxical in view of Parnell's career as a parliamentarian. Parnell's power was that of an individual leader, whereas Sinn Féin stressed individual self-reliance.[53] Joyce considered the movement strong because it put its trust in neither priest nor politician. As an anonymous pamphleteer put it, 'leaders may betray their fellows', (or, in Joyce's view, people may betray their leaders), 'the people can never betray themselves.'[54] Joyce realised, however, that Griffith was no Parnell, and makes Bloom concede that Griffith 'is a squareheaded fellow' but has 'no go in him for the mob' such as Parnell had (*163–4; 207*).

Joyce indicated which policy he considered to be the correct one in his usual indirect manner. When the 1902 Municipal Elections took place, the major issue of the campaign consisted in whether or not to present a loyal address to the visiting monarch, Edward VII. Griffith took the occasion to pour his scorn on the parliamentarians who were in favour of doing so, and advised his supporters to vote only for those candidates who opposed the projected royal visit. Since Sinn Féin was not a political party, Griffith came out openly for the candidacy of James Connolly, the founder of the Irish Socialist Party in 1896, and supported most of the labour candidates in other wards, and did so again in the 1903 elections.[55] Connolly, however, stood unsuccessfully for the Wood Quay Ward on both occasions. His defeats were mainly due to the fact that the Irish hierarchy vehemently opposed him, portrayed him as an anti-Christ, and prohibited any Catholic to vote for him under pain of excommunication.[56]

In 'Ivy Day in the Committee Room' Joyce's exposure of the Irish Party's futility and their treasonous dishonour to Parnell's memory is made clear. There is an oblique reference to Connolly in the form of the labourite Colgan's policies, endorsed by Hynes:

' – The working-man, said Mr Hynes, gets all kicks and no

halfpence. But it's labour produces everything. The working-
man is not looking for fat jobs for his sons and nephews and
cousins. The working-man is not going to drag the honour of
Dublin in the mud to please the German monarch.
(136) (*121*)

There is no allusion to the factors surrounding Connolly's
candidacy, nor to the outcome of the election. But Joyce's tact
enables the reader to presuppose that the Church-backed Nationalist
candidate will easily win out, as in fact he did. The 'paralysis' in Irish
political life arises out of the inability of the parliamentary party to
wrench itself free from the hold of the Church and the British State.
By focusing on the ineptitude of parliamentary action as a weapon
for independence, and by evincing sympathy for the labour party's
stand against the royal visit, Joyce tacitly takes Griffith's view of the
election and of the Parnell controversy.

Although Griffith admitted there was a 'tincture of expediency' in
his support for Labour, Joyce's position was not as equivocal. He
welcomed socialism as a counterpoise to the Church's political
power, and he suspected that one reason why an order like the
Dominicans opposed the 'quite unheretical theory of socialism' was
because they knew that 'one of its items is expropriation'.[57] The
interest he took in socialism was not predominantly Marxist,
however, for according to Herbert Gorman, Joyce found the first
sentence of *Das Kapital* 'so absurd that he immediately returned the
book to the lender'.[58] Instead he read Italian translations of Lassalle.[59]
Lassalle differed most from Marx in conceiving the State as the
manifestation of the will of the people whose spirit the working class
embodied. In Dublin too, where Joyce had frequented meetings of
socialist groups similar to those attended by Mr Duffy in 'A Painful
Case',[60] other socialists rather than Marx were discussed.[61]

Griffith rejected socialism outright, and Joyce's main objection to
Sinn Féin was this avoidance of the social question: 'What I object to
most of all in his paper is that it is educating the people of Ireland on
the old pap of racial hatred whereas anyone can see that if the Irish
question exists, it exists for the Irish proletariat chiefly.'[62] Joyce also
understood that the success of Griffith's policy would be, in effect,
the substitution of Irish for English capital. 'But', he commented in
another letter to Stanislaus, 'no-one, I suppose, denies that
capitalism is a stage of progress. The Irish proletariat has yet to be
created.'[63] These comments indicate that political independence was

not enough, and that Joyce desired socialism in an Irish context, the very thing James Connolly had been trying to initiate.

In 1897 Connolly had published his first major theoretical work, *Erin's Hope*, which treated the conflict between the Irish clan system of common ownership of land and the introduction of the feudal system by the English conquerors. This theme was later developed in his *Labour in Irish History* (1910), the first Marxist analysis of Irish history. Connolly also pioneered the concept of industrial unionism in Ireland,[64] and it is curious that Labriola should have reminded Joyce only of Griffith, for syndicalism played no part in the 'Sinn Féin Policy'. Connolly's political beliefs were much closer to Labriola's than Griffith's ever were.*

Griffith, meanwhile, did not limit his combativeness to the political sphere. He intensified his quarrel with his literary compatriots which had begun with the skirmish over *In the Shadow of the Glen*. When Synge's new play, *The Playboy of the Western World*, was staged at the Abbey Theatre in 1907, Griffith unleashed a vitriolic attack:

> Mr Synge's play as a play is one of the worst constructed we have witnessed. As a presentation on the public stage it is a vile and unhuman story told in the foulest language we have ever listened to from a public platform.[65]

Joyce had anticipated that Synge would be condemned from the pulpit as a heretic by Griffith's paper and by the pietistic *Leader*, and he strongly urged, in a letter to Stanislaus, that Fred Ryan in particular should start another paper in defence of free thought for a little while.[66] But Joyce surprisingly sided with the nationalists against Yeats. He did so not because he was in favour of censorship, but partly to prove his point that the alliance between nationalism

---

* In 1900 Connolly attacked the President of the Irish Trades Union Congress, Mr George Leahy, for his advocacy of the slogan 'Ireland sober is Ireland free.' Connolly ridiculed his contention that if the workers 'were only sober their masters would not oppress them – they and their country would be free!!' (*James Connolly: Selected Political Writings*, ed. Owen Dudley Edwards and Bernard Ransom (London, 1973), pp. 366–8). In 'Cyclops' (*311; 401–2*), Bloom's approval of the temperance movement is scoffed at by the narrator, who recalls a musical evening given by the antitreating league when Bloom was supposedly put off by the serving of lemonade. In *Finnegans Wake*, Joyce intimates that the 'Erin Go Dry' mentality (462) leads to 'Ireland sober is Ireland stiff' (214). In altering the slogan, Joyce was perhaps recalling Connolly's jibe at the equation of Irish sobriety with social freedom.

and art works to the detriment of the latter, and partly to show his resentment towards the Irish writers.

Joyce, however, could not have agreed with Griffith's strictures on literature. A leader in the *Sinn Féin* edition of 27 February 1909 on 'Literature and Politics' compared Whitman's *Democratic Vistas* with the cultural aspirations of the Gaelic League. Whitman's harping on the primary need of a national literature dovetailed with the desires of the Irish-Ireland movement for their artists. Joyce believed that the social and religious problems of humanity were to be met and treated by literature, and he could proclaim, in Whitman's words, 'The priest departs, the divine literatus comes.' Democrat though he was, when Whitman looked upon the conditions of contemporary America, he perceived that the people were in need of liberation through the imagination more than through the franchise. This perception concurs with Joyce's idea of 'spiritual liberation' of the people made possible by art. Joyce could not condone, however, the 'democratic' spirit in poetry which rejected a great deal of European tradition in order to foster a native culture. Griffith took Whitman's pronouncements to mean that literature was an instrument for the nationalist cause.[67] As a result, he chided Yeats for relinquishing 'the propaganda that made him the first of our lyric poets to become an artist in English'. Yeats, on the other hand, still accused Griffith of that 'obscurantism' of the politician 'who would reject every idea which is not of immediate service to his cause'.[68] At heart, Joyce upheld with unswerving courage Yeats's stand in not allowing art to be subordinated to the national cause, and in preserving its right to project its own ideal.

Joyce recoiled, in addition, from the racism he detected in *Sinn Féin*. In this regard he was thinking mainly of his old nemesis, Oliver Gogarty. He wrote to Stanislaus,

> You complain of Griffith using Gogarty and Co. How do you expect him to fill his paper: he can't write it all himself. The part he does write, at least, has some intelligence and directness about it. As for O.G. I am waiting for the *S.F.* policy to make headway in the hope that he will join it for no doubt whatever exists in my mind but that, if he gets the chance and the moment comes, he will play the part of MacNally and Reynolds. I do not say this out of spleen. It is my final view of his character: a very native Irish growth, and if I begin to write my novel again it is in this way I shall treat them.[69]

It is implied in this statement that Joyce's treatment of Gogarty in *Ulysses* would have strong political implications, and Buck Mulligan is indeed portrayed as 'Ireland's gay betrayer' as well as Stephen's.

Joyce read three of Gogarty's articles in *Sinn Féin* on 'Ugly England' with critical interest. Being a renegade artist, Joyce said he was amused by Gogarty's description of the English middle-class, with reference to the 'slattern comediennes':[70] 'For them [the English] the sea must receive their shapeless skeleton pier with its bands, promenade and side shows; the nigger minstrel must shout and grin, and the slattern comediennes must dance and smile.'[71] But he became irritated by Gogarty's hypocrisy in denouncing the British Army's 'venereal excess', and he recommended that 'some unkind person' should write a book about the venereal condition of the Irish which he suspected to be worse than that of the English. Gogarty's dusty phrase, moreover, should be replaced by the unscientific expresion, 'venereal ill-luck'. The exasperated Joyce demanded, 'Am I the only honest person that has come out of Ireland in our time?'[72]

Joyce became even more annoyed when *Sinn Féin* took up the 'venereal excess' cry, and derisively suggested that Skeffington could write something on the subject, since he was a '*pure* man'. But he added,

> If I put down a bucket into my soul's well, sexual department, I draw up Griffith's and Ibsen's and Skeffington's and Bernard Vaughan's and St Aloysius' and Shelley's and Renan's water along with my own. And I am going to do that in my novel (inter alia) and plank the bucket down before the shades and substances above mentioned to see how they like it: and if they don't like it I can't help them.[73]

He also found Irish intellectuals, like Griffith, 'very tiresome' because their views seemed always to be thinly-disguised anti-English propaganda. For example, in an editorial on 'The Immorality of the British Army', Griffith referred to it as 'the only mercenary and most diseased army in civilisation.'[74] Joyce commented, 'I suppose he prefers the conscription system because it is French.'[75] For him neither kind of army was warranted. Gogarty produced another tirade on 'our' glorious army in *Sinn Féin*, this time under the pseudonym of 'Mettus Curtius'.[76] And Griffith continued to pour out articles, complete with statistics, on the same topic as late as April 1907. Bloom notes this fact in 'Lotus-Eaters'

(72–3; 88): 'Griffith's paper is on the same tack now: an army rotten with venereal disease: overseas or halfseasover empire.'

Gogarty endorsed Griffith's view in his articles and asserted strongly, 'the facts of the case are only too clear to anyone who has the unblinded eye to see them.'[77] The Citizen, ironically, repeats this statement when he tells Bloom defiantly, 'there's no-one as blind as the fellow that won't see, if you know what that means' *(326; 423)*. And his reference to the 'syphilisation' of the English seems to be a deliberate echo of Gogarty's and Griffith's remarks on 'venereal excess'. But Joyce corrects these partial perspectives in 'Circe', which is set in the red-light district of Dublin, as if to highlight his point that syphilis is not an English innovation. 'The Irish consider England a sink: but, if cleanliness be important in this matter, what is Ireland?' he asked Stanislaus.[78] Joyce's Homeric analogue to Circe's changing of men into swine is not only a joke being played at Gogarty's expense, but also a rebuttal to his *Sinn Féin* articles, a political sleight-of-hand featuring 'Ugly Ireland' instead of 'Ugly England'.

Joyce reacted most vehemently to Gogarty's last instalments in *Sinn Féin*, dismissing them as 'stupid drivel'.[79] Gogarty was convinced that the 'Jew mastery of England' explained such things as the gross materialism of the English and their underhanded methods of enacting justice when the Irish refused 'to bring upon themselves the moral ruin and physical decay which joining the English mercenary forces certainly involves'. Gogarty saw these as 'signs' of the decline and fall of England, and ended his final article by saying, 'I can smell a Jew . . . and in Ireland there's something rotten.'[80] In *Ulysses* Haines and Deasy hold the same views, and Buck Mulligan is hostile to Bloom because he is a Jew. Joyce's indictment of Irish nationalism covered not only its provincialism, but its arrant prejudice as well.

Gogarty was not the first in this unfortunate ranting; he had been anticipated by Griffith. When the anti-Semitic outburst took place in Limerick in 1904, Griffith defended Father Creagh, the priest who had warned the people against the 'usurious toils' of the Jews, in the front-page 'All Ireland' column of the *United Irishman*:

> The Jews of Great Britain and Ireland have united, as is their wont, to crush the Christian who dares to block their path or point them out for what they are – nine-tenths of them – usurers and parasites of industries. In this category we do not include the Zionist

minority of the Jews, who include those honest and patriotic Jews who desire the re-establishment of the Hebrew nation in Palestine – the last thing on earth the majority desire. Attack a Jew – other than a Zionist Jew – and all Jewry comes to his assistance. Thus, when France condemned a Jew, Captain Dreyfus, to perpetual imprisonment for high treason, all Jewry combined and spent over ten millions sterling seeking to ruin France. . . .

In all countries and in all Christian ages he has been a usurer and a grinder of the poor. The influence he has recently acquired in this country is a matter of the most serious concern to the people. In Dublin, half the labourer population is locked up in his toils. Father Creagh deserves the thanks of the Irish people for preventing the poor of Limerick being placed in a similar predicament. The Jew in Ireland is in every respect an economic evil. He produces no wealth himself – he draws it from others – he is the most successful seller of foreign goods, he is an unfair competitor with the ratepaying Irish shopkeeper, and he remains among us, ever and always an alien. We have spoken pretty freely about the Jew, since we observe that there is not even one of our great Catholic papers to stand up against the Grand Jewish League with the Limerick priest who has had the spirit to denounce his methods of training. But for the small minority – the Zionist Jews – the patriotic men who desire to reconstruct the Hebrew nation, and who feel bitterly the humiliation of their race through the sordid pursuit of gold by the majority – we have the same esteem we have for all patriotic and lofty-minded men.[81]

Bloom and Stephen counter the tenor of these libellous statements in *Ulysses*. Stephen pointedly tells Mr Deasy, 'A merchant . . . is one who buys cheap and sells dear, jew or gentile, is he not?' (*34; 41*) And Bloom takes issue with the argument that the presence of Jews signifies a nation's decay:

– Jews, he softly imparted in an aside in Stephen's ear, are accused of ruining. Not a vestige of truth in it, I can safely say. History – would you be surprised to learn? – proves up to the hilt Spain decayed when the Inquisition hounded the jews out and England prospered when Cromwell, an uncommonly able ruffian, who, in other respects, has much to answer for, imported them. Why? Because they are practical and are proved to be so . . . But in the economic, not touching religion, domain, the priest spells poverty. Spain again, you saw in the war, compared with goahead

America. Turks, it's in the dogma. Because if they didn't believe they'd go straight to heaven when they die they'd try to live better – at least, so I think. That's the juggle on which the p.p.'s★ raise the wind on false pretences (*643–4; 746*)

In this way, Bloom offsets the violent rhetoric not only of the Citizen and Father Creagh, but that of Gogarty and Griffith as well.

Fred Ryan, on the other hand, condemned the boycott of the Jews in the very first issue of *Dana*. Griffith protested in the *United Irishman* feebly and naïvely, 'But the Jew in Limerick has not been boycotted because he is a Jew, but because he is a usurer.' Ryan sent a firm reply to the *United Irishman*: 'The Limerick disturbance distinctly began in an incitement *against Jews as Jews*.' He objected, moreover, to Griffith's remarks on Dreyfus:

Does any intelligent person now believe that Zola was bribed to ruin his country? Or Clemenceau, or Millerand, or Jaures, or, in fact, the bulk of the democratic leaders? . . . since the Republican and Democratic parties who were mostly 'Dreyfusard' have *now* succeeded in beating down the Chauvinists and Clericals and converting a majority of the French electorate to their side, are we to conclude that France is irretrievably ruined? . . . The plain fact of the matter is that the much-discussed Dreyfus case simply resolved into a phase of the fight between the clericals and the French Republic, which in one form or another has been going on since the Republic was established. It was not the 'Dreyfusards' who wished to 'ruin' France; it was the anti-Dreyfusards who thought they had found a good pretext in the Dreyfus case to overthrow the Republic. They chose the side of fanaticism and fraud, and they were beaten. That is the whole story. Dreyfus, to both sides, was more a shuttle-cock than anything else. Anti-Semitism, in short, is the refuse of the Continental reactionary parties. It may seem good tactics on the part of corrupt militarists and capitalists to set the mob at the heels of rich Jews. But the cause of true liberty has nothing to gain by being associated with such tricks, and the very *personnel* of the parties who resort to them ought to warn us of their objects. Let us fight for liberty as liberty and put down capitalist greed as capitalist greed, but let us resolutely shut our eyes to questions of race and creed, which are

★ parish priest's.

only raised by the reactionaries to create disorder in the camp of progress.[82]

Griffith now moderated his tone but, missing the drift of Ryan's argument, still persisted obstinately in his objection to the 'Jew trader' not because of his creed or beliefs, but with his 'character and actions':

> We are unable to understand how Mr Ryan has arrived at the belief that the capitalists set the mob at the heels of rich Jews. The major part of the capitalists of the world are Jews, and we have never yet heard of a great anti-Jewish capitalist in any quarter of the globe. There is no greater existent danger to civilisation than the growth of capitalism, the accumulation of the world's wealth – or what men are pleased to consider wealth and starve amidst plenty for lack of – and that few human birds of prey – proceeds unchecked. We cannot, nor can Mr Ryan, view without apprehension the power wielded in Europe by the Jewish financier. A world ruled by the Jewish capitalist would eventually invite the destruction which an oppressed and brutalised proletariat wreaks upon a debauched civilisation. So far as Ireland is concerned, she sees the Jews swarming in while her children are going out. The fault lies in the fact that we are ruled not by ourselves but by foreigners, to whom our interests are diametrically opposed. But when an attempt is made to alleviate the situation – when a priest is courageous enough to sound a note of alarm, and in consequence assailed by all the ramifications of the Jewish bond – it is, we firmly hold, the duty of Irishmen to stand by him, and we only regret that in other cities in Ireland, suffering from the Jewish usurer, priests as courageous as Father Creagh have not warned the unthinking people on when the harpies prey.[83]

It now becomes clear why Griffith allowed Gogarty's bigoted attack on the Jews to be published in *Sinn Féin*. Bloom grappled with the Citizen for similar warped views. He concurred with the sketch of the 'new Jew' who, in *Zionism and the Jewish Future* (a book Joyce had with him), proclaimed that 'If nationalism means hostility, the persecution of other nations, narrow-mindedness and racial fanaticism, I reject it.'[84] Joyce demonstrated that if there was something rotten in Ireland, the Jew was not the cause for it, but political and clerical prejudice.

Ironically, Gogarty regarded the portrait of Mulligan as a

'betrayal' on Joyce's part.[85] Joyce's prophecy about Gogarty's betrayal of Sinn Féin turned out to be, according to Gogarty's biographer, Ulick O'Connor, wide of the mark.[86] When Joyce lived briefly at the Martello Tower Gogarty rented in 1904, one of the frequent weekend visitors was Arthur Griffith, who swam regularly with Gogarty. In the phrase 'To ourselves . . . new paganism . . . omphalos' (7; 7) ('Omphalos' was Gogarty's name for the Martello Tower)[87] Stephen mocks the Celtic revival and links Mulligan with Sinn Féin. When Griffith outlined his policy at the first annual convention in 1905, Gogarty supported it. Only Gogarty's speech was reported in the *United Irishman*.[88] Gogarty had in fact been writing for the paper since 1899, and he remained Griffith's close friend until the latter's death in 1922. He even embalmed him. Just before Griffith died, he had expressed his wish to make Gogarty rather than Tim Healy the first Governor-General of Ireland.[89]

In *Ulysses*, however, Mulligan toadies to the Englishman Haines and the Church he blasphemes against. And Joyce detested Gogarty on these political grounds too: 'Gogarty would jump into the Liffey to save a man's life but he seems to have little hesitation in condemning generations to servitude.'[90] But he was not as typical of that 'stupid, dishonest, tyrannical and cowardly burgher class' as Joyce made him out to be. Writing under the pseudonym of 'Alpha and Omega' Gogarty unleashed his boldest attack on the establishment in a play entitled *Blight: The Tragedy of Dublin* (1917), which Joyce read. Gogarty, before Sean O'Casey, exposed the deteriorating conditions of Dublin slums, and lampooned talk of Christian 'charity' when social reform was required.

Not all Sinn Féin sympathisers were as staunch supporters of Griffith as Gogarty was, or as moderate in their political objectives. The more militant Cumann na nGaedheal recruited many members, and 'advanced' nationalist societies called the Dungannon clubs began flourishing in Belfast. These were more rigidly separatist and extremist in tone, and were generally dissatisfied with what they considered to be Griffith's compromising attitude towards England as evidenced in his 'dual monarchy' theory. The first open rift between these organisations and Griffith occurred at the second annual convention of the national council in September 1906, which Joyce was reading about in *Sinn Féin*. Non-resident members, like P. S. O'Hegarty and Bulmer Hobson, one of the initiators of the nationalist movement in the North, felt Griffith was rejecting complete separation from England in favour of the mere partial independence advocated in the Hungarian Policy.[91] As a result, Hobson, determined to advance the republican cause, launched his Belfast weekly, the *Republic*, on 13 December 1906. Joyce felt the split important enough to warrant sending Stanislaus a copy of Hobson's paper from Rome.[92]

Griffith and Hobson differed not only in ultimate objectives, but also on the methods whereby to attain them. Hobson, although prepared to sanction passive resistance as a temporary measure, believed that a republic could only be achieved by physical force.[93] He felt his view was justified by the examples of armed resistance in Irish history, and that Griffith's policy broke with the Fenian tradition. A series of articles running from February to April 1907 on 'Fenianism in Practice', written pseudonymously by 'Sarsfield' – the leader of James II's army defeated at the Battle of the Boyne in 1690 – pushed for an Irish-Ireland.

'Sarsfield' attributed the success of the Irish Revival to the assertion of the principle of aggressive nationalism, of which Fenianism was taken to be a symbol. All movements and organisations working for the realisation of an independent Irish nation were manifestations of Fenianism in practice. The Irish-Ireland movement represented 'the fullest and most complete expression of militant Irish Nationalism yet reached', not merely in politics, 'but in language, in industries, in the arts, in all the internal and external functions of a nation'. The national instinct had not confined itself to the physical realisation of the nation, but also to its 'spiritual' realisation, inspiring all spheres of national activity.[94] Hence the 'Language Fenian' in the Gaelic League is 'political in the bedrock nationalist sense; [he] fights English civilisation at its root, and it is a war to the death'. The restoration of native culture precipitates 'that irresistible native power of assimilation'.[95] The 'Gaelic Athletic Fenian' enters into combat against another aspect of the Anglicisation of Ireland, and proves victorious because he is applying 'Fenianism in practice in the games section of the national life':

> We were at one time a race of fine physique, and, though most of it has emigrated, we can be so again – ay, and we *shall!*[96]

The 'Sinn Féin Fenian', 'Sarsfield' maintains, represents the culmination of the Irish-Ireland philosophy:

> The Sinn Féin man supports and works not only for his own

particular section of the movement, the political side, but for every section – every movement which aims at the realisation of any portion of the national life by action within Ireland has his support, and he welds them all together. His position is, that the Irish people, and no other people, possess all rights within Ireland, and should exercise them, and *will* exercise them. He says, in effect, 'We will not have in this country English laws, or the English language, or the English economic system, or educational system, usage, institution, or actually whatever, save such as are in accordance with our national characteristics, developed by ourselves, evolving unrestrainedly from our own civilisation; if any such there be, of foreign origin, let them go – or wait to be forcibly expelled.' Fenianism said, 'We will not have in this country English laws or government, or English landlords, or any who would conspire against the liberties and rights of the people; if any such there be, let them go – or wait to be forcibly expelled.' The principle in each case is identical, the method and the scope of its application differ, but *the principle remains unaltered*, hence the Sinn Féin policy is Fenianism in practice – on the lines of passive resistance, the clogging of the machine of British government, the building up of the intellect of the nation, as well as its muscle. Hence the Sinn Féin Fenian who heads this article.[97]

The Sinn Féin, Language, Gaelic Athletic, Industrial and other Fenians all stand on the same level, all employ 'fighting methods'. On this basis, 'Sarsfield' made the incredible claim that they are all physical force men, all rely on coercion, 'for the physical force principle is not the less physical force because it calls itself "passive resistance".'[98] Their common goal remains the destruction of English civilisation in Ireland.

For Joyce patriotism militant represented the twin symptom, with the Church militant, of the same disease. He objected to the application of the principle of physical force to any phase of national life. The practice of Fenianism had taken hold of Ireland, and it is in this context that Joyce makes 'Fenian' the symbol of the 'Cyclops' chapter. It is the Sinn Féin philosophy, employing violent rhetoric, proclaiming 'We'll put force against force' (*329; 427*), that Joyce is primarily attacking. That is why the Citizen, a Sinn Féin Fenian, is hostile to Bloom even though Bloom is purported to have given Griffith the idea for the Hungarian Policy. Griffith's moderate objectives are not adequate for the Citizen, who desires complete separation from England by force. Confusion as to the object of Joyce's satire has led many critics to argue that he is denouncing the Sinn Féin movement outright. But Joyce is exposing the dangers of militant nationalism which extreme Sinn Féiners were advocating. Joyce's article on 'Fenianism' for *Il Piccolo della sera* in 1907, probably based on his reading of the *Republic*, also makes this point quite clear:

> Now, it is impossible for a desperate and bloody doctrine like Fenianism to continue its existence . . . and in fact, as agrarian crimes and crimes of violence have become more and more rare, Fenianism too has once more changed its name and appearance. It is still a separatist doctrine but it no longer uses dynamite. The new Fenians are joined in a party which is called Sinn Féin (We Ourselves). . . .
> From many points of view, this last phase of Fenianism is perhaps the most formidable. Certainly its influence has once more remodelled the character of the Irish people.[99]

Joyce evidently preferred passive resistance and economic boycotts to what he termed 'the persuasive faculty of the knife or the bomb'. Although he had reservations about Griffith's policies, Joyce basically agreed with his non-violent credo and his moderate views.

'Nations have their ego, just like individuals', Joyce announced in his lecture on 'Ireland, Island of Saints and Sages'. He then proceeded to apply this precept to the political chapter of *Ulysses*, where it is embodied in the Fenian Cyclops. The Sinn Féin policy of 'We ourselves', which Joyce feared would go out of control, reflected national vainglory.* In the narrator's 'I' Joyce may have been obliquely satirising *The Ego and His Own*, in which the second section bears the simple title 'I' to express Stirner's radical notion of egoism. The patriotism described by national figures, like Skeffington and D. P. Moran, represented other extremes to be avoided. In Skeffington's novel about the 1798 uprising, *In Dark and Evil Days*, Esmond, the protagonist, pronounces the lofty ideal, 'It is better to die in Ireland, for Ireland, than live elsewhere.'[101] Joyce abhorred sentimental patriotism and preferred to live in exile than to

---

* In attacking the sentiment of 'My country, right or wrong', Joyce may have been adapting Herbert Spencer's argument in *The Study of Sociology*, a book he had with him in Trieste. Spencer, like Joyce, asserted that 'Patriotism is nationally that which egoism is individually', and maintained that emancipating ourselves from 'national vanity' constitutes a vital step towards achieving true patriotism.[100]

die for Ireland. Moran's *Tom O'Kelly*, on the other hand, extolled Irish virtue by denigrating the English, and the Anglo-Irish ascendancy. Whereas Tom O'Kelly leaves Ireland as an 'economic exile'[102] Joyce made his leave-taking a truly patriotic mission, a call to forge the conscience of his race. He becomes one of Ireland's 'most favoured children', a 'spiritual' exile. Joyce agreed with Wilde in *The Soul of Man under Socialism* in rejecting a disproportionate egoism and replacing it with an unselfish 'Individualism'.*

Although sceptical in outlook, Joyce did not want his work to appear cynical: 'I don't want to hurt or offend those of my countrymen who are devoting their lives to a cause they feel to be necessary and just.'[103] One of Joyce's friends, Dixon, needled him on this point, as Joyce's brother, Charles, informed Stanislaus:

> Dixon . . . said it was a pity that Jim did not use his 'undoubted' talent for a better purpose than writing a book like *Dubliners*. 'Why did he not use his talents for the betterment of his country and his people?' Jim replied that he was probably the only Irishman who wrote leading articles for the Italian press and that all his articles in 'Il Piccolo' were about Ireland and the Irish people. He said also that he was the first to introduce Irish tweeds into Austria although that business was not the least in his own line.[104]

Joyce insisted that his work was a patriotic undertaking.

Many critics have argued that Joyce remained aloof from politics even while in exile. Joyce's work as an Italian journalist bears witness to the contrary. Not only did he keep abreast of the Irish political scene, but Joyce staunchly defended Griffith's line of argument on key issues. When the Liberals returned to power in 1906 with a huge majority, the Home Rule question came to the fore once again. Joyce took the opportunity to scourge the parliamentarians for their betrayal of Parnell. He also branded them as a self-seeking lot who were bankrupting Ireland. How closely Joyce was following *Sinn Féin* is indicated by the titles of his three articles for *Il Piccolo*. Joyce borrowed the title for his article 'Home Rule Comes of Age' from an editorial in *Sinn Féin*:

> The infant [Home Rule] born on the morrow of its publication has come of age. He is a man – he demands his birthright – that Irish

---

* See below, p. 220.

Parliament and that regenerated Irish nation the Irish
Parliamentary Party declared it had won on the day his mother
bore him.[105]

Similarly, Joyce took the title of 'The Shade of Parnell' from a
political cartoon in *Sinn Féin* which depicted a member of the Irish
Party bowing at the feet of the English Prime Minister with Parnell's
shade hovering in the background. It bore the title, 'The Shade of
Parnell' and had for caption, 'And this is how they block the way
when I am gone.'[106] The article on the 'Home Rule Comet' was also
inspired by another cartoon in *Sinn Féin* entitled 'The Comet'. The
comet has 'the budget' (a recent budget inflicting a taxation of two
millions per annum on Ireland) written on it, with a crowd of people
observing it through telescopes. The caption reads, 'Can anybody
find the promised Home Rule Tail?'[107]

Joyce also adapted some elements of Griffith's rhetoric in his
article on Home Rule. He introduces his first paragraph, before
tracing the progress of successive Home Rule Acts since the initial
measure of 1886, with the number of years elapsed since that date:
'Twenty-one years ago'. The next paragraph begins with the same
technique: 'Seven years ago'.[108] This stylistic tactic renders Joyce's
argument, that parliamentary agitation is ineffectual, more convincing. Griffith's editorial on 'Devolution' employed identical
stylistic techniques, as his two opening paragraphs begin in exactly
the same way:

> Twenty one years ago the British Prime Minister, faced by the
> alternative of ruling Ireland by the sword, or re-establishing a
> Legislature in Dublin chose the Legislature. . . .
>   Seven years later the British Liberal Party was returned to
> power by the votes of the Irish Parliamentary Party.[109]

More importantly, the arguments put forward by Joyce are those
which Griffith was continually making in the *United Irishman* and
Sinn Féin. For example, Joyce claims that 'the most fervid enemy of
the Irish Catholics is the head of English Catholicism, the Duke of
Norfolk.'[110] He does not substantiate this charge, and one might
conclude that he is merely giving vent to one of his frequent tirades
against Rome. But he is following *Sinn Féin*'s regular comments on
English machinations against Ireland at the Vatican:

> At present what takes place is this: the Duke of Norfolk visits the
> Vatican three times each year as the representative of the Catholics

of the 'United Kingdom'. Of course this mean-souled man whose hatred of Ireland and the Irish is perhaps the most intense part of his nature – and whose revenues, by the way, are derived from confiscated Catholic Church property – does not 'represent' the Irish Catholics; but he is accepted in Rome as embracing them in his representation, because an Irish Catholic layman is quite unknown in Rome as a representative. Every slander this man pours out on Irish Nationalism is accepted at the Vatican as the views of an accredited representative. The position is one that cannot be tolerated if the Irish national cause is to be carried to success. The attempt to undermine the Irish-Ireland movement is the last proof needed to show that Ireland must, for her own protection, take steps to establish and accredit a permanent representation at the Vatican.[111]

When Joyce attacks the Irish Party, he says

For twenty-seven years it has talked and agitated. In that time it has collected 35 million francs from its supporters, and the fruit of its agitation is that Irish taxes have gone up 88 million francs and the Irish population has decreased a million.[112]

A typical extract from the *United Irishman* reveals how much Joyce based his politics on the intransigent press:

We are content to wait . . . to ask him [Redmond] how the circumstances of Ireland have altered since 1896 when he declared it the duty of the Irish members of the British Parliament to oppose the Liberals whenever they regained power, unless they made Home Rule the first plank of their platform. Ten years have passed. In the interim, Ireland has paid to maintain the Irish Party at Westminster, £120,000, has lost 250,000 of her people and has had the taxation of the remainder increased by millions of pounds.[113]

It would be difficult, faced with these twin statements, to distinguish between the Irish and Italian press, except for the different statistics.

Joyce was also concerned about Ireland's image before the world. In 'Ireland at the Bar' he complained: 'Abroad there is no talk of Ireland except when uprisings break out.'[114] And he chided the European press for presenting a distorted picture of Ireland. There had been a few violent deaths in 1907, Joyce conceded, but, as mentioned earlier, at the hands of British troops in Belfast who opened fire on an unarmed crowd and killed two people.[115] On that occasion, *Sinn Féin* had criticised the Irish Party vehemently for not making a formal protest to the British Government.[116] In later years Joyce still defended his race against those, like Wyndham Lewis, who insisted that the Irish were pugnacious. 'Would you say they were pugnacious?' Joyce asked. 'That's not been my experience', he concluded, and added – 'a very gentle race'.[117] In 'Ireland at the Bar', he viewed Ireland as a weak nation 'unable to appeal to the modern conscience of England and other countries'.[118] Joyce interpreted his role as an exile as presenting to the European nations a more balanced picture of Ireland. His task had two aspects. While in his art he was attempting to instil a foreign conscience into Ireland, in his journalistic exploits he was introducing the Irish predicament to foreign nations. Joyce's commitment might appear paradoxical, but Joyce considered it patriotic. He was implementing Kettle's proposal that Ireland become European in both the cultural and political spheres. In his own way he was taking up arms for Ireland and raising her to respectability.

Joyce made it clear to Stanislaus, when the latter urged him to be friends with Kettle, that he took no interest whatsoever in parliamentarianism.[119] But Joyce still respected Kettle and kept himself informed of his career. Kettle had become the first Professor of National Economics in the new National University of Ireland in 1908. When his *Home Rule Finance: An Experiment in Justice* was published in 1911, Joyce had a copy sent to him promptly by George Roberts.[120] Kettle's figures indicated that England was running Ireland at a loss to herself, and that Home Rule would necessitate a subsidy. Griffith pounced immediately on what he considered to be a grave political blunder on Kettle's part. He claimed that Kettle had completely misunderstood the figures, and in so doing he 'supplied the Unionists in England with the argument that Home Rule would mean a subsidy out of England's pocket', and simultaneously 'played right into the hands of the Irish Unionists'. Griffith proposed that the collection of the entire revenues of Ireland be placed instead in the hands of an Irish Government.[121]

As Joyce indicated to Stanislaus in 1906, he approved of Griffith's measures for Ireland's economic woes. He now followed Griffith's merciless attack on Kettle's 'arithmetical ignorance and political folly' in the columns of *Sinn Féin*. When a third Home Rule bill was presented in the House of Commons and eventually passed in May 1912, Griffith published two pamphlets, which Joyce purchased, on

The Finance of the Home Rule Bill and *The Home Rule Bill Examined*.
The Bill reduced the number of Irish members from 103 to 42 and
not 40 as Joyce claims in 'The Shade of Parnell'. Griffith wondered
how the Irish Party, which professed to follow Parnell's directives,
hoped to reconcile 'the acceptance of an enormous reduction in Irish
representation at Westminster whilst Westminster holds Irish
services and Irish revenues in its hands with Parnell's refusal to
consent to a reduction of representation under such
circumstances'.[122] In financial terms, Griffith feared that increased
taxation would inevitably lead to dire political consequences:

> The Unionist manufacturer and man of commerce will accept
> Home Rule and maintain it if he realises that his earned income is
> not so heavily taxed as it would be under Westminster rule. The
> Irish Government starting with a 'deficit' of two millions alleged
> against it, must as its first duty reconcile all sections in Ireland to its
> existence and rally them to its support. But if it does so, it takes
> serious financial risk. If it does the opposite, it must face the
> hostility of the Orange North with an economic footing for its
> bigoted opposition. It must face an industrial antagonism in the
> urban South and a general dissatisfaction amongst all classes. In
> short, no Irish Government can vindicate the finance of the
> proposed measure without committing political suicide.[123]

Joyce ignored the adverse political effects of the Bill described by
Griffith, and stressed instead the hostility of the classes in 'The Shade
of Parnell'. At the same time, he summarised Griffith's argument
against the financial clauses of the Bill:

> Into its tangle of financial qualifications, there is no chance of
> penetrating. At any rate, the Irish government about to be born
> will have to cover a deficit ably created by the British treasury,
> either by manipulation of local and imperial taxes, or by a
> reduction of its administrative expenses, or by an increase in direct
> taxes, in any case provoking the disillusioned hostily of the middle
> and lower classes. The Irish separatist party would like to reject
> this Greek gift, which makes the Chancellor of the exchequer in
> Dublin a titular minister fully responsible to the taxpayers and at
> the same time dependent on the British cabinet, one who has the
> power to tax without being able to control the collections of his
> department – a transmitter which cannot work unless the dynamo
> at London sends a current of the necessary voltage.[124]

Joyce affirms yet again in 1912 that the solution to Ireland's economic ills resides in Griffith's policies.

Griffith's paper provided Joyce with material not only for his political articles but also for his art. When the Citizen says '*Sinn féin amhain*' (*306; 396*) ('Ourselves alone forever'), he is probably referring to a poem of the same title which appeared in the very first issue of *Sinn Féin*; it ended with the lines: 'Here we strive, and, fighting, for the land we own, / And we hope for freedom, trust Ourselves alone.'[125] The question of evicted tenants, one of whose holdings the Citizen has bought, was not only a topical issue during the early Land League days, but also a going concern of *Sinn Féin*. The Parliamentary Party, according to the Sinn Féiners, was not providing relief measures for them. The vote of evicted tenants did not seem to count, *Sinn Féin* pointed out, and offered to help with their reinstatement.[126] *Sinn Féin*'s position renders the Citizen's buying up the holding of an evicted tenant all the more ironical.

Another unexpected source is an article on 'Esperanto and Irish'. The anonymous writer suspected that Esperanto had been taken up in Ireland to stifle the growth of Gaelic. And he accused a certain Dr Traill of using the universal language as a weapon with which to fight Irish-Ireland.[127] In 'Circe' an unknown sinister-looking figure watches Bloom suspiciously from 'under a wideleaved sombrero'. Bloom asks the lady in Spanish what street he finds himself on, and the figure responds in Gaelic that it is Mabbot Street. Bloom thanks her in Gaelic and mutters, 'Haha . . . Esperanto . . . Gaelic league spy' (*436; 568*). The mysterious figure is a Gaelic Leaguer. Bloom suspects that she dresses in Spanish attire in order to spy on exponents of esperanto, like himself. Bloom's advocacy of esperanto (*490; 610*), then, indicates subtly his opposition to Gaelic and to aggressive aspects of Language Fenianism.

This was Joyce's position also, for, as he told Stanislaus, 'If the Irish programme did not insist on the Irish language I suppose I could call myself a nationalist. As it is, I am content to recognize myself an exile: and, prophetically, a repudiated one.'[128] He still separated himself from the nationalists by his exile and by his socialism. Griffith held at first a moderate view on the language issue. Although he expressed the wish to see an 'Irish-tongued Ireland', he thought a politically independent Ireland was 'a thousand times more important'.[129] Griffith made this statement in the *United Irishman* in 1902. By 1909, however, he no longer held that view: 'Time and circumstances could regain and restore the liberties and political institutions of Ireland, but if she lost her language she lost something that could never be restored.'[130] In 1904 Fred Ryan had argued that to make Irish the test of nationalism would exclude the achievements of such men as Parnell. What in fact gave a nation its noble distinction was its culture, science, and art.[131] Joyce had attended classes in Irish for a while in Dublin, but he gave them up because Patrick Pearse, the instructor, exalted Irish by denigrating English.[132] Joyce did not approve of Pearse's political writings either. These were the 'pearse orations' referred to anachronistically in Anna Livia's monologue (620). Pearse gave an oration on Wolfe Tone in 1913, two on Robert Emmet in 1914, and a final one on the Fenian O'Donovan Rossa in 1915. He thought Robert Emmet's last words were 'the most memorable words ever uttered by an Irishman'.[133] Joyce parodies Pearse's view by having Bloom break wind on reading Emmet's last words in 'Sirens'. Pearse described Emmet's death in a sentimentally patriotic style:

> And his death was august. In the great space of Thomas Street an immense silent crowd; in front of Saint Catherine's Church a gallows upon a platform; a young man climbs to it, quiet, serene, almost smiling, they say – ah, he was very brave; there is no cheer from the crowd, no groan; this man is to die for them, but no man dares to say aloud 'God bless you, Robert Emmet.' Dublin must one day wash out in blood the shameful memory of that quiescence. . . . He was saying 'Not yet' when the hangman kicked aside the plank and his body was launched into the air. They say it swung for half-an-hour, with terrible contortions, before he died. When he was dead the comely head was severed from the body.[134]

Joyce may also have aimed at deflating Pearse's oration in 'Cyclops' (*308–310; 399–402*), when he satirically describes an Irish revolutionary's execution, probably Emmet's as well as the Croppy Boy's.

Joyce's sympathy for Sinn Féin in his articles for *Il Piccolo* was unwittingly repaid. A parliamentarian like Kettle had reproached *Chamber Music* in a review written in 1907 for its lack of 'national feeling': 'The inspiration of the book is almost entirely literary. There is no trace of the folklore, folk dialect, or even national feeling that have covered the work of practically every writer in contemporary Ireland.'[135] Now he came out against *Dubliners* by warning Joyce, 'I'll slate it.'[136] Such a story as 'An Encounter' he considered 'beyond anything in its outspokenness he had ever read'.[137] Griffith proved more amenable. In 1911 Joyce sent a public letter, which contained a history of his difficulties in publishing *Dubliners* and the controversial passage about King Edward VII, to newspapers in Ireland. Only two newspapers published the letter, and of these two only Griffith did so at the risk of libel by publishing it in full. The next year, when Joyce visited Dublin to settle the contract disputes over *Dubliners* with George Roberts, the publisher, he consulted Griffith who, as he informed Stanislaus in a letter,

> received me very kindly and remembered my letter. He says I am
> not the first person from whom he has heard this story. He says
> Roberts has been playing that game for years. He says the idea of
> Maunsel sueing me is simple bluff and believes that they will not
> come into court and that if I get a strong solicitor on my side they
> will yield. He gave me a note to a first-class solicitor in
> Westmoreland Street. He asked me also to send him copies of my
> articles in P.d.S.[138]

Just as he had defended Joyce's right of independent thinking in *The Day of the Rabblement*, Griffith now asserted Joyce's freedom of political comment on Edward VII against 'one-eyed' printers. An ardent nationalist could scarcely have done more for Joyce at this stage than Griffith did.

Griffith probably saw Joyce's letter as a good stick with which to beat the English. His hatred of England overrode all other concerns. In 1909 a daily edition of *Sinn Féin* appeared for a short while. The front page of the issue of 8 January carried a cartoon depicting the King of England walking over Ireland with a sword on which is written the word 'Anglicisation' with the caption 'Plague'. Joyce punned, in answer, that 'there's no plagues like rome' in *Finnegans Wake* (465). He was not alone in considering Rome a greater threat to Ireland than England. An Orangeman writing in the *Republic* complained that Griffith's paper which at one time described Vaticanism as the 'bane of Ireland and demanded that Ireland should be freed from Vatican rule, now . . . screeches with all its force for a closer union with the Vatican'.[139] He went on to argue,

> If you clear Vaticanism out of Ireland, neither Englishman nor
> sectarianism will remain a generation. When the Irish Roman
> Catholic becomes nationalist enough to refuse to heed the Pope
> when he meddles in Irish political affairs, then England will cease

to go to the Vatican when she wants an Irish movement crushed. When the Irish Roman Catholic becomes nationalist enough to join a nationalist movement neither England nor the Pope will be able to crush it.[140]

Joyce, like Stephen in *Ulysses*, concurred with these views. He desired separation from England, but, although he never stated it, without alienating the Protestant North. He, like the Protestants, also opposed 'Rome Rule' in both temporal and spiritual matters. 'Sarsfield' attempted to quell Protestant fears in his articles on Irish-Ireland by stating that he too saw the chief danger of the movement as lapsing into sectarianism. The remedy lay in fighting the Church in Ireland and forcing it to recognise that its function was spiritual, not political.[141]

In 'Circe' (*490; 610*), Bloom agreed, in his own way, that 'a free lay church in a free lay state' was preferable. Bloom is recalling Cavour's famous formula, 'Libera Chiesa in libero stato', which attempted to reconcile the apparently conflicting aims of nationalism and religion. O'Connell had advocated essentially the same doctrine by endorsing the view that 'the Irish take their politics from Ireland and their religion from Rome.'[142] The idea of a liberal state held a peculiar significance for Ireland in the 1860s. When the Irish hierarchy pressed for the disestablishment of the Protestant Church of Ireland, this action, as E. R. Norman points out, unwittingly and paradoxically placed them at odds with the Vatican:

> They were working for the establishment in Ireland of the very principles over which Pius IX had joined issue with the Italian Liberals in his excruciating endeavour to preserve the connexion of Church and State and prevent the secularization of ecclesiastical property. The Irish bishops therefore flew in the face of the *Syllabus of Errors* in a campaign to attain that which the Papacy most dreaded: a 'free church in a free state'.[143]

In Bloom's statement, then, Joyce ironically points out once again the necessity of eliminating the Church's political power. Just as he had welcomed the advent of socialism as a counterpoise to the Church's political power, Joyce conceived of his art as a weapon with which to supplant its spiritual dominance. Joyce not only exposed the shortcomings of Sinn Féin, but his politics went beyond Griffith's and consisted in Anna Livia's motto, 'Ourselves, oursouls alone' (623).

2 'Zürichschicken': Waging the Inkbattle

> In the midst of deviation and destruction lies the Beauty of
> Switzerland, undeviating and undestroyed. Here a secure
> harmonious home of peace unites that which beyond the
> boundaries is cleft by hate. Here the desire to love first uttered its
> deed–word: Help. Here more than in places which the war
> profanes, we hope to find courage for our commencing.
>
> *(The International Review,*
> vol. I, 5 July 1915)*

When war broke out in July 1914, Joyce faced the threat of having to
interrupt work on *Ulysses*, which he had then just begun. He
persevered at his task, however, perhaps fortified by the idea, as he
later told Georges Borach in Zürich in 1918, that some of the best art
in the world was produced in conditions of war:

> Consider: Renaissance Italy gave us the greatest artists. The
> Talmud says at one point, 'We Jews are like the olive: we give our
> best when we are being crushed, when we are collapsing under the
> burden of our foliage.'[144]

The olive is the symbol of peace but also of resistance. While others
displayed their heroism in armed combat, Joyce remained content to
act as paladin of the written word.

Joyce considered himself a 'prisoner of war' in Zürich. He was
released on 'parole' in July 1915 by the Austrian Government in
Trieste for reasons of health.[145] When a gift from the Civil List was
obtained for him, Joyce, according to Frank Budgen, decided to
'further the Allied cause by cultural propaganda in the shape of his
work for the English Players'.[146] Joyce, however, was not working
to please the English Government from whom he had received his
grant. He had no intention of breaking the promise that he had made
to the Austrian authorities, as he said, that he would remain neutral
in return for his exit permit. His work for the English Players would
not violate his principle of freeing art from propaganda either.

What began as allegedly pro-British propaganda ended instead
with Joyce being forced to conduct a private war against the British.
The Consul General, A. Percy Bennett, tried to shame him into
enlisting in the British Army, while Henry Carr, an employee of the
British Consulate, threatened to 'wring his neck' over a salary
dispute. Joyce protested to Bennett and to Sir Horace Rumbold, the

British Minister in Berne, but neither replied. He then wrote to the Prime Minister, Lloyd George, who skirted the issue and wished the English Players every success. Joyce's attitude was one of defiance: 'These people look upon themselves as representatives of the King, and expect me to go to them cap in hand, but I look upon them as functionaries who are paid by my father to look after my interests while I am abroad.'[147] He looked upon the British functionaries as bullies and they are treated accordingly in *Ulysses*. Sir Horace Rumbold appears as the English executioner who hangs Irish revolutionaries and Henry Carr as the British soldier who bashes Stephen in the jaw. Bennett is the sergeant-major, with authority over Private Carr, who however refers to him by uttering a profanity.

Joyce regarded the British State as violent and brutal, and he preferred instead the old Austrian Empire. When Trieste finally achieved its political liberation in 1918, and united itself to Italy, Joyce unexpectedly pointed out that the Austro-Hungarian emperor had been a lenient ruler. 'They called it a ramshackle empire', he later told Padraic Colum, 'I wish to God there were more such empires.'[148] He labelled those Allies who had failed to support the French in opposing the Italian move to grab Trieste 'cowardly'.[149] These comments represent one of the paradoxes of Joyce's political views, since he resented British oppression of Ireland. What Joyce meant apparently, was that, as Padraic Colum noted, the Austro-Hungarian Empire 'tried to impose so little upon its own or upon other people. It was not war-like, it was not efficient, and its bureaucracy was not strict, it was the country for a peaceful man.'[150] Joyce had always loathed war, even as a young man. When in 1899 one of his fellow-students delivered a paper on 'The War Machine, A State Necessity' before the University College Literary and Historical Society, Joyce attacked the paper by modifying the eight beatitudes to suit what he considered to be the British mentality.[151] In *Ulysses* (*424; 556*), these 'British Beatitudes' are itemised as 'Beer, beef, bibles, bulldogs, battleships, buggery and bishops.'

Joyce judged his presence in Zürich with a cold sense of humour, remarking that 'the official position of an Irishman at war with England is now that of a British citizen at war with Austria. It is not easy to accept and less easy to deny.'[152] Joyce was alluding to the fact that Irishmen resented British rule; but as British subjects they were expected to conduct war against the Austrians rather than the British, whom they considered to be their real enemies. The position of Irishmen in Ireland was no less difficult. Redmond failed in his efforts to enlist Irishmen as a distinct unit under the Irish flag. Kettle, out of sympathy for small nations like Belgium, volunteered for service with the British Army in France. This contradiction did not escape him: 'England goes to fight for liberty in Europe but junkerdom in Ireland.'[153] Although some 100,000 Irishmen eventually served the Allied cause, many more held serious reservations about this course of action. This attitude can be understood by reference to some arguments put forward in A. R. Orage's *An Englishman Talks it Out with an Irishman*, a title which Joyce found interesting and which he bought. The 'Irishman' states his case clearly:

> Some do not deny that the principle for which Britain is con-
> tending in this war may be right. . . . But others, and the
> majority, think that as a war for the rights of the little nations it is
> the greatest fraud in all history. . . . Must it not appear hypo-
> critical to Ireland for England to undertake such a crusade with
> just such a victim at her own door?[154]

Griffith's *Sinn Féin*, in the last issues before it was suppressed under the Defence of the Realm Act on 2 December 1914, maintained that Ireland was not at war with Germany or with any other Continental power:

> England is at war with Germany, and Mr Redmond has offered
> England the services of the National Volunteers to 'defend
> Ireland.' What has Ireland to defend and whom has she to defend it
> against? Has she a native Constitution or a National Government
> to defend? All know she has not. All know both were wrested
> from her by the power to whom Mr Redmond offers the services
> of Nationalist Ireland.

Bloom makes a similar point in 'Eumaeus' (*641; 743*)[155], where he reminds Stephen that 'Irish soldiers had as often fought for England as against her, more so, in fact. And now, why?' Griffith accused the press in a column entitled, with Joycean aptness, 'The All-lies', of distorting the war picture for propagandistic purposes.[156]

In this attitude Griffith found an unexpected ally in Zürich. Joyce's perspective on the war was equally paradoxical. Although he was supposedly indifferent to the war's outcome, his difficulties with Consular officials led him to praise the German offensive, and to express satisfaction at Britain's troubles in Ireland.[157] At the same time, Joyce cherished his 'neutrality'. When the sometime Professor of Economics in Vienna, Sigmund Feilbogen, started his *International Review* in Zürich in 1915, he employed Joyce as a translator. The neutralist periodical had a programme which Joyce could at least partially accept:

1 We combat lying and the inciting of the peoples one against the other. We desire to oppose to the campaign of lies a war of minds which shall shatter the unholy legends that are forming around us. We shall refute pamphlets directed against the honour of any nation whatsoever.

2 We are persuaded that every nation produces not only 'atrocities' but also acts of nobleness even towards the foe. These are what we glean and treasure up. We are grateful to everyone who communicates to us well-attested facts relating to considerate treatment of prisoners, magnanimity towards the wounded, chivalry in the fight, ingenious charitable arrangements for war-time.

3 We want to prepare ourselves for peace on the lines of national economy, and with this object in view, to profit by the experience of war. Questions such as these of the arrangements of war-socialism, short military service, customs and coinage unions between related states will be subjected to expert examination.[158]

In view of Joyce's British citizenship, which he never wished to renounce, the claim of the *International Review* that 'Our passport bears no party colour, and is stamped by no government' must have seemed amusing.[159] But it accorded with Joyce's basic pacifism.

Feilbogen contributed occasional articles for the *International Review*. Joyce described him to Frank Budgen as haunting the Café des Bouques, 'with an eartrumpet which he orients and occidents night and day to catch rumours of peace anywhere at any hour'.[160] Feilbogen put both his economic expertise and desire for peace to good use in his work. As early as 1915, he laid down as the first duty of the belligerents after the war to renovate those districts rendered unserviceable for production purposes. As a remedial measure for the crisis of the unemployed and of falling wages, he suggested the co-operation of employers and trades-unions with civil and military authorities. Feilbogen also urged the warring nations to transform trades-unions from organisations of class struggle into instruments of the common good. The final task consisted in developing all areas of trade into one unified world economy.[161] Feilbogen stresses the economic motives for wars. Bloom espouses the same viewpoint in 'Eumaeus':

> All those wretched quarrels, in his humble opinion, stirring up bad blood – bump of combativeness or gland of some kind, erroneously supposed to be about a punctilio of honour and a flag – were very largely a question of the money question which was at the back of everything, greed and jealousy, people never knowing when to stop. (*643; 746*)

Bloom avers that only by mutual co-operation can enmity be overcome.

Bertrand Russell's stirring 'Appeal to the Intellectuals of Europe' also appeared in the *International Review* in October 1915, and doubtless caught Joyce's eye. Russell lamented the fact that philosophers, professors, and writers generally felt it their duty to make out a case for their own country. He cited Romain Rolland and Bernard Shaw as honourable exceptions. He contended that the intellectuals should use their reputations and their freedom from political entanglements 'to mitigate the abhorrence with which the nations have come to regard each other, to help towards mutual understanding, to make the peace, when it comes, not a mere cessation due to weariness, but a fraternal reconciliation, springing from realisation that the strife is a folly of blindness'.[162] D. H. Lawrence, in a vitriolic letter of 14 September 1915, accused Russell of hypocrisy in presenting himself as an 'angel of peace': 'The enemy of all mankind you are, full of the lust of enmity. It is *not* the hatred of falsehood which inspires you. It is the hatred of people, of flesh and blood.'[163] Later, in a letter of 11 December 1916 to Cynthia Asquith, Lawrence avowed that 'Fusty, fuzzy peace-cranks and lovers of humanity are the devil. We must get on a new track altogether. Damn Humanity, let me have a bit of inhuman, or non-human truth, that our fuzzy human emotions can't alter.'[164] Joyce, on the other hand, endorsed Russell's viewpoint on the war, and so does Bloom when he says 'he was only too conscious of the casualties resulting from propaganda and displays of mutual animosity and the misery and suffering it entailed as a foregone conclusion on fine young fellows, chiefly, destruction of the fittest, in a word' (*657; 764–5*). Bloom, moreover, would uphold the letter of the law against 'all orotund instigators of international persecution, all perpetuators of international animosities' (*716; 843*).

One of the instigators of international strife, according to a writer for the *International Review*, was Henri Bergson. Joyce, perhaps as a result, obtained Bergson's *The Meaning of War*. Bergson claimed that the war was an instance of Life and Matter in conflict, with Germany representing a mechanical and materialistic force. The reviewer laid the blame for the contemporary trend in France of a union between chauvinism and religious mysticism on Bergson's philosophy of 'sentiments', which inevitably led to a politics ruled by sentiments. Although in his book Bergson does not speak either of revenge or of the arch enemy, he became unpopular because when war broke out he had described it as 'a holy war on behalf of culture and civilisation'.[165] For Joyce all wars were unholy, and destructive of culture and civilisation.

Joyce had more respect for Russell's *Principles of Social Reconstruction*, which he purchased probably in 1917. Russell's countrymen accused him of being unpatriotic, since he opposed the war. His battle with the authorities grew so intense, in fact, that in 1918 he was imprisoned. Russell's philosophy of politics was based on the belief that impulse has more effect than conscious purpose in moulding men's lives. Most impulses may be divided into the creative and the possessive, those that make for life and those that make for death. Russell claimed that the State, war and property are the chief political embodiments of the possessive impulse. He endorsed the creative impulses and saw those of art as being the more civilised: 'Many artists have remained wholly untouched by the passions of war, not from feebleness of feeling, but because the creative instinct, the pursuit of a vision makes them critical of the assault of national passion, and not responsive to the myth in which the impulse of pugnacity clothes itself.'[166] Russell's statement is the key to Joyce's position. Joyce included the Church as well as the State as embodiments of the possessive impulse tending towards death. By combating their effort to hamper individual growth through his art, Joyce asserted the creative impulse.

'Dooleysprudence', written in 1916, crystallises Joyce's stance. Although Mr Dooley appears indifferent to the war, he is in fact indicting both Church and governments as causes for the bloodshed by preaching that 'the only way to save all human souls / Was piercing human bodies through with dumdum bulletholes.' The collusion between Church and State is indicated by the epithet,

'Jingo Jesus'. As a pacifist, Mr Dooley, like Joyce, disapproves of both sides since he disbelieves that 'British Tar is water from life's fount' (that is, Bishop Berkeley's theory that tar water is the panacea for all ills), and refuses to be taken in by 'the gospel of the German on the Mount'. Joyce stresses his anarchistic distrust of the legal codes and structures of society and, as a result, he 'won't salute the State / Or serve Nabuchodonesor or proletariat'. In paddling his own canoe, the artist represents the common man who relies on his own good sense rather than on the folly of those nations and institutions which perpetrate enmity among men.[167]

Although for Joyce all governments were 'pirates',[168] he felt like Russell,[169] that the most important purpose of existing political institutions was to foster individual creativity. Jacob Schwartz maintains that Joyce as a young man had hoped that 'society in general would support all artists because they were supermen.'[170] In a letter to Stanislaus in 1905, Joyce had welcomed the rise of socialism also in order to gain a subsidy for his work: 'Some people would answer that while professing to be a socialist I am trying to make money: but this is not true at least as they mean it. If I made a fortune it is by no means certain that I would keep it. What I wish to do is to secure a competence on which I can rely, and why I expect to have this is because I cannot believe that any State requires my energy for the work I am at present engaged in.'[171] Joyce did not always strictly hold this view. A Marxist State was not better disposed than the bourgeois State to subsidise its artists; a Marxist State would substitute old guidelines only to impose new ones for artists to follow. When he realised that his ideal was not possible under any State, Joyce became more sympathetic to the anarchist position. Errico Malatesta had argued that governments oppressed mankind even indirectly by 'denying them the means of life and thus reducing them to a state of surrender'.[172] Joyce allied himself with collectivist politicians like Kropotkin because they aimed to fulfill the artist's needs. The anarchists believed that a revolution would free all men from base preoccupations with money, enabling the individual to pursue his own interests without intellectual restraints. As Elisée Reclus asserted in his preface to Kropotkin's *The Conquest of Bread*, 'the artist will no longer prostitute his ideal of beauty to gain a livelihood; and thenceforth, as friends, we shall be able to realize in harmony the great things of which the poets have caught only glimpses.'[173] In Zürich Joyce appeared to Frank Budgen as 'the Mr

Dooley . . . who had turned his back alike upon Marx and Engels and upon "Jingo Jesus".[174]

What may also have appealed particularly to Joyce about the *International Review* was that it printed some of Tolstoy's work. We do not know which translations from the German Joyce made or helped with, since only Cecil Palmer's name is given as a translator. But I suspect that Joyce had a hand in translating *How Much Land Does a Man Need?*, since in a letter to his daughter he remarked, 'In my opinion *How Much Land Does a Man Need* is the greatest story that the literature of the world knows.'[175] Feilbogen included this folk tale because 'its application beyond the scope of an individual's fate, gives food for reflection'.[176] Tolstoy explored the universal theme of how an individual's insatiable greed for riches results in personal disaster; Feilbogen, like Joyce, attributed international calamities to the lust for money and power which infected all nations.

Joyce's views dovetailed with Tolstoy's at many points. Tolstoy's political writings, along with those of Tucker, were the ones Joyce admired most.[177] Joyce was acquainted with his anarchist philosophy in Eltzbacher's book on *Anarchism*. In Trieste, Joyce had also come across an article by Tolstoy in a London paper, and he immediately came to Tolstoy's defence in a letter to Stanislaus in 1905:

> I see that he wrote a 13 column letter to *The Times* of London attacking governments. Even the English 'liberal' papers are indignant. Not merely does he attack armaments, he even alludes to the Tsar as a 'weak-minded Hussar officer, standing below the intellectual level of most of his subjects, grossly superstitious and of coarse tastes.' The English liberals are shocked: they would call him vulgar but that they know he is a prince. A writer in the *Illustrated London News* sneers at Tolstoy for not understanding WAR. 'Poor dear man!' he says. Now, damn it, I'm rather good-tempered but this is a little bit too much. Did you ever hear such impudence? Do they think the author of *Resurrection* and *Anna Karénin* a fool? Does this impudent, dishonourable journalist think he is an equal of Tolstoy, physically, intellectually, artistically or morally? The thing is absurd. But when you think of it, it's cursedly annoying. Perhaps that journalist will undertake to revise Tolstoy more fully – novels, stories, plays and all.[178]

Tolstoy had attacked the violence of the government in its so-called administration of justice and the law, and condemned the hypocrisy and repression of the orthodox Church in *Resurrection*. In *Stephen Hero*, as has become clear, Joyce upbraided his contemporaries for upholding English liberalism (in which he discovered nothing save the administration of law and of bullets) and its ally the Catholic Church. In *Anna Karenina*, Levin accused the government for thrusting the Russo–Turkish War on an ignorant populace. Joyce, like Tolstoy, renounced violence outright.

Tolstoy's main thesis in his article entitled 'The One Thing Needful', which Joyce refers to, is that no government can really be better than the people who allow it to control them. Bloom echoes this idea when he tells Stephen in 'Eumaeus' (*643; 745*), 'every country, they say, our own distressful included, has the government it deserves.' The reviewer in the *Illustrated London News* found Tolstoy's repudiation of all governments 'deliberate wrong-headedness' and his onslaught on monarchy 'pathetically naive'.[179] Tolstoy indicted both the party politics of democracies and the irresponsible will of the despot because their actions lacked any real principle:

> The history of the European Christian nations from the time of the Reformation . . . is an uninterrupted enumeration of the most dreadful, senselessly cruel crimes committed by representatives of the Government against their own and other nations and against each other. . . . Our contemporary Governments – i.e. the men who at present compose Governments (whether these Governments be autocratic or limited Monarchies or Republics) – do the same thing; they cannot but do it because in it consists their function.
>
> Their function consists in grasping the greater part of the property of the labouring classes by means of violence in the form of direct or indirect taxation, and of using these means according to their discretion – i.e. always for the attainment of party or their own personal avaricious ambitions and vain aims. Secondly, in maintaining by violence the right of a few men to possess the land taken from the whole nation. Thirdly, to organize by hire or conscription an army – i.e. professional murderers – and at their will to send these murderers to kill and rob this people or that. Or, lastly, to institute laws which would justify and consecrate all these villanies.[180]

Proudhon had made a similar statement in *What is Property?*:

'Whatever forms it takes, – monarchic, oligarchic, or democratic – royalty, or the government of man by man, is illegitimate and absurd.'[181] Wilde also claimed that 'there is no necessity to separate the monarch from the mob; all authority is equally bad.'[182] In his essay on 'Force', as we have seen, Joyce considered all forms of subjugation to be detestable. He dismissed, moreover, all forms of government except a socialistic utopia:

> My political faith can be expressed in a word: Monarchies, constitutional or unconstitutional, disgust me. Kings are mountebanks. Republics are slippers for everyone's feet.
> Temporal power is gone and good riddance. What else is left? Can we hope for monarchy by divine right? Do you believe in the Sun of the Future?★

In rejecting democracy as well as autocracy the anarchist shows no inconsistency. As George Woodcock points out, democracy advocates the sovereignty of the people whereas anarchism upholds the sovereignty of the individual. Parliamentarianism is inadmissible to the anarchists because a person hands over his sovereignty to a representative, whom he can no longer control, and who makes decisions in his name. The ballot is therefore spurned by the anarchist because he considers it a symbolic and actual betrayal of freedom.[183]

Tolstoy believed that patriotism is an 'unnatural, irrational, and harmful feeling' and the cause for a great part of the world's ills. Like Joyce and Russell, he observed that for the sake of patriotism nations are ready to perpetrate 'on other peoples the very same deeds that their oppressors have perpetrated and are perpetrating on them'.[184] But at the same time he defined real patriotism as the 'wish for spiritual benefits for one's own people'.[185] Joyce conceived of his art as fulfilling this purpose. Tolstoy indicted all governmental activity on the grounds that it was supported by a false patriotism:

> People construct this terrible machine of power, they allow anyone to seize it who can . . . they slavishly submit to him, and are then surprised that evil comes of it. They are afraid of anarchists' bombs, but are not afraid of this terrible organization which is always threatening them with the greatest calamities.[186]

★ As Richard Ellmann has pointed out (*JJ*, p. 394 fn.), 'That is, do you believe in socialism? The Sun of the Future is a phrase from the Italian Socialist anthem.'

Joyce noted the following point for 'Cyclops': 'Anarchists: who accuse them? Kriegshetzer [warmongers].'[187] In a similar vein he told Georges Borach:

> I can't approve of the act of the revolutionary who tosses a bomb in a theatre to destroy the king and his children. On the other hand, have those states behaved any better which have drowned the world in a blood-bath?[188]

Wilde had answered the question of what form of government is most suitable for an artist to live under by stating forcefully, 'The form of government that is most suitable to the artist is no government at all. Authority over him and his art is ridiculous.'[189] For this reason political terminologies left Joyce indifferent.[190] If, as George Woodcock maintains, Tolstoy represents the anarchist as moralist while Wilde is the anarchist as aesthete, Joyce cannot belong to either category. Tolstoy subjected art to a propagandistic end, that of social and moral renewal, while Wilde is supposed to have regarded art as an end in itself. Joyce, however, walked a tightrope between these positions. He agrees with Wilde that art is above all else in society, but holds that a political theory such as anarchism can shape artistic endeavour, such as in *Stephen Hero*. Joyce also believed with Tolstoy that literature can usher in the spiritual liberation of the people, but this must be done through innuendo rather than through ponderousness.

To extirpate the legalised violence sanctioned by governmental structures, Tolstoy employed what he called the 'tactic of love'.[191] To resist injustice and oppression by the 'tactic of violence', he claimed, forces one to implement the same devices of violence implanted by the unjust oppressor. A stateless society would be brought about instead by refusing obedience to the existing order. Joyce found the doctrine of non-resistance to evil by force congenial, and he indicates this sympathy in his early review of Hall's book on Buddhism written in 1903:

> Our civilization, bequeathed to us by fierce adventurers, eaters of meat and hunters, is so full of hurry and combat, so busy about many things which perhaps are of no importance, that it cannot but see something feeble in a civilization which smiles as it refuses to make the battlefield the test of excellence.[192]

When John Wyse Power urges Bloom to stand up to injustice 'with force like a man', Bloom responds instead with moral vigour by

defining life as 'Love . . . I mean the opposite of hatred' (*333; 432*).*
He meets ferocity by attempting to promote 'a little goodwill all
round', as he later tells Stephen (*643; 745*). The Citizen is bent
on upholding by force his immediate goal of political independence
to the exclusion of everything else. Even Griffith, as Richard Davis
points out, while advocating non-violent resistance, never embraced
it as a full-blooded policy 'with its emphasis on human brotherhood,
self-sacrifice and love for opponents so clearly stated in the writings
of his contemporary Tolstoi'.[193] For Joyce and Tolstoy, however,
nationalism can only justify itself when it moves towards that higher
ideal, human kinship.

Joyce was aware that his actions might be misconstrued. He could
be accused, like Shem, of cowardice, of being a 'zürichschicken'
(70), or a 'chicken' of Zürich, for not taking part either in the Easter
Rebellion of 1916 or in the World War. Instead, 'without having
struck one blow', he 'kuskykorked himself up tight in his inkbattle
house' with his booze and writing materials, 'hemiparalysed by the
tong warfare and all the shemozzle' (176–7). But Joyce, like
Earwicker, 'anarchistically respectsful of the liberties of the non-
invasive individual', does not answer to the abusive names he is
called. The 'passive resistant' made 'no mocks for his grapes' (72).

Joyce, as has become clear, found the non-violent aspect of
anarchism, rather than the terrorist one, to be the most congenial.
Joyce, like Earwicker, bases his reaction on the philosophy of
Benjamin Tucker (who also advocated passive resistance) as well as
on Tolstoy. Tucker defined government as 'the subjection of the
non-invasive individual to an external will', and the State as 'the
embodiment of the principle of invasion in an individual, or a band
of individuals, assuming to act as representatives or masters of the
entire people within a given area.'[194] Eltzbacher gathered Tucker's
statements on this point:

> 'By "invasion" I mean the invasion of the individual sphere,
> which is bounded by the line inside of which liberty of action does
> not conflict with others' liberty of action.' This boundary-line is in
> part unmistakable; for instance, a threatened act is not an invasion,
> 'a man has a right to threaten what he has a right to execute.' But
> the boundary-line may also be dubious; for instance, 'we cannot
> clearly identify the maltreatment of child by parent as either

---

* See below, pp. 232–3.

invasive or non-invasive of the liberty of the third parties.'
'Additional experience is continually sharpening our senses of
what constitutes invasion. Though we still draw the line by rule of
thumb, we are drawing it more clearly every day.' 'The nature of
such invasion is not changed, whether it is made by one man upon
another man, after the manner of the ordinary criminal, or by one
man upon all other men, after the manner of an absolute monarch,
or by all other men upon one man, after the manner of a modern
democracy.'

'On the other hand, he who resists another's attempt to control
is not an aggressor, an invader, a governor, but simply a defender,
a protector.' 'The individual has the right to repel invasion of his
sphere of action.' 'Anarchism justifies the application of force to
invasive men' . . . . 'defensive associations acting on the
Anarchistic principle would not only demand redress for, but
would prohibit, all clearly invasive acts. They would not,
however, prohibit non-invasive acts, even though these acts
create additional opportunity for invasive persons to act
invasively: for instance, the selling of liquor.' 'And the nature of
such resistance is not changed whether it be offered by one man to
another man, as when one repels a criminal's onslaught, or by one
man to all other men, as when one declines to obey an oppressive
law, or by all other men to one man, as when a subject people rises
against a despot, or as when the members of a community
voluntarily unite to restrain a criminal.'[195]

Tucker defined anarchism succinctly as 'the belief in the greatest
amount of liberty compatible with equality of liberty; or, in other
words, as the belief in every liberty except the liberty to invade.'[196]
The individual, then, has the right to resist invasion of his sphere of
action. As Joyce told Georges Borach, he admired Odysseus because
he was 'the only man in Hellas' who opposed the war, and because he
thought up the stratagem of the wooden horse.[197] At the end of the
First World War, when the Allies were convinced that in winning
they had made the world 'safe for democracy', Joyce asked
pointedly, 'Who won this war?'[198] For Joyce that war, or any war,
never benefited mankind. He never considered brute force to be profoundly human. As an artist, he repelled the theory of physical force
in life and in literature by adopting a 'suave philosophy' which
permitted him to use only the non-violent weapons of silence, exile,
and cunning.

3 'The Reawakening'

He [Joyce] told me in Salzburg that Finnegan's dream would have
a sequel, a reawakening. I urged him to finish off *Work in Progress*
and get on with the *Reawakening*.'

(Stanislaus Joyce)[199]

One of the principal reasons why Joyce supported the early Sinn Féin
movement was that although it still advocated separatism, as
Fenianism had done, it no longer used dynamite to achieve that end.
Griffith had opposed violent revolution as impractical because of
England's superior military strength. In *The Resurrection of Hungary*
he had argued that although physical force was used at opportune
moments in its history, Ireland had always benefited most from a
policy of passive resistance. This statement was a keynote of
Griffith's programme. It therefore must have puzzled Joyce when
the Rising of Easter 1916 was being described as a *Sinn Féin*
rebellion. Had Sinn Féin reverted to what Joyce called the 'desperate
and bloody doctrine' of Fenianism?

The fact that individual Sinn Féiners participated in the fighting
helped to confound the issue. But these men went out as Irish
Volunteers or soldiers in the Citizen Army, not as members of Sinn
Féin. The Irish Volunteers had been established in 1913 in answer to
the Ulster Volunteer Force, which had been formed to uphold the
constitution of the United Kingdom as it then stood. The object of
the Irish Volunteers was also a defensive and protective one. It was
the Irish Republican Brotherhood, whose members held influential
positions in the Irish Volunteers, that decided an insurrection should
take place before the end of the war since England would now be in a
weaker position. Connolly's Citizen Army concurred with this
view. Griffith, however, was kept in the dark about these plans until
the Saturday before the Rising. It is difficult, however, to ascertain
Griffith's actions during the Rising itself. One account has him
offering to join the insurgents but being held back so that a future
civil government could be headed by him.[200] But judging from the
fact that Griffith was still prepared to voice his opposition to the
Rising as late as September 1917, it seems highly unlikely that he
could have even temporarily approved of it.[201] The British
Government, though, associated the name Sinn Féin with the
physical force movement and it was felt that Griffith's anti-British
propaganda (*Sinn Féin* had been suppressed in 1914 for opposing

recruitment) helped foster an atmosphere of revolution. Perhaps for this reason, Joyce also links the insurrection of 'eireweeker', or Easter 1916, with Sinn Féin, indicated by the slogan 'Sonne feine, somme feehn avaunt!' in *Finnegans Wake* (593).

Among the insurgents was Patrick Pearse, who had conceived of a 'blood sacrifice' to achieve independence. Skeffington, although opposed to violence, sympathised with the aims of the Republicans. He organised a Citizen's Defence Force to stop looting, but was arrested and shot by a firing-squad at the command of the insane British Captain Bowen-Colthurst. Later, at the battle of the Somme in September 1916, Thomas Kettle was killed in action leading his company of Dublin Fusiliers.

Joyce's attitude to this drastic turn of events was complex. He regretted the deaths of his friends Kettle and Skeffington. According to Herbert Gorman, Joyce is reported to have answered the question of whether he was looking forward to an independent Ireland with the curt rebuff, 'So that I might declare myself its first enemy?' But would Joyce not die for Ireland? 'I say,' came the reply, 'let Ireland die for me.'[202] The only response Joyce would give he indicated in a letter to Fanny Guillermet of the *Journal de Genève* for which he refused to analyse the Irish situation:

> le problème de ma race est tellement compliqué qu'on a besoin de tous les moyens d'un art élastique pour l'esquisser – sans le résoudre. Je suis de l'avis qu'une prononciation personelle ne m'est plus permise. Je suis contraint à la faire moyennant les scènes et les personnages de ma pauvre invention.
>
> (The problem of my race is so complicated that one needs to make use of all the means of an elastic art to delineate it – without solving it. I am of the opinion that I am no longer permitted to make a personal pronouncement. I am restricted to making one by means of the scenes and characters of my poor art.)[203]

Joyce realised that he could no longer make direct political statements, as he had done for *Il Piccolo della sera*, in what was already a highly sensitive situation. As he says, he was now restricted to enumerate his views only in the scenes and characters in his art.

The movement of *Ulysses* is against violence, and Joyce opposed Pearse's Messianism because it was violent. Stephen makes the same remark to Private Carr that Joyce made about the Rising: 'I say: Let my country die for me.' But he adds, 'Up to the present it has done so. I don't want it to die. Damn death. Long live life!' (*591; 689*). The Fenians had argued that 'love of country was in itself a transcendent virtue and that man who was ready to die for his country ought not to be convicted of mortal sin.'[204] Joyce dismissed the violent sacrifice of self for country, seeing it as a destructive impulse. His art would offer his country instead new life by preserving the integrity of body and soul. That Joyce was anti-British did not mean he supported the Irish Rebellion. He must have thought it absurd, as Conor Cruise O'Brien says now – an inculcation of extremism that has dyed Irish politics ever since.

After Easter 1916 the cause of Sinn Féin did indeed advance, but the principles it now espoused were not entirely those which Joyce had earlier endorsed. Originally Griffith did not intend Sinn Féin to be a new political party determined to oust the parliamentarians in elections. The organisation was then based on local government bodies, not on parliamentary representation. But the failure of Redmond to obtain the long-awaited Home Rule measure and the menacing prospect of conscription helped turn the tide in Sinn Féin's favour after the executions of the sixteen insurrectionaries. In January 1917 Griffith's old abstentionist policy became a reality when a Sinn-Féin backed candidate, Count Plunkett, won a by-election in North Roscommon and refused to take his seat at Westminster. For the first time in Irish politics an entirely new situation existed.

In the next few months the position of the parliamentary party weakened steadily as Sinn Féin candidates won three successive by-elections. The most significant victory was the one in East Clare by the senior serving Commanding officer of the Easter Rising, Eamon de Valera. His platform was the Proclamation of the Irish Republic for which Pearse and the other leaders had fought. A vote for de Valera, then, was not just a vote against Redmond and the Home Rule movement, but a vote for Easter 1916.[205] This has become a shibboleth ever since. His election marked a turning point in the history of Sinn Féin and of Ireland. Acclaimed as a national leader, de Valera now succeeded Griffith as President of Sinn Féin at its *Ard Fheis* or Convention in October 1917. Of more immediate consequence, from Griffith's and perhaps from Joyce's point of view, was de Valera's election as President of the Volunteers the day after the Convention. The merger of the political and physical force movements was now complete. As a result, the label 'Sinn Féin' was applied to the resurgence of nationalism after 1916 and became a symbol for revolution. For Joyce the accession of de Valera could only mean a triumph of the old doctrine of Fenianism.

The militant Sinn Féin party set up her own parliament, Dáil Eireann, in Dublin in 1919. It was backed by the Volunteers, or the Irish Republican Army as they now called themselves. Lloyd George counteracted this move by sending two paramilitary groups, the 'Black-and-Tans' and the 'Auxiliaries' ('Auxies'), as reinforcements to the Royal Irish Constabulary. A bloody and bitter Anglo-Irish war ensued. The guerrilla warfare reached its climax on 'Bloody Sunday', 21 November 1920, when Michael Collins' 'Squad' shot eleven British Intelligence officers. The Black-and-Tans took revenge on a football crowd at Croke Park by opening fire on them without warning. Joyce's reaction to Bloody Sunday is recorded in the 'Shem' chapter: on that 'surprisingly bludgeony Unity Sunday' when 'the roth, vice, and blause met the noyr blank and rogues and the grim white and cold bet the black fighting tans' Shem shut himself up tight in his inkbottle house (176). Joyce alludes to the combatants of the First World War in the colours red, white, and blue, of the flags of both France and England, and the black, white, and red of the flag of Germany. Meanwhile, the Irish green, white, and gold ('grim white and cold') took on the Black-and-Tans. In the 'roth, vice, and blause' Joyce includes his own literary battles with Samuel Roth, the pirate of *Ulysses*, and with the vice leagues in the United States, who conducted a campaign against *Ulysses*.

Joyce was not indifferent to Ireland's plight. He regretted the death of George Clancy (Davin in the *Portrait*) who was dragged out of bed by the Black-and-Tans and shot in the presence of his wife.[206] When the Lord Mayor of Cork, Thomas MacCurtain, was assassinated in 1920 Terence MacSwiney succeeded him. MacSwiney, while presiding at a City Hall meeting of the IRA, was arrested for possession of treasonous documents. He was imprisoned in Brixton Jail and went on a hunger strike as a protest against the incessant arrests of the 'Republic's' representatives. After 73 days he died. The day of his burial was declared an official day of mourning by the Dáil. Joyce followed the hunger strike with compassion, and wrote a poem identifying his fight with British Consular officials in Zürich with MacSwiney's:

The Right Heart in the Wrong Place

Of spinach and gammon

Bull's full to the crupper,
White lice and black famine
Are the Mayor of Cork's supper
But the pride of old Ireland
Must be damnably humbled
If a Joyce is found cleaning
The boots of a Rumbold.[207]

Joyce shared his countrymen's hatred of British coercion and their refusal to submit to British domination. During the final two years of the drive for Irish independence, MacSwiney's hunger strike was the only incident that moved him.

The protracted hostilities ceased with the signing of a treaty between Ireland and England on 6 December 1921 which would create the Irish Free State. The question of Ulster and partition was to be settled later by a Boundary Commission. De Valera, who was in favour of creating a Republic, adamantly rejected the terms agreed upon by his plenipotentiaries, Griffith and Michael Collins, and bitterly accused them of having failed to consult him before signing the agreement. When the Treaty was ratified by the Dáil on 7 January 1922, de Valera resigned, and Griffith was elected the first President of Ireland the following day. The country split into two camps: pro-Treaty and anti-Treaty, Free State troops and the 'Irregulars'. As a result, civil war raged in Ireland for nine months.

'That blackguard Lloyd George knew what he was doing when he gave them the Free State; he knew they'd make a mess of it'[208] could have expressed Joyce's attitude to the new developments in Ireland as much as it did that of his father. The hen who sounds the 'peacefugle' in the opening chapter of *Finnegans Wake* is described as a 'Parody's bird' announcing that 'it's the armitides too-nigh, militopucos and there's to be a gorgeups truce for happinest childher everwere' (11). The 'gorgeups truce' refers to Lloyd George's peace offer to the Irish. The civil war confirmed Joyce's worst suspicions about his countrymen. He still believed in the malevolence of certain people in Dublin towards him. When Nora Joyce and the children left for Galway in April 1922 against his wishes he spent his time in Paris brooding, expecting to hear of what he termed the 'assassination' of his family.[209] The warehouse opposite their lodgings had been seized by the I.R.A. while Free State troops invaded their bedrooms. Nora and Lucia managed to escape in a train but had to lie prone to protect themselves from the fusillade. Giorgio had trouble sleeping at night afraid that the 'Zulus', as he called them, would take him out of bed and shoot him.[210] Joyce, embittered, interpreted the assault as being really aimed at himself, and, consequently, he became disenchanted with both sides in the Sinn Féin party. Although he had supported Griffith's early programme, the political situation had now gone out of control. His position was similar to Dante's who, though a Guelph in his youth, detached himself in exile from party factionalism. Joyce wrote to his Aunt Josephine that he was willing to hear of matters that would interest him but 'wrathful epistles should be addressed preferably . . . to the president of your free fight or the leader of the irregulars or to the parish priest of Fairview or to the Sacred Heart to whom Ireland is dedicated and not to me.'[211]

In *Finnegans Wake* Joyce claims half-mockingly that he had foreseen the political events dating from 1916. In his absence from home Shem is said to have 'cutely foretold . . . death with every disaster, the dynamitisation of colleagues, the reducing of records to ashes, the levelling of all customs by blazes, the return of a lot of sweetempered gunpowdered didst unto dudst' (189–190). The disasters include the burning of the Four Courts and the Customs House in the civil war of 1922. For this reason Shem is said to have run away 'with hunself and became a farsoonerite, saying he would sooner muddle through the hash of lentils in Europe than meddle with Irrland's split little pea' (171). In other words, Shem left Ireland because of the future partition of his country, or the split arising from those in favour or against the Treaty leading to the civil war. Joyce is seeking to justify his exile after the fact and in doing so he follows Dante, who, in *The Divine Comedy*, refers to political events occurring before his exile as yet to take place in order that, as Cacciaguida tells him, it will be his honour to have constituted a party by himself.* Joyce employs events occurring after his exile to the same effect.

In *Ulysses* there is constantly at work a double motive which Joyce is not at pains to make single or crystal clear. The desire to bring Ireland to a new self-awareness is matched by the equally urgent need of preventing its acceptance of any rigid control by Church and State. The first enables him to state, in Stephen's words in *A Portrait*, 'This race and this country and this life produced me. I shall express myself as I am' (207) (*203*). This individuality permits Joyce at the

---

* See below, p. 198.

same time to turn to the Irish social question and to early Sinn Féin. In this pursuit he is represented by Bloom who at first espoused the radical causes of the 1880s in supporting Davitt, Parnell and Gladstone, and who in 1904 sees a solution to Ireland's problems in Griffith's policies. Joyce shares Bloom's personal utopianism as expressed in his concern for the general welfare of all, unimpeded by warfare and other forms of strife. The positive aspect of this position, however, is countered by its apparently negative dimension. Bloom's plans for affording economic security to all are not Marxist since they do not assert the necessity of mass political organisation of the working classes for the purpose of gaining power. Bloom is not a party man (Sinn Féin was not a *party* in 1904) and, like the anarchists, he will not entrust the realisation of his ideals to the State. This is not to say that he has no sense of civic responsibility or does not hold any views about how to regenerate Dublin. Bloom insists on the importance of 'civic self help' (*666; 777*), by which he presumably means the improvement of the city through free and independent individual action rather than through State intervention. In this sense Bloom corroborates the view of Samuel Smiles who in 1859, in *Self-Help*, declared, 'Even the best institutions can give a man no active help. Perhaps the most they can do is to leave him free to develop himself and improve his individual condition.'[212] Joyce doubted whether the relationship he had established between himself and his country would change with the emergence of an independent Irish State and, as we have seen, he said he would declare himself its first enemy. In 1919, during the British campaign against the Irish, he told Frank Budgen bluntly, 'Ireland is what she is and therefore I am what I am because of the relations that have existed between England and Ireland. Tell me why you think I ought to wish to change the conditions that gave Ireland and me a shape and a destiny?'[213] The possibility of independence threatened to take the edge off his portrait of the political paralysis of Ireland under British rule.

These statements pose problems in determining Joyce's attitude to the new Irish State that came into being in 1922. Their negative import makes it difficult to imagine that, as Richard Ellmann maintains, Joyce put behind his socialism and anarchism in order to hail the Irish Free State. The controversy between Valery Larbaud and Ernest Boyd over *Ulysses*, on the other hand, has been put forward to confirm the opposing view.[214] In his lecture on *Ulysses* held at the bookshop of Adrienne Monnier on 7 December 1921,

Larbaud claimed that with Joyce's new work 'Ireland makes a
sensational re-entry into European literature.' When Boyd, who had
written a history of *Ireland's Literary Renaissance*, took exception to
this remark by pointing to the work of Yeats, Synge and Moore,
Larbaud clarified his position by saying he meant 'Young Ireland',
the Ireland after 1914 (since that was when Joyce started working on
his book). He added that his lecture had been delivered only a few
hours after the armistice declared between Ireland and Britain, on the
day following the signing of the Treaty. His lecture had been
delivered in the spirit created by the armistice.[215] Larbaud's
statements *seem* to indicate that *Ulysses* not only coincided with the
formation of the new Irish government, but that it also endorsed it.
Yet in his lecture Larbaud intended something altogether different:

Comme Irlandais, James Joyce n'a pas pris effectivement parti
dans le conflit qui a mis aux prises, de 1914 à ces derniers jours,
l'Angleterre et l'Irelande. Il ne sert aucun parti, et il est possible
que ses livres ne plaisent à aucun et qu'il soit également désavoué
par les Nationalistes et les Unionistes. Quoi qu'il en soit, il ne fait
pas figure de patriote militant, et n'a rien de commun avec ces
écrivains du Risorgimento qui étaient surtout les serviteurs d'une
cause et se presentaient comme les citoyens d'une nation opprimée
pour laquelle ils réclamaient l'autonomie, et en faveur de laquelle
ils demandaient l'aide des patriotes et des revolutionnaires de tous
les pays. Autant que nous en pouvons juger, James Joyce présente
une peinture tout à fait impartiale, historique, de la situation
politique de l'Irelande. Si, dans ses livres, les personnages anglais
qu'il introduit sont traités en étrangers et quelquefois en ennemis
par ses personnages irlandais, il ne fait nulle part un portrait
idéalisé de l'Irlandais. En somme, il ne plaide pas. Cependant, il
faut remarquer qu'en écrivant *Gens de Dublin, Portrait de l'Artiste* et
Ulysse, il a fait autant que tous les héros du nationalisme irlandais
pour attirer le respect des intellectuels de tous les pays vers
l'Irlande. Son oeuvre redonne a l'Irelande, ou plutot donne à la
jeune Irlande, une physionomie artistique, une identité
intellectuelle; elle fait pour l'Irlande ce que l'oeuvre d'Ibsen a fait
en son temps pour la Norvège, celle de Strindberg pour la Suède,
celle de Nietzsche pour l'Allemagne de la fin du XIXe siècle, et ce
que viennent de faire les livres de Gabriel Miró et de Ramon
Gómez de la Serna pour l'Espagne contemporaine.

(As an Irishman, James Joyce has not, in actual fact, taken sides in
the conflict which, from 1914 to recent times, has pitted Ireland
against England. He does not serve any party, and it is possible
that his books do not please anyone and that he is equally
repudiated by the Nationalists and Unionists. Be that as it may, he
does not cut a figure as a militant patriot, and has nothing in
common with these writers of the [Irish] Renaissance who were
above all the servants of a cause and who presented themselves as
citizens of an oppressed nation for which they demand
independence, and for which they asked the aid of patriots and
revolutionaries of all countries. As far as we can judge, James
Joyce presents an altogether impartial, historical portrait of the
political situation in Ireland. If, in his books, the English
characters that he presents are treated as strangers and sometimes
as enemies by the Irish characters, he does not anywhere present
an idealised portrait of the Irishman. In short, he does not plead.
Meanwhile, it should be mentioned that in writing *Dubliners*, *A
Portrait of the Artist* and *Ulysses*, he did as much as all the heroes of
Irish nationalism in gaining the respect of intellectuals from all
countries for Ireland. His work gives once again to Ireland, or
rather gives to Young Ireland, an artistic physiognomy, an
intellectual identity; his work does for Ireland that which Ibsen's
work did in its time for Norway, that of Strindberg for Sweden,
that of Nietzsche for Germany at the end of the nineteenth
century, and that which the books of Gabriel Miró and of Ramon
Gómez de la Serna have just done for contemporary Spain.)[216]

Larbaud's statement about the writers of the Irish literary renaissance
is in keeping with what Joyce said of them in a letter to Stanislaus in
1906: 'If it is not far-fetched to say that my action, and that of men
like Ibsen &c, is a virtual intellectual strike I would call such people as
Gogarty and Yeats and Colm the blacklegs of literature. Because
they have tried to substitute us, to serve the old idols at a lower rate
when we refused to do so for a higher.'[217] *Ulysses* was in Larbaud's
view, then, an impartial, historical portrait of the political situation
in Ireland after 1914. It was not written in the service of a cause, and,
according to Larbaud, Joyce did not take sides in the Anglo-Irish
conflict. Joyce's works, and *Ulysses* in particular, had put fresh life
into the Ireland of Sinn Féin by giving it an artistic physiognomy and
intellectual identity in the manner that Ibsen and Strindberg had
done for their countries. Ibsen had forged an intellectual identity for

Norway without hailing either Liberals or Conservatives. In *Giacomo Joyce* (15), in fact, *Ulysses* is referred to as the 'symbol of the intellectual conscience' of Ireland. Larbaud, of course, overlooked the fact that Joyce was not pro-English or a Unionist, and if nationalism meant being opposed to the English government in Ireland, then Joyce was a nationalist in that sense. In demonstrating the tension between non-violent Sinn Féin, as represented by Griffith's moderate policy, and the militancy which later dominated the movement, Joyce encapsulated the spirit of Ireland after 1914. By creating the new Irish conscience coincidental to the formation of the Irish Free State, Joyce had accomplished as much as the Irish patriots in drawing the respect of intellectuals from all countries towards Ireland.

That Molly makes two references to Griffith, however, should not override the reservations Joyce had about Sinn Féin, and some of Griffith's views. As far as political independence was concerned, Joyce supported Griffith's plan for economic self-reliance, and his non-violent methods. So when Molly informs us that her husband singled out Griffith as the coming man, Joyce *is* complimenting Griffith's efforts in the construction of the new State: 'he was going about with some of them Sinner Fein lately or whatever they call themselves talking his usual trash and nonsense he says that little man he showed me without the neck is very intelligent the coming man Griffith is well he doesn't look it thats all I can say still it must have been him he knew there was a boycott I hate the mention of politics' (*748; 886*). Joyce had predicted in 1906 that either Sinn Féin or British imperialism would conquer Ireland. The Ireland of 1906, however, differed from the one after 1916. Sinn Féin had conquered Ireland but not in the way Joyce had foreseen. Sinn Féin after 1916 became associated with the physical force idea, and Griffith relinquished his position as head of the movement in favour of de Valera, until the Treaty debates put Griffith in the limelight once again. The Sinn Féin that triumphed was the one the Citizen in 'Cyclops' represented. What permitted the Irish representatives finally to negotiate for independence was the armed struggle Irishmen had been carrying out against Britain since the Easter Rising. Bloom, 'the least pugnacious of mortals' (*657; 764*), would not have gone out in 1916 or afterwards. He would have given the new Sinn Féin militant patriots '(metaphorically) one in the gizzard' (*657; 764*) in the manner he had administered to the Citizen. Stephen is of the same mind. In 'Circe' he refuses to make use of the dagger

Old Gummy Granny or Ireland thrusts towards his hand against the British soldiers (*600; 696*). (Mother Grogan had earlier thrown her boot at Bloom after he promulgated his political platform (*489–90; 610*).) The Citizen, on the other hand, would have obeyed his country's demand 'To slit the throat / Of the English dogs / That hanged our Irish leaders' (*593; 691*). Stephen, after proclaiming mental warfare instead against the British, is promptly knocked down. It is more than likely, therefore, that Joyce would have been out of sympathy with the methods adopted by Sinn Féin in the Easter Rising and after.

That Griffith represented the best possible alternative to the parliamentary party or to the militants in his own movement, however, does not necessarily mean that his programme was the ideal one in Joyce's view, or that it represented the 'culmination of his hopes'. Even Archbishop Walsh voted for the radical party in 1917. The question remains, then, could Joyce have realised his vision of life in a State where the Church was still dominant? If Joyce exaggerates Bloom's vague humanitarian goals in 'Circe', he does not shrink from mocking Bloom's supposed advocacy of the Hungarian Policy either. King Leopold I of Ireland is no less absurd than Bloom as the world's greatest reformer. Stephen had pointed out in *Stephen Hero*, as we have seen, that the Hungarian analogy was a political absurdity. Furthermore he objected to Griffith because he only looked to Europe to report any signs of Philocelticism. Joyce wished that Ireland be Europeanised but not that Europe be Celticised. In *Ulysses* Stephen realises that Sinn Féin, rather than the Irish Party headed by Redmond, is the movement most political extremists, like Kevin Egan, in the Ireland of 1904 support, as he thinks 'Of Ireland, the Dalcassians, of hopes, conspiracies, of Arthur Griffith now' (*43; 53*). But just as his dialectical art failed to save Socrates from 'the archons of Sinn Féin and their noggin of hemlock' (*190; 243*), so too Stephen fears that Sinn Féin will poison his moral fibre and art and put him away in the process. In the first version of *A Portrait of the Artist* Joyce aimed his attack at 'the joint government of Their Intensities and Their Bullockships'; that is, of Sinn Féiners and priests.[218] The socialistic vision will supplant these joint forces as well. Bloom's socialism, however vague, could not coexist with Griffith's view of the labour question as put forward in *Sinn Féin*: 'If there be men who believe . . . that the path to redemption for mankind is through universalism, cosmopolitanism, or any other ism other than nationalism, I am not of their company. . . . The free nation I desire to see rise again upon the soil of Ireland is no offspring of despair – or neo-feudalism – with Marx and Lasalle and Proudhon as its prophet.'[219] Joyce insisted, on the other hand, that if the Irish question existed, it existed for the Irish proletariat chiefly. His ill-defined socialism, moreover, was not of the democratic type. Nor could Bloom's humanitarian goals have acceptance in the new Ireland. In his preface to John Mitchel's *Jail Journal*, Griffith made it essential to distinguish between the case for Irish independence and theories of universalism:

> The right of the Irish to political independence never was, is not, and never can be dependent upon the admission of equal right in all other peoples. It is based on no theory of, and dependable in nowise for its existence or justification on the 'Rights of Man', it is independent of theories of government and doctrines of philanthropy and Universalism. He who holds Ireland a nation and all means lawful to restore her the full and free exercise of national liberties thereby no more commits to the theory that black equals white, that kingship is immoral, or that society has a duty to reform its enemies than he commits himself to the belief that sunshine is extracted from cucumbers.[220]

Negro slavery and Irish subjection to foreign rule were separate cases for Griffith.

Griffith's anti-Semitic tendencies, moreover, like the Citizen's, would hardly have endeared him to Bloom. The 'boycott' Molly mentions is not, I think, the boycott of English goods, as Richard Ellmann suggests, but the boycott of Jewish merchants in Limerick which took place shortly before 16 June, and which Griffith clearly supported. Bloom asserts that he is as good an Irishman as the Citizen by advocating an egalitarian society embracing all creeds and classes:

> I want to see everyone, concluded he, all creeds and classes *pro rata* having a comfortable tidysized income, in no niggard fashion either, something in the neighbourhood of £300 per annum. That's the vital issue at stake and it's feasible and would be provocative of friendlier intercourse between man and man. At least that's my idea for what it's worth. I call that patriotism. (*644; 747*)

If Bloom's support of Griffith was overwhelming, he would tell Stephen so openly, as he does here in revealing his pacifist and socialistic ideals. Instead he dwells on the bigoted attack hurled against him by the Sinn Féin patriot. Just as the Citizen could not tolerate Bloom's freemasonry, Griffith could not have done so either. He maintained that masonic influence had betrayed the Boer cause, and would exclaim 'Great is masonry' on hearing anything untoward.[221] So when Molly tells us that her husband mixes company with 'those Sinner Fein or Freemasons' (*772; 918*), there is an implicit irony in the statement and Joyce underlines Bloom's secret activity or what the Church would have regarded as subversive activity. Stephen and Bloom come together, therefore, in their radicalism and their heterodoxy, not because of their support for Sinn Féin (Stephen does not engage actively in political debate) or their putative approval of the Irish Free State. Turgenev's *Fathers and Sons* had treated the clash between generations, that of reactionary fathers and their revolutionary sons. The theme of the son in search of a father in *Ulysses* is enhanced by the political connotations too. Bloom and Stephen, unlike the families in Turgenev's book, are not divided by political issues but share 'an inherited tenacity of heterodox resistance' which leads them to profess their 'disbelief in many orthodox religious, national, social and ethical doctrines' (*666; 777*). Joyce hints that political independence is not enough, and that the new Ireland must also accommodate the ideals of its artists, and not vice-versa.

Ulysses was not a national epic in the manner of the *Aeneid*. Joyce did not celebrate the exploits of the national heroes or exalt the new State as Virgil had glorified the Roman Empire. Yet Joyce claimed he had written for the benefit of his race. Would the Irishmen of Griffith's new State be kindly disposed towards *Ulysses* then? Apparently not, and Joyce was always afraid to return because of his book. Ireland was the last of nations to allow its entry. On this point Joyce's second motive, his wariness of rigid control by Church and State, takes precedence. A statement Joyce purportedly made to Arthur Power illustrates this central concern:

In the Dublin of my day there was the kind of desperate freedom which comes from a lack of responsibility, for the English were in governance then, so everyone said what he liked. Now I hear since the Free State came in there is less freedom. The Church has made inroads everywhere, so that we are in fact becoming a bourgeois nation, with the Church supplying our aristocracy . . . and I do not see much hope for us intellectually. Once the Church is in

command she will devour everything . . . what she will leave will
be a few rags not worth the having.[222]

In *Ulysses*, as in *Dubliners* and in *A Portrait*, Joyce subjects his
countrymen to a subtle examination of conscience with respect to
their submission to a restricted lifestyle imposed on them by the
Church. Both Stephen and Bloom defy its jurisdiction. Joyce
remained sceptical of an Irish Free State which still paid homage to
what he considered to be spiritual tyranny. He remained loyal to the
conscience of his race which he had just forged and which alone
safeguarded individual sovereignty over mind and body from the
stranglehold of external authority.

4 Forged Documents

The historian, essentially, wants more documents that he can
really use; the dramatist only wants more liberties than he can
really take.

(Henry James)

Joyce's political views did not alter greatly, even after 1922. His
concerns, ranging from Ireland's economic development, which he
had displayed as early as 1903 in his critical review of Stephen
Gwynn's *Today and Tomorrow in Ireland*,* to the role of Church and .
State in society and that of Irish nationalism, remain constant
throughout. His sympathy for socialism and anarchism, although
more subdued than in his early writing, did not diminish either as the
international situation claimed his attention more and more.

Not everyone in the Irish Free State or in Britain was as hostile to
Joyce or his work as he had feared. He was gratified that Winston
Churchill, who had taken part in the Treaty negotiations, had
subscribed to *Ulysses*.[223] In February 1922, after the publication of
Ulysses, the Minister for Publicity of the Irish Free State, Desmond
Fitzgerald, paid him a visit in Paris and he told Joyce that he intended
to nominate him for the Nobel Prize. Joyce explained the situation in
a letter to Robert McAlmon:

The *Dail Eireann* minister of propaganda called on me and wished
to know if I intended to return to Ireland – to which I returned an

---

* See *CW*, pp. 90–2.

evasive answer. He is proposing me, it seems, for the Nobel prize in his capacity of cabinet minister as soon as the treaty is ratified in Westminster though not in the name of his cabinet. I will take on a small bet that if he does not change his mind when he sees the complete text he will lose his portfolio while I have not the faintest chance of being awarded the prize.[224]

It is curious that Joyce should have felt Griffith's cabinet would disapprove of *Ulysses* in view of Griffith's earlier help.* The answer perhaps lies in his letter from Paris to Stanislaus on the same subject in which he said that he would not return to Dublin as 'one redeemed city (and inhabitants thereof) will last me for a few years more'.[225] He still believed that Ireland, although it was on the road to political independence, had not been 'redeemed' from the stranglehold of the Church.

What was Joyce's reaction to de Valera? That the Shaun of *Finnegans Wake* represents in part de Valera, a theory first introduced by John Garvin, has now become a generally accepted view in *Wake* criticism. It is more than likely, then, that various words containing 'dev' may allude punningly to the former Irish President. Joyce toys with the 'Luciferian' as well as the 'divine' aspects of de Valera. The Molochy wars that bring the 'devil era' (473) mark out the Irish leader as the anti-Christ.[226] 'D. V. (527) can be the abbreviation for 'Deo Volente' or for de Valera. Dublin is itself the very essence of de Valera, or 'deblinity devined' (373). Joyce's treatment is ironical since Ireland is also described as 'von Demon's land' (56), with de Valera as the local Tasmanian devil.

Joyce associates de Valera in the *Wake* with warlike activity. The signal of war announces that 'the Baddelaries partisans are still out to mathmaster Malachus Micgranes' (4). On one level the phrase includes the 'mathmaster' (de Valera left his post as a teacher in mathematics to take part in the Easter Rising) as well as 'Malachus' ('Moloch' and possibly 'Malachi' Gogarty who vehemently opposed de Valera). The authors of *A Skeleton Key* indicate that 'mathmaster' can mean 'to overpower by cutting down men and annihilating their homes and monasteries'.[227] And as John Garvin suspected, the twin Primas who 'was a santryman and drilled all decent people', and later Kev who 'coached rebelliumtending mikes' (287) represent de Valera.[228] With the twin Caddy, who wrote 'o peace a farce', Joyce

---

* It is not known whether Fitzgerald made his proposal to the Cabinet, and, if so, what the Cabinet's reaction was.

contrasts his own peaceful activity with the activity of de Valera.

Joyce did not exonerate the pro-Treaty belligerents either. He refers to the Free Staters invariably as 'frayshouters' (378) and 'three shouters' (329). The signing of the Treaty is described as a day of jubilee for

> Freestouters and publicranks, hafts on glaives. You could hear
> them swearing threaties on the Cymylaya Mountains, man. And
> giving it out to the Ould Fathach and louthmouthing after the
> Healy Mealy with an enfysis to bring down the rain of Tarar . . .
> The grandest bethehailey seen or heard on earth's conspectrum
> since Scape the Goat, that gafr, ate the Suenders bible. (329–330)

Although the Treaty brought an end to the 'Reign of Terror' of the Black and Tans, as Healy seems to have maintained, the Free Staters were in fact swearing threats against 'publicranks' or republicans. Joyce links the aftermath of civil war, or 'blooders oathes' (325), with Skin-the-Goat's action as an accomplice in the Phoenix Park murders. Similarly, when the 'attackler' makes peace with Earwicker the terms of negotiation are a satire on the Treaty:

> the queer mixture exchanged the pax in embrace or poghue puxy
> as practised between brothers of the same breast, hilleluia,
> killeluia, alenalaw, and . . . ratified before the god of the day their
> torgantruce which belittlers have schmallkalled the treatyng to
> cognac. (83)

The 'blood brothers', after exchanging a kiss of peace, do not conclude a political pact, but instead an entreaty to cognac, whereby the Irishman, because of his weakness for drink, is worsted by the 'Adversary'.

Earwicker, like Ireland, seems to have been short-changed. The 'attackler' offers to pay back the sum he formerly pickpocketed from Earwicker, 'six vics odd', and asks if he can get some change for a ten-pound note. Earwicker replies that he can only give him four shillings and sevenpence (or seven shillings and fourpence). The gunman leaves, however, without paying the ten pound note. The transaction is an allegory of the consequences of the Treaty: partition. The 'intruder' asks de Valera (by his nickname 'the Long Fellow'),[229] about the transaction, 'Was six victolios fifteen pigeon takee offa you, tell he me, stlongfella, by pickypocky ten to foul months behindaside?' (82). The latter part of the question looks forward to the Butt and Taff episode where Joyce comments on the result of the deal as fulfilling St Columcille's prophecies (and that of the *Book of Kells*) whereby Ireland, instead of achieving freedom, becomes 'Erin gone brugk' (347). Consequently Jaun, in his platform speech about ways to improve Dublin, complains that voters are advising him to retire on a pension. But he does not know where the money is to come from on account of 'the sanguine boundary limit' (448). Jaun is therefore linked with Earwicker or de Valera who lost his money (or six counties) in the deal involving partition. Joyce puns on de Valera's name in terms of valuation in 'de valure' (478) and 'Da Valorem' (342). Earwicker, in boasting about his civic achievements, explains that in the midst of civil strife he 'devaleurised the base fellows for the curtailment of their lower man' (543). The result of 'Hireling's puny wars' (270) and devaluation is Dublin as 'A phantom city, phaked of philim pholk, bowed and sould for a four of hundreds of manhood in their three and threescore fylkers for a price partitional of twenty six and six' (264). Joyce resented the unnecessary bloodshed arising from the civil strife which split his country into twenty-six and six counties as much as Dante resented the factionalism of his native Florence. His statement also carries the bitter overtones of Parnell's betrayal when he told his followers, 'When you sell, get my price!' At the cost of the death of her own people Ireland did not get the full price in her negotiations with Britain.

Johnny MacDougal of Connaught says at one point that he saw Matty Armagh at the 'darkumound numbar wan' (386). Later Matty asks Johnny if he knows a young student named Kevin who was shooting the hen 'that found the dogumen number one . . . an illegible downfumbed by an unelgible' (482). The 'unelgible' is Document No. 2 (since it was not approved by the Dáil)[230] with which de Valera sought to replace the Treaty, or Document No. 1 as it was called. But de Valera's document offered no alternative proposals for Ulster. Johnny replies that of course he knows the sainted sage and that he needs no prompting from Matty: 'Your too farfar a cock of the north there, Matty Armagh, and your due south so.' He tells Matty that freedom in the south is preferable to loyalty to Britain in the north: 'You're up-in-Leal-Ulster and I'm-free-Down-in-Easia, this is much better' (482). The 'Brain Trust' in Dublin, however, think the problem of the 'aglo iris of the vals' and Britain is more complicated:

there's all the difference in Ireland between your borderation . . . and me . . . Doggymens' nimmer win! . . . We bright young chaps of the brandnew braintrust are briefed here and with maternal sanction compellably empanelled at quarter sessions under the six disqualifications for the uniformication of young persons . . . removal act by Commitalman Number Underfifteen. (528–9)

Joyce claims that Dublin was irritated with the boundary question ('borderation'), and he takes to task the Boundary Commission in 1925 which failed to make the necessary alterations to the border area. 'Doggymens' nimmer win' refers to Document No. 1, but 'nimmer' means 'never' in German. Joyce is perhaps suggesting, therefore, that the Documents (either No. 1 or No. 2), 'ducomans nonbar one . . . come on now . . . whichever won of you wins!' (358), could not and did not succeed in unifying the country. And he equates the Dublin Brain Trust which sanctioned 'the six disqualifications for the uniformication' of Ireland with the members of Parnell's party in Committee Room 15 who split and voted against their leader and he charges them with betraying the national destiny. The shade of Parnell still haunts the proceedings of New South Ireland.

Joyce associated England's attempt to enforce a boundary on Ireland's territory with that of literary critics like Wyndham Lewis to delimit his experiments with the English language in *Work in Progress*. Distorting Parnell's famous statement, 'no man has a right to fix the boundary to the march of a nation', Joyce claims that 'no mouth has the might to set a mearbound to the march of a landsmaul' (292)★ and the footnote reads, 'Matter of Brettaine and brut fierce.' The writer's efforts notwithstanding, there will always be the 'beast of boredom' (or Wyndham Lewis) to tell one that 'you must, how, in undivided reawlity draw the line somewhawre' (292). Joyce avers that just as the English had no right to set a limit to the march of his nation, literary critics should not pontificate against his experiments with language. Although Shaun accuses Shem of intending to 'wipe alley english spooker . . . off the face of the erse' (178), Joyce did not revert to the policy of the Gaelic League. Shem's 'disunited kingdom' is thereby placed in opposition to the United Kingdom.

★ The Norwegian *Landsmaal* movement was in some ways similar to the Gaelic Revival. 'Mear' or *Meer*, is German for 'sea'.

Although Joyce told Stanislaus that he was not interested in politics but only in style, it becomes clear that the two are interrelated. Joyce would not replace English with Irish but would at once extend his language beyond national boundaries. Yet he wished his work to be looked upon as deeply Irish.

Writing, therefore, becomes the most important activity in the *Wake*. Joyce scatters references throughout his work to political events taking place in Ireland during the 1930s, such as the Eucharistic Congress in 1932, the appointment of the new Governor General Donal Buckley, and the Economic War against Great Britain. But he refers outstandingly to and concentrates on the political documents or document surrounding the signing of the Treaty. When Arthur Power explained to Joyce his uncertainty about how to write, Joyce recommended that he study the *Book of Kells*, maintaining, 'It is the most purely Irish thing we have.'[231] On the *Tunc* page the illuminated manuscript carries the mystery of a Greek interpolation, XPI (Christos), in the phrase, 'Tunc crucifixerant XPI cum eo duos latrones' ('There were two thieves crucified with him.') Joyce asks if the addition to the Latin text was written by the scribe 'with a tongue in his (or perhaps her) cheek as the case may have been then' (122). Perhaps in light of the question of whether there was an authoress of the *Odyssey*, Joyce asks ironically if the interpolation was written by a woman. The *Book of Kells* represented the culmination of early Irish Catholicism while Document No. 1 represented the most Irish piece of writing of Joyce's day since it created the Irish Free State, a new political entity. Document No. 2 provided a personal alternative expression of Ireland's national destiny inserted by de Valera into the discussion after Document No. 1 had been signed by the plenipotentiaries. But Document No. 2 contained its own mystery, at least to Michael Collins, who was the originator of the name given to de Valera's proposal:

> The document was not drafted by Mr de Valera. There is little difficulty in guessing the author. Dominionism tinges every line. No Irishman who understands the tradition and history of Ireland would think or write of his country's aspirations in the terms used in this document. . . . The outlook of the author of the document is bounded entirely by the horizon of the British Empire.[232]

But who is the author Collins has in mind? Erskine Childers? The *Book of Kells* and Document No. 2 invite the possibility of multiple authorship. In *Finnegans Wake* Anna Livia's 'mamafesta' encourages similar speculation: 'Closer inspection of the *bordereau* would reveal a multiplicity of personalities inflicted on the documents or document' (107), since we have to concentrate equally on 'the enveloping facts themselves circumstantiating any document' (109). '*Bordereau*' alludes at once to the Dreyfus case, since the *bordereau* or schedule was the unsigned letter of 1894 which enumerated a number of documents about to be sent to the German military attaché in Paris. The letter was stolen from the German embassy and handed to the French Ministry of War and, because of the similarity of the handwriting to that of Dreyfus, he was arrested and eventually convicted. But *bordereau* alludes to the Irish border dispute as well, and identifies Document No. 1 or the Treaty as well as Document No. 2. Shem certifies the reliability of the document:

> while we in our wee free state, holding to that prestatute in our
> chapter, may have our irremovable doubts as to the whole sense of
> the lot, the interpretation of any paraphrase in the whole, the
> meaning of every word of a phrase so far deciphered out of it,
> however unfettered our Irish daily independence, we must vaunt
> no idle dubiosity as to its genuine authorship and holusbolus
> authoritativeness. (117–8)

But the question remains, 'who in hallhagal wrote the durn thing anyhow?' (107–8)

Joyce indicates that his work (in the form of the postscript of the night letter) must have inspired 'the tenebrous *Tunc* page of the Book of Kells' (122). On one level such a statement reveals Joyce's pride in his craftsmanship, but it carries a mischievous intent. Joyce's claim parallels de Valera's own assertion that his Document No. 2 contained a 'greater reconciliation with Irish national aspirations' than Document No. 1. One of the peculiarities of the text uncovered by the hen is the '(probably local or personal) variant *maggers* for the more generally accepted *majesty* which is a trifle and yet may quickly amuse' (120). Griffith had referred to de Valera's alteration of the oath to the British King as 'a quibble of words' and Collins argued that 'Plain people will see no difference between these oaths.'[233]* In

---

* Treaty oath: 'I . . . do solemnly swear true faith and allegiance to the Constitution of the Irish Free State as by law established and that I will be faithful to His Majesty George V, his heirs and successors by law, in virtue of the common citizenship of Ireland with Great Britain and her adherence to and membership of the group of nations forming the British Commonwealth of Nations.'

his conclusion of his analysis of Document No. 2 Collins reserved harsh words for de Valera:

> As an improvement on the Treaty Document No. 2 is not honest. It may be more dictatorial in language . . . It merely attaches a fresh label to the same parcel, or, rather, a label written, of purpose, illegibly in the hope of making belief that the parcel is other than it is.[234]

In *Finnegans Wake* the original document is described as 'illegible' (119), while Shaun accuses Shem of being an 'illegible clergimanths' (421). And it is Shaun who accuses Shem of 'always cutting my phrose to please his phrase' and calls him 'Digteter!' (dictator!) (423). But then Document No. 1 is also described as 'illegible' (482). All the documents are thereby fused and so are the charges and counter-charges.

A major confrontation between Shem and Shaun involves their abilities as writers. As Kev, Shaun asks Dolph (Shem) to help him 'construct ann aquilittoral dryankle' and to 'concoct an equangular trillitter' (286). Dolph tells Kev that he should 'first mull a mugfull of mud, son.' Kev, scandalised by the obscene overtones of Dolph's suggestion, replies impatiently, 'What the D.V. would I do that for? . . . what the Deva would you do that for?' (287). D.V. can be the abbreviation for Deo Volente, 'disorded visage' (as footnote 3 suggests on page 286), or de Valera,[235]★ the 'mathmaster'. Kev becomes increasingly angry while Dolph by the aid of his creative mind offers to liberate the mass from 'the booty of fight' (300). In order to calm Kev down Dolph suggests that one should compliment his writing and tell him, 'sure you could wright anny pippap passage, Eye bet, as foyne as that moultylousy Erewhig, yerself, mick!' (301). He then guides Kev in the manner of composing 'all the charicatures in the drame': 'Pose the pen, man, way me does', Dolph says, and uses as his models the Irish artists and politicians Wilde, Swift, Sterne, Steele, Burke, Yeats, Shaw, Parnell, O'Connell, and Connolly (303). Kev's rage at Dolph's impertinence finally leads him to strike his brother (with the 'cawraidd's blow' later dealt by Taff to

---

Mr de Valera's oath: 'I . . . do swear to bear true faith and allegiance to the Constitution of Ireland and to the Treaty of Association of Ireland with the British Commonwealth of Nations and to recognize the King of Great Britain as Head of the Associated States.' (*Times*, 21 December 1921).

★ 'Deva' means 'God' or 'heavenly' in Sanskrit.

Butt (344)). Private Carr, representing the British State, had bashed Stephen in the jaw in *Ulysses*. Kev, like Shaun and other characters in *Finnegans Wake*, undergoes various personality changes and cannot be said to represent de Valera consistently. But insofar as he is the Irish politician at home, Kev represents the new Irish State rejecting Dolph's or Joyce's writings. Dolph, however, still urges Joyce to 'Forge away, sunny Sim!' (305)

The brother battle also revolves around the discovery of the manuscript by the hen. Originally we are told that Kevin appropriated the find and tried to pass it off as his own discovery (110). We learn later that the manuscript in question was Document No. 1 and that Kevin was found shooting the hen by Matt Gregory (482). The letter represents all writings and all documents, particularly *Finnegans Wake* itself. What I want to emphasise, however, are the aspects of the letter as the Treaty or as Document No. 2. Collins had referred to Document No. 2 as not being an 'honest' improvement on the Treaty. Similarly, the Four Old Men cast 'strong suspicion on counterfeit Kevin'. The penman's tale is 'the gist of Shaun but the hand is the hand of Sameas' (483). Earlier Butt had hoped that the dawn would shed some light on 'the darkumen (scene as signed, Slobabogue)' (350) which alludes to a forged order against Irish prisoners at Scullabogue in the 1798 rebellion. There are also rumours that the letter, 'decumans numbered too' (369) was written by a secretary with 'authorsagastions from Schelm the Pelman' (autosuggestions from Shem the Penman). Shaun is asked by Shem if he had read 'the strangewrote anaglyptics of those shemletters patent for his Christian's Em?' Shaun replies that he has and that 'it is not a nice production. It is a pinch of a scribble . . . Overdrawn! Puffedly offal tosh!' and the foulest piece of writing he has ever witnessed. He claims that he could write much better and 'play the sem backwards like Oscan wild . . . with my eyes thickshut and all' (419). Shaun as Kevin is a student of 'psychical chirography' (482), while as Yawn he attempts to wriggle out of the probings by the Four Old Men by claiming that he does not speak English and evading questions about Document No. 1:

> – He no angly mo, me speakee Yellman's lingas. Nicey Doc Mistel Lu, please! Me no pigey ludiments all same numpa one Topside Tellmestoly fella. (485)

He seems to claim that 'number one' is pidgin English for 'Tell me a story'. It is becoming clear that the original document is *Finnegans*

Wake and that Joyce allows the 'devil era' to win out before the dawn comes:

> Ay, already the sombrer opacities of the gloom are sphanished! Brave footsore Haun! Work your progress! Hold to! Now! Win out, ye divil ye!

The question remains, who is the original author?

'Well it is partly my own, isn't it?' says Shaun (422). He hates Shem because of his 'root language' (424) and the thundering hundred letter word leads him to offer peace in 'vealar penulti-matum', indicating by an anagram of 'Valera' that the speaker is probably de Valera.[236] Shaun claims that 'every dimmed litter in it is a copy. . . . The last word in stolentelling! And what's more rightdown lowbrown schisthematic robblemint!' (424). *Finnegans Wake* is the last word in plagiarism for Shaun and he boasts that he could outdo Joyce for his 'authordux Book of Lief would, if given to daylight, (I hold an almost incredible faith about it) far exceed what the bogus bolshy of a shame' (425) produced.* Shaun here merges with de Valera, Wyndham Lewis, as well as Stanislaus Joyce who referred to *Finnegans Wake* in a letter as 'literary bolshevism' and claimed that some of the ideas for *Ulysses* were pilfered from him.[237]† 'The Book of Lief' includes both the Book of Liffey and the Book of Life mentioned in *Apocalypse* 20: 12–15, where those whose names are not found written in the Book of Life are thrown into a lake of fire representing a second death. That is why Shaun says 'I will commission to the flames any incendiarist whosoever or ahriman howsoclever who would endeavour to set ever annyma roner moother of mine on fire' (426). At the same time Joyce is probably echoing the attack on him in *Time and Western Man*, where Lewis stated, '*Chamber Music* would certainly not have secured its author a place 'among the english poets' – it would hardly even have set the Liffey on fire for five minutes!'[238] Shaun therefore becomes the inquisitor for Shem whose name is not in the Book of Life or the Book of Lief and who intends to make the Liffey a second Hell like the lake of fire in the *Apocalypse* through his 'bolshevist' writings.

---

* 'Authordux' may refer to Arthur, Duke of Wellington, as well as to King Arthur; but the more obvious meaning is 'orthodox'.

† Ironically enough, Oliver Gogarty, in a review of *Finnegans Wake* in the *Observer*, also referred to the language of the book as 'literary Bolshevism' (see *James Joyce: The Critical Heritage*, ed. Robert H. Deming (London: Routledge & Kegan Paul, 1970), vol. II, p. 675).

Stanislaus too attacked the installments of *Work in Progress* bitterly in his letters and asked Joyce 'when he intended to take down the scaffolding, and whether it was likely to go on until somebody asked a question in Parliament about it'.[239]

The idea of de Valera writing an orthodox *Finnegans Wake* might appear ludicrously funny, but I think Joyce is satirising de Valera's attempt at outdoing Document No. 1 after it had already been drawn up and signed. Collins declared that the main difference between the Treaty and Document No. 2 was that one was signed and the other was not.[240] At the same time the fact that Joyce presents the *Book of Kells* as a work of art deriving from *Finnegans Wake* and de Valera's Document No. 2 as receiving inspiration from the same source might again appear gratuitous. But Joyce is indicating that his work is the most native document, the conscience of his race, the conscience inaccessible to a document reflecting early Irish Catholicism or one purporting to contain Ireland's national aspirations more adequately.

But why does Shem make Shaun the custodian of 'that letter selfpenned to one's other, that neverperfect everplanned' (489)★ and why is he anxious that Shaun should receive the installments of *Work in Progress* before its final publication? I think that Joyce is here re-enacting the history of the signing of the Treaty in an ironical manner. By submitting *Finnegans Wake* for de Valera's and Shaun's perusal before applying his personal signature to the whole work Joyce is doing the very thing the Irish plenipotentiaries had forgotten to do. Joyce is acting as Ireland's envoy plenipotentiary abroad 'wiping english spooker off the face of the erse' and even Shaun considers himself an unworthy bearer of such a document and admits that 'It should of been my other with his leichname for he's the head and I'm an everdevoting fiend of his' (408).† In this way de Valera as Shaun could not complain that he has not seen Ireland's most native document before its actual publication and consequently de Valera as Shaun becomes ironically Joyce's envoy to Dublin. Joyce's point seems to be that playing with words and documents in the daytime world incurs serious political consequences, whereas in the night world such activity quietly amuses.

★ Shem's letter also alludes to Davitt's 'Pen Letter', See Clive Hart, *Structure and Motif in Finnegans Wake* (London, 1962), pp. 200 ff.

† 'Everdevoting fiend' is an ironical reference to Wyndham Lewis who used to sign the letters he wrote to Joyce, 'your everdevoted friend'.

Joyce knew, however, that Shaun would reject *Finnegans Wake* just as de Valera had rejected Document No. 1 and that he would draft an alternative proposal. After the civil war de Valera's image as a rebel gradually changed into that of a statesman. In 1932 as 'Fianna's foreman' (76) of his new party, Fianna Fáil, de Valera replaced William Cosgrave's governing Fine Gael party. Dissatisfied with the constitution of the Irish Free State, de Valera drafted almost singlehandedly a new constitution which was put into effect in 1937 and created the Irish Republic of Eire. Eire claimed 'the whole island of Ireland' as its territory, the North as well as the South. But until the country was reunited Eire's laws would apply only to the South. The Head of Government would be the Prime Minister or Taoiseach (Chief). I think that a possible answer to the puzzle as to the number relationships in Earwicker's family of five (285–6), 'Equal to-aosch', may actually be the Irish Prime Minister or Taoiseach.

The new constitution, or possibly Shaun's 'Book of Lief', was a tour de force for de Valera as he finally succeeded in scrapping Document No. 1, although the six county area in Northern Ireland remained the same as it still does today. The preamble displayed a peculiarly Catholic flavour: 'In the name of the most Holy Trinity, from whom all authority and to whom, as our final end, all actions both of men, and states must be referred.'[241] Anna Livia's untitled mamafesta, also 'memorialising the Most Highest', begins 'In the name of Annah the Allmaziful, the Everliving, the Bringer of Plurabilities' (104). We are told that the 'proteiform graph itself is a polyhedron of scripture' (107). In de Valera's new constitution Irish independence is associated with Christian redemption, for the constitution embraced in part the theocratic notion of the State. For this reason 'Deblinity' is 'devined' and Shaun succeeds to the Irish throne by divine nomination:

> I heard a voice, the voce of Shaun, vote of the Irish, voise from afar (and cert no purer puer palestrine e'er chanted pangelical mid the clouds of Tu es Petrus. (407)

It might be said that here Wyndham Lewis is intended as part of the Shaun figure, but de Valera remains a major model too. Under the new constitution Ireland has become an island of the sainted sage, de Valera. Joyce is uncomplimentary about de Valera's Ireland after 1937, labelling it 'Valgur Eire' (256), as distasteful as when Tim Healy had been Governor-General until 1927 in Healyopolis.

The result of the alliance between de Valera and the Church is

'Christ in our irish times! Christ on the airs independence! Christ hold the freedman's charewoman! Christ light the dully expressed!' (500), a decidedly Catholic influence in the daily political and social affairs of Irishmen. Shaun's daylight book his 'trifolium libretto' (which suggests the shamrock as well as the Trinity) is 'authordux' to say the least. With the dawn of the advent of the new era (as opposed to the devil era), 'Procreated on the ultimate ysland of Yreland in the encyclical yrish archipelago' (605), of Kevin is celebrated. The Shaun of Irish politics, at first a rebel and denounced as Luciferian, is now the respectable Kevin 'of increate God the servant' (604), a man leading two political and social lives. In previous times the Church was suspected of collusion with the British State; now its alliance with Eire is enshrined in the constitution and is made official. Joyce viewed de Valera's pact with the Church as, in effect, a pact with the devil.

Joyce places some of the details of Earwicker's dream after the creation of the Free State. Earwicker's death, for instance, is attributed to the MacMahon chaps, and it has been shown that the reference is to Fitz Urse, one of the assassins of Thomas à Becket who allegedly fled to Ireland and founded the MacMahon family.[242] But the killing described is of more recent occurrence. In 1922 Michael Collins was shot in an ambush during the civil war. After his death, the cruel lines, 'Turn over Mick, make room for Dick, and Willie follows after',[243] were painted on a city wall. Richard Mulcahy succeeded Collins as Commander-in-Chief of the Irish Free State Army and William Cosgrave the subsequent President. A variation of the phrase, 'Move up Mackinerny! Make room for Muckinerny!' (264), appears as a gloss on Joyce's statement about partition. The first version is 'Stand up, mickos! Make strake for minnas!' (12), and later as 'Quake up, dim dusky, wook doom for husky' (593), and 'Move up, Mumpty! Mike room for Rumpty! By order, Nickekellous Plugg' (99). In this last passage Joyce describes the phrase as being 'inscribed in the national cursives . . . turreted and envenomoloped in piggotry' (99). The ambush is similar to the Piggott frame-up and this associates Earwicker (and Collins) at once with Parnell, and as an 'expatriate' (100) perhaps with Joyce. The inference seems to be that Joyce feared the same thing might happen to him if he returned to Ireland.

Joyce, in fact, wrote to his friend Curran saying that he would not consider returning to Ireland before he had completed his book.[244] Mary Colum stated her view that 'up to nearly the end of his life

Joyce was waiting patiently, I think, for a signal from the Irish government, inviting him back to place bay leaves in his hair.'[245] Joyce's letters to Harriet Shaw Weaver and Giorgio certainly indicate that if a reconciliation was to take place between him and Ireland the initiative would have to come from his country. Lucia, in fact, was the one who attempted to bring about an accord in a conversation recorded by Joyce:

L How long will your country refuse to recognise what
   you have done?
I How long indeed?
L I want to reconcile you. It is time for some great person of
   your country to come forward and hold out a hand to you and
   to us.
I Hear, hear.[246]

In a letter written to T. S. Eliot in 1932 shortly after John Joyce's death, Joyce stated these reasons for not returning home:

An instinct which I believed in held me back from going, much as I longed to. *Dubliners* was banned there in 1912 on the advice of a person★ who was assuring me at the time of his great friendship. When my wife and children went there in 1922, against my wish, they had to flee for their lives, lying flat on the floor of a railway carriage while rival parties shot at each other across their heads and quite lately I have had experience of malignancy and treachery on the part of people† to whom I had done nothing but friendly acts. I did not feel myself safe and my wife and my son opposed my going.[247]

The fear that his countrymen would not welcome a prodigal son, that they would drive a knife into his heart, as he told Italo Svevo more bluntly,[248] and the spectre of having quicklime thrown into his eyes, like Parnell, also prevented Joyce from returning. And the invitation from 'the great person' of the 1930s never came.

While Joyce waited in silence and in exile de Valera as Shaun becomes the 'spickspookspokesman of our specturesque silentiousness!' (427), using the radio as his medium for direct talks to the Irish people. Accordingly, the customers in Earwicker's pub chip in to buy 'their tolvtubular high fidelity daildialler' in the doom of 'the

---

★ Thomas Kettle.
† Michael Lennon.

balk of the deaf' (or talk of the dev) (309). Earlier, in the study chapter, the question 'while the dail are they doodling dawdling over the mugs and grubs?' (306) was asked. But can Joyce and de Valera, as Shem and Shaun, ever be reconciled? Dolph and Kev were temporarily appeased (305), but dear dirty Dublin has been transformed into 'dim delty Deva' (614), or de Valera's Dublin, and Anna Livia is 'still her deckhuman amber too' (619), or Document No. 2. This passage, as well as others which involve de Valera, is in part playful, and Joyce is not at this stage eager to plump for or against de Valera. He is more concerned with showing the 'will gens wonts' – the conflict of opposites – as a permanent part of human life. There is plenty of tension no matter how much one longs for relief from tension or peace. Adversaries are as necessary as proponents, and as inevitable. Shaun and Shem – as the fable of the Ondt and Gracehoper says – depend upon each other for existence, and between them constitute 'Homo Vulgaris', or the common man: '*These twain are the twins that tick* Homo Vulgaris' (418).

This is not to say, however, that because Joyce urges us to be 'tolerant of antipathies' (163), he did not have preferences between the ideals of life represented by Shaun and those represented by Shem. Both points of view are always faithfully presented in *Finnegans Wake*, but it cannot be said that Joyce approves of Shaun-like politics. To maintain that he does is to say that in the end Joyce accepted those very ideas and conventions he had spent a lifetime fighting against. He could not accept, for instance, de Valera's Constitution or Shaun's daytime 'Book of Lief' since it fostered the Church's influence on Irish society, a main reason for which he had originally left. His own night book was inspired by the Liffey, to which Shaun attests: 'She, the mammy far, was put up to it by him' (421). 'To part from Devlin is hard' (24) as Joyce knew, but 'so they parted. In Dalkymount nember to' (390). Even Anna Livia as she passes through Dublin and back to the sea blames her parting on de Valera, for 'dev do espart' (626), and she finds Ireland's 'lintil pea' (625) on her journey outward. In this way they are 'devourced' (370). But Joyce told Mrs Skeffington, 'There was an English queen who said that when she died the word 'Calais' would be written on her heart. 'Dublin' will be found on mine.'[249] He left his readers free to choose which book of Liffey contained Ireland's true conscience and who was its most native author.

At the same time, Joyce did not agree with Shaun who advises the girls, 'The soil is for the self alone. Be ownkind. Be kithkinish. Be bloodysibby. Be irish' (465). To be Irish did not mean bloodthirsty involvement in the movement for independence or the narrow nationalism represented by 'dogmestic' – or dogmatic and domestic – Shaun (411). Joyce preferred to be outward-looking. As a young man he had aimed to Europeanise Ireland. With *Finnegans Wake*, he not only Europeanised, but *internationalised* Ireland. In this sense, it can be said that in the end Joyce hibernicised Europe too, since he had accomplished as much as Irish politicians in drawing the attention of people from all countries towards Ireland.

Chapter 5

Literary Politics

1 Dublin's Dante

Joyce's political consciousness was not based solely on scrutiny of political writings. He was especially alive to how his predecessors had treated politics in art. One of the first books to stamp itself indelibly on him was *La Divina commedia*. The crises faced by Dante in relation to his city, his faith, and love invited irresistible comparisons to Joyce's own. The turning point in Dante's life, which later impelled him to write *The Divine Comedy*, was a political one. Dante's preoccupation with politics revolved around his enforced exile from his native Florence in 1302. For half a century prior to this event the city had been embroiled in civil wars between the Guelfs, who nominally supported the Papacy, and the Ghibellines, who made alliance with the German Emperors. From 1266 onwards Guelf supremacy in Florence became firmly established and their power consolidated at the battle of Campaldino in 1289, at which Dante was present. The ruling Guelf party, however, soon split into 'Black' and 'White' factions, with Dante's family supporting the latter group. The 'Whites' wanted Florence to be a strong city free from Papal influence, whereas the 'Blacks' were willing to compromise with the Pope in order to gain complete control of the government. At this time, about 1295, Dante joined one of the powerful local guilds, from whose members public officials were chosen. In 1300 he became politically active by being appointed one of the six guild representatives to govern the city. The crucial question of Dante's priorate concerned whether or not to send military aid to Papal armies and help them quell a rebellion in Sicily. The refusal of the priors to do so caused resentment among Papal adherents and, on account of this, the conflict between the

'Blacks' and 'Whites' was intensified. Pope Boniface VIII at first threatened reprisals but then decided to send Charles de Valois, brother of the French King, ostensibly as a peacemaker. Dante opposed the papal initiative as unwarranted interference in an internal civic dispute. To make matters worse, Charles sided with the 'Blacks' and removed the 'White' priors, including Dante, from office. The priors were subsequently tried and sentenced to exile on trumped up charges of fraud. Their opposition to the Pope and the coming of Charles was also cited as sufficient cause for their expulsion from the city.

Joyce's expatriation lacked the purely political circumstances surrounding his hero's exile. Although Joyce claimed in 'Gas from a Burner' that his country always sent 'her writers and artists to banishment', Ireland did not deport him as Florence deported Dante. Joyce left of his own accord. Still, he felt that the artistic soul in Ireland suffered the danger of suppression and stunted growth. The sensitive artist, therefore, experienced a sentence of banishment no less severe than the one imposed on Dante. But he resorted to his art, as his Italian master had done, to vindicate himself under the challenge of betrayal and ostracism. In a letter to the Emperor Henry VII Dante described himself as a 'Florentine undeservedly in exile', but he held this exile for honour (L'esilio, che m'è dato, onor mi tegno), as he says in the *Canzone dell' esilio*. Brunetto Latini is made to emphasise this point in Canto XV of the *Inferno*:

La tua fortuna onor ti serba
  che l'una parte e l'altra avranno fame
  di te; ma lungi fia dal becco l'erba.

(Thy fortune holds for thee such honour that the one party and the other shall be ravenous against thee, but the grass shall be far from the goat)[1]

Away from his native Florence, the poet will be beyond the reach of Guelfs and Ghibellines. The strife between these Florentine factions had its parallel in Irish politics. The most immediate political event prior to Joyce's departure caused the Parnellite split, which resulted in victory for the anti-Parnellite faction and which plunged Ireland into a state of political paralysis.

Dante's reflections on politics centred on the city which had expelled him. This focus for his art provided an insight which Ibsen, another model of the exiled writer for Joyce, did not afford. A character in George Moore's *Evelyn Innes* remarks that 'You cannot understand Paris until you have read Balzac. Balzac discovered Paris; he created Paris.'[2] The same can be said of Dante and Florence, of Joyce and Dublin. In a letter to Grant Richards, Joyce emphasised, 'I do not think that any writer has yet presented Dublin to the world.'[3] Joyce was more of a Dubliner than an Irishman. As he informed Arthur Power, 'I always write about Dublin, because if I can get to the heart of Dublin I can get to the heart of all the cities of the world.'[4] Dante wrote what Joyce called 'Europe's epic'[5] from a similar point of view. Dante's early technique in *La Vita nuova*, however, differed from Joyce's. In the interest of universality he suppressed all picturesque detail about the city even to the exclusion of the name itself.[6] Florence is simply referred to as *'la sopradetta cittade'* ('the above-mentioned city'), perhaps out of bitterness. On his first visit to Dublin in *A Portrait of the Artist* (68) (*66*), Stephen wanders through the city streets making a 'skeleton map of the city in his mind'. And it was Joyce's boast about *Ulysses* that if Dublin were to be destroyed it could be reconstructed out of his work.

Yet the art of Dante and Joyce shared a common 'moral' purpose in relation to the inhabitants of their native cities. The circles of the *Inferno* are occupied to a large extent by Dante's contemporaries, his friends, acquaintances and the people with whom he waged his political battles:

> Godi, Fiorenza, poi che se' sì grande
> che per mare e per terra batti l'ali
> e per lo 'nferno tuo nome si spande!
>
> (XXVI. 1–3)

> (Rejoice, Florence, since thou art so great that over land and sea thou beatest thy wings and through Hell thy name is spread abroad!)

Dante's stricture arises from his concern for what he considered to be the moral and political deterioration in Florence. In writing *Dubliners* Joyce similarly expressed a moral aim: 'My intention was to write a chapter of the moral history of my country and I chose Dublin for the scene because that city seemed to me the center of paralysis.'[7] Joyce's Dantesque cast of mind is revealed most clearly in a passage from *Stephen Hero* (164) (*158–9*), where Stephen spending a social evening at the Daniels', makes this mental outburst:

The ugly artificiality of the lives over which Father Healy was comfortably presiding struck this outrageous instant out of him and he went on repeating to himself a line from Dante for no other reason except that it contained the angry disyllable 'frode'. Surely, he thought, I have as much right to use the word as Dante ever had. The spirits of Moynihan and O'Neill and Glynn seemed to him worthy of some blowing about round the verges of a hell which would be a caricature of Dante's. The spirits of the patriotic and religious enthusiasts seemed to him fit to inhabit the fraudulent circles where hidden in hives of immaculate ice they might work their bodies to the due pitch of frenzy. The spirits of the tame sodalists, unsullied and undeserving, he would petrify amid a ring of Jesuits in the circle of foolish and grotesque virginities and ascend above them and their baffled icons to where his Emma, with no detail of her earthly form or vesture abated, invoked him from a Mohammedan paradise.

Dante reserved the eighth circle, known as 'Malebolge' (or Evil Pouches) for those guilty of simple fraud, and he divided them into ten separate categories. As he enters the first ditch Dante observes a double file of sinners, panders and seducers, and he ironically compares them to the pilgrims making their way to Rome for Pope Boniface's celebration of the Church's Jubilee in 1300 (XVIII. 25–33). Stephen's hell will not be based on the same moral principles but will rather be a caricature of Dante's, as he makes clear. Indeed to have Emma, the Irish Beatrice, invoke Stephen from a 'Mohammedan' paradise is a caricature of Dante, who considered Mahomet a sower of discord and placed him in the ninth bolgia of the fraudulent. But Stephen underlines the fact that he has as much right as Dante to use the word 'frode' because of the ugly artificiality of the lives of those Dubliners who are patriotic and religious enthusiasts. In *Ulysses* the ultra-patriotic Citizen blasphemes against Christ in whose name he attacks Bloom, while Private Carr utters a profanity against the King in whose name he assaults Stephen. In 'The Day of the Rabblement' Joyce condemned the members of the literary movement for compromising their art in order to gain commercial success. Falsity of purpose was for Joyce, as Stanislaus said, 'the literary sin against the Holy Ghost', or literary simony.[8] When Dante asks Cacciaguida at the end of *Paradiso* XVII whether he should be cautious in setting down what may be for many bitter truths, his ancestor firmly urges him to 'rimossa ogni menzogna, /

tutta tua vision fa manifesta; / e lascia pur grattar dov'è la rogna.'
('put away every falsehood and make plain all thy vision, – and then
let them scratch where is the itch'). Like Dante, Joyce set out to
expose what he deemed false in Dublin life and desired to liberate his
contemporaries from their spiritual paralysis by having them take a
good look at themselves in his 'nicely polished glass'.[9] He wrote
Dubliners with the conviction that 'he is a very bold man who dares
to alter in the presentment, still more, to deform, whatever he has
seen and heard.'[10] Like Dante, he came to the conclusion that 'I
cannot write without offending people.'[11] And like Dante too, he
wanted to save his own soul and that of his city.

Dante placed the blame for the moral and political decadence of his
times on the Church. In particular, he considered the intervention of
Pope Boniface VIII in Florentine politics a main reason for his
personal miseries and those of his city. In *Paradiso* Cacciaguida
forewarns Dante of his dismissal from Florence and refers indirectly
to the person behind the plot:

> Questo si vuole, e questo già si cerca
>   e tosto verrà fatto a chi ciò pensa
>   là dove Cristo tutto dì si merca.

(XVII. 49–51)

(This is determined, nay is already contrived and will soon be
accomplished, by him who meditates it in the place where Christ
is bought and sold all day.)

Dante hears an account of the coming strife between Blacks and
Whites from his fellow-citizen Ciacco in the *Inferno* and allusion is
made once again to the reigning Pope as the cause of civic turmoil:

> Dopo lunga tencione
> verranno al sangue, e la parte selvaggia
> caccerà l'altra con molta offensione
> Poi appresso convien che questa caggia
> infra tre soli, e che l'altra sormonti
> con la forza di tal che testè piaggia.

(VI. 64–9)

(After long strife they shall come to blood and the party of the
rustics shall drive out the other with much offence; then, by force

of one who is now manoeuvring, the party is destined to fall within three years and the other to prevail.)

That Pope Boniface was already plotting against Dante *personally* at Easter 1300 is disputable. But Dante's sense of his own political destiny and importance leads him to make such a claim. Before leaving his country Joyce suspected his friends of brewing plots against him and he interpreted their treachery as a national symptom. Gogarty, for example, is *Ireland*'s gay betrayer. In a letter to Elkin Matthews in 1913 Joyce insisted that the banning of *Dubliners* and the burning of a thousand copies all ready for publication was due to 'a deliberate conspiracy of certain forces in Ireland to silence me'.[12] Stanislaus identified these forces as a certain vigilance committee presided over by the Viceroy's wife and widely represented by the Jesuits.[13] Later incidents, such as the one involving Nora and the children during the Irish civil war, Joyce also understood to be aimed at him *personally* by his countrymen. Free Staters and Republicans had acquired the ravenous characteristics of Blacks and Whites.

Joyce distrusted the alliance between Catholicism and nationalism, and he commented in *Stephen Hero* (58) (*53*) that 'working hand in hand with the priests had over and over again ruined the chances of revolutions.' He also indicated obliquely in 'Aeolus' that the Irish Church, through its representative Archbishop Walsh, meddled in Dublin politics. In Dante's time the Papacy had enhanced its political power through the expansion of the Papal States. Clement V, a successor to Boniface VIII, moved the Holy See from Rome to Avignon, since he owed his election as Pope to Philip of France. Dante reprimanded the Papacy because of its subservience to the French Kings for he thought this action detrimental to the political interests of Italy. He reserved the third bolgia of the *Inferno* for simoniacal Popes with political pretensions. In *Finnegans Wake* Shaun, while lecturing to the girls, gives them his consent to 'skim over through Hell with the Papes (mostly boys) by the divine comic Denti Alligator (exsponging your index) and find a quip in a quire arises aream' (440). Nevertheless, Shaun is surprised to learn that Dante put Popes in hell. But Dante proved even bolder when he characterised the Church as a 'puttana sciolta' in Canto XXXIII of the *Purgatorio*, identifying it with the harlot in the *Apocalypse*. Joyce remembered Dante's epithet when he spoke of the Church to Francini of being as big as a 'whore'.[14] Just as Dante had accused the

Pope in Avignon of working against Italy, so too Joyce attributed the source of Ireland's woes to Adrian IV's Bull, *Laudabiliter*, which allegedly made Ireland a fief of England. From this action he continually suspected the Vatican of working in collusion with the British Government against Irish interests.

In 'Grace', where Joyce parodies the tripartite division of *The Divine Comedy*, he again takes the Church to task. Four well-meaning friends attempt to rehabilitate Tom Kernan by accompanying him to a spiritual retreat. At one point there is an informal discussion among them on Church history highlighting the proclamation of papal infallibility. In political terms the Vatican always represented a reactionary force for Joyce. As he told Frank Budgen, 'In the nineteenth century, in the full tide of rationalist positivism and equal democratic rights for everybody, it proclaims the dogma of the infallibility of the head of the Church and also that of the Immaculate Conception.'[15] Joyce points out the irony of the position of John MacHale, Archbishop of Tuam, who opposed the doctrine of infallibility until the Vatican Council approved it (192) (*170*). When the conversation turns to the so-called mottoes of the various Popes, Pope Leo XIII is referred to as 'The Prisoner of the Vatican' (187) (*165*). Joyce borrowed this epithet from William Barry's *The Papacy and Modern Times: A Political Sketch 1303–1870*, which traces the origin of the Vatican's temporal power through to its decline. In his conclusion the author cites approvingly the Church's contemporary position as an exclusively spiritual force:

> It remains always true, as Auguste Comte perceived, that society rests on a creed, explicit or latent, in which its members are united; that its law is ethics and standard conscience. True likewise it is that the Pope cannot deny his origin, which was not a victory of the strong arm, but was due to the free immortal spirit. He never can be absorbed by the absolute State, for he is the pilgrim of eternity. And thus, a prisoner in the Vatican, without kingdom or army, Leo XIII, succeeding immediately to Pius IX, began and ended a reign of twenty-six years the most brilliant in its manifestations and most fruitful in results of any since the sack of Rome.[16]

Joyce opposed the temporal power of the Vatican and had adopted socialism as an effective countermeasure to it. He was fond of equating the secular interests of the Church with the offence of simony, the same charge that Dante had levelled against the Papacy of his time. In 'Grace' Father Purdon is described as a priest who will spare his listeners 'the depths and heights of religious experience'. He compares his office inappropriately to that of a 'spiritual accountant' come to 'open the books' of the faithful. In so doing he deforms the theological concept of 'grace' by equating it with good deeds in a commercial sense. In medieval terminology, 'grace' expressed the concept of a concession made by divinity and was used by the Popes in the governmental sense, as in the phrase 'The King by the grace of God.'[17] It was an essential principle in the argument in favour of theocratic forms of government. There is a twofold irony, then, in Joyce's title, since the theological concept of 'grace' is perverted in its usage as a commercial term and in its allusion to a medieval political ideal.

Dante's concentration on the politics of his native city in relation to the Church and Empire, therefore, was of particular significance to Joyce since he shaped his artistic consciousness with reference to the same political determinants. *The Divine Comedy* takes place at Easter 1300, a date of central importance to Dante because, in addition to its appositeness as a religious metaphor, it marked the beginning of his political misfortune, his own 'crucifixion' so to speak. The 'resurrection' theme in *Finnegans Wake* fuses with Easter 1916, when the course of Irish history changed dramatically. Joyce meanwhile was engaged in writing *Ulysses* and was not directly involved, but he too was 'in honour bound to the cross of [his] own cruelfiction' (192). When Charles Martel asks Dante in Canto VIII of the *Paradiso* whether it would not be worse for man on earth if he were not a citizen, the reply is an unequivocal 'yes' since his status as a citizen unites man with different forms of life. Joyce's response to a similar question posed by Frank Budgen was a modified affirmative in that he believed the artist should be a passive rather than active member of the State having at his disposal the agency of beauty and not politics to better and save the world.[18] He nevertheless felt compelled to serve his race through his art. Just as Florentine mothers told their children fabulous stories 'de' Troiani, di Fiesole e di Roma' (*Paradiso* XV), so too Stephen, as we have seen, is initiated into the world of Parnellite politics at an early age. Dante's mission is urged upon him by his ancestor Cacciaguida, whom Dante calls 'father', in Cantos XV–XVII of the *Paradiso*. Similarly, Stephen invokes his 'spiritual' ancestor and father Dedalus for confirmation of his calling. Stephen, moreover, marks his affinity with Dante's destiny in 'Telemachus' (*20; 24*) when he thinks that the moment he gives Buck Mulligan the key to the tower he too must 'eat his salt bread' in exile.

When Stephen declares later on in 'Circe' that 'in here it is I must kill the priest and king' tapping his brow, he is again following a precedent set by Dante.[19] At the end of Canto XXVII of the *Purgatorio* as Dante is about to enter the Garden of Eden, scene of man's first innocence, Virgil tells him that since his will has attained freedom and his spirit purification, the poet is now king and priest over himself:

> Non aspettar mio dir più nè mio cenno:
>> libero, dritto e sano è tuo arbitrio,
>> e fallo fora non fare a suo senno:
> per ch'io te sovra te corono e mitrio.

> (No longer expect word or sign from me. Free, upright and whole is thy will and it were a fault not to act on its bidding: therefore over thyself I crown and mitre thee.)

Dante had indicated in *De Monarchia* that before the Fall man did not need the institutions of Church and Empire to direct him. His soul now having been cleansed of sin, he no longer needs the control of these outward authorities. Dante associated with the White Guelfs in exile, but in 1304 he separated himself from 'la malvagia compagnia'. At the same time he was not willing to join the Ghibellines, as the sixth canto of *Paradiso* (97–105) makes clear. The political consequences for Dante, as Cacciaguida informs him, are that 'it shall be to thine honour to have made a party by thyself' ('a te fia bello averti fatta parte per te stesso') (*Paradiso* XVII). He will rise above party factionalism. Stephen too becomes his own priest through his art, a priest of the eternal imagination. In *Finnegans Wake* Shem is also accused of being 'a clerical party all to yourself' (190). Having cut himself off from the Church and State, Joyce devoted himself to the family. As Frank Budgen relates, Joyce praised the position of the Jewish father who is priest and king in his own household.[20]

Dante's independence is still subject to the Christian moral order, whereas Joyce regarded such an order to be an impediment to that higher freedom which he sought. Dublin, the seventh city of Christendom, is described in *A Portrait* (171) (*167*) as 'no older nor more weary nor less patient of subjection than in the days of thingmote', the Danish council which ruled it in ancient times. In Joyce's view man's fallen nature did not demand his submission to *any* external authority. There is a fundamental distinction in these positions. When Dante attacks the Church he does so by the Church's own standards. Its corruption led him to urge Henry VII of Luxembourg to march into Italy (*Paradiso* XXX). Dante considered himself a spiritual as well as a political exile in the sense that he was a pilgrim on earth exiled from God's sight, from his true native land of heaven. He retained his basic faith in both secular and spiritual institutions as aids to man in his struggle for salvation. Dante sees politics, then, as a 'moral' factor in human existence. He places a distinct emphasis on the continuity between good morals and good politics. Dante, moreover, vindicates himself as a faithful Christian in *Paradiso* (XXIV–XXVI) where, after a rigorous examination by Saints Peter, James and John, his orthodoxy is asserted and he is received into the Church Triumphant and the Church Militant. Hence whereas he is still working within the supernatural Church Joyce dissociates himself from its moral jurisdiction. In the Joycean world view, man, instead of attempting to harmonise his will with that of God, asserts the freedom of his will. It is no longer the Church but art which is seen to minister to the spiritual needs of mankind. Nor does the State ensure the stability and physical security for the artist to fulfill his mission. Consequently, the artist envisages a 'moral' order exclusive of that imposed by Church and State. In this way he remains a continual 'spiritual' and 'political' exile.

These differing perspectives on politics stem from the role Dante and Joyce assigned to the moral question in art. Dante conceived of the poet not only as spiritual leader of his people but also as moral teacher. He claims that *The Divine Comedy* is ''l poema sacro / al quale ha posto mano e cielo e terra' ('the sacred poem to which both heaven and earth have set their hand') (*Paradiso* XXV, 1–2; XXIII, 62). In his essay on 'Catilina' Joyce stated that the modern generation preferred instead to wander amid the 'shapeless hells and heavens' of Balzac, 'a Dante without the unfortunate prejudices of Dante'.[21] His aesthetics did not sanction a moral or didactic end. Since the good, the true, and the beautiful are interrelated, the purpose of art transcends conventional morality. While conceding that the poet is the spiritual focus of his time, Joyce insisted that he should not preach. He had in mind a poet like James Clarence Mangan,

one of those strange abnormal spirits who believe that their artistic

life should be nothing more than a true and continual revelation of
their spiritual life, who believe that their inner life is so valuable
that they have no need of popular support, and thus abstain from
proffering confessions of faith, who believe, in sum, that the poet
is sufficient in himself, the heir and preserver of a secular
patrimony, who therefore has no urgent need to become a
shouter, or a preacher, or a performer.[22]

The poet, having no need of popular support, is sufficient in himself,
or a party by himself in Dante's words, but his patrimony is secular.

Joyce asserted in his review of 'Catilina' that the work of the
modern era consisted in the breaking-up of tradition.[23] Joyce's
complaint about Ireland, as evidenced in the Trieste notebook, was
that its art was 'in the hands of blacklegs who still serve those ideas
which their fellow artists in Europe have rebelled against'.[24] In
Stephen Hero it is proclaimed that 'No esthetic theory is of any value
which investigates with the aid of the lantern of tradition' (217)
(*212*). Feudal terminology would therefore have to be supplanted by
a modern aesthetics. Stephen explains to Cranly that unlike the
serious love verses of Dante's *Vita Nuova* he is compelled to express
his love a little ironically. It is this ironical note that distinguishes
what Stephen calls the 'feudal spirit' from the 'spirit of humanity'
(179) (*174*). Joyce identified this spirit of humanity with the
Renaissance, claiming it had put the journalist in the monk's chair.
The Renaissance had 'deposed an acute, limited and formal mentality to give the scepter to a mentality that is facile and wide-ranging
(in the parlance of theater journals), a restless and rather amorphous
mentality'.[25] Stephen describes this modern spirit as 'vivisective'.

Cranly, however, labels Stephen's distinction between ancient
and modern a mere trick of words, and argues that human nature is
constant. Stephen maintains that making a wreath of songs is 'the
simple rhythmic liberation of an emotion' (181) (*176*). He agrees
with Renan that a man is 'a martyr only for the things of which he is
not quite sure' (180) (*175*). As a result, modern art entails the paradox
that in the midst of this doubt 'the spirit of man makes a continual
affirmation':

> The age, though it bury itself fathoms deep in formulas and
> machinery, has need of these realities which alone give and sustain
> life and it must await from those chosen centres of vivification the
> force to live, the security for life which can come to it only from
> them. (85) (*80*)

Joyce named Blake and Dante as examples of these chosen centres of vivification.[26] Stephen believes, therefore, that there exists a relationship between civil and individual life, that the life of the community is in constant interaction with that of the artist. In this way Joyce took it upon himself to smash feudalism not only in the political sense, but also aesthetically.

Dante's high, original purpose proved as intense at the end of his life. The constant concern of the exile, no matter how bitter his experience, is his *nostos*, the wistful memory of the homeland. Odysseus, after numberless wanderings, returned to his native soil to vindicate himself against domestic usurpers. Ibsen, the voluntary exile, also returned home to Christiania. Dante indicated in *Convivio* (I. 3) that he wished to rest his tired soul and to end his days in Florence. In *The Divine Comedy* he declared that if his sacred poem should ever overcome the cruelty of the Florentines who sent him into exile, he would take the poet's laurel crown at the font where he was baptized (*Paradiso* XXV. 1–10). In *De Vulgari Eloquentïa* (I. 6) he admitted that 'as regards our own pleasure or sensuous comfort, there exists no more agreeable place in the world than Florence.' Joyce too in his less virulent moments expressed an indulgent view of Ireland. 'Sometimes thinking of Ireland,' he confided in a letter to Stanislaus, 'it seems to me that I have been unnecessarily harsh.' The stories in *Dubliners*, he continued, conveyed 'none of the attraction of the city, for I have never felt at my ease in any city since I left it, except in Paris'. He had failed to reproduce its virtue of 'ingenuous insularity and its hospitality'.[27] But a return to the native city would have to be an honourable one. In 1315 the Angevin vicar in Florence issued a decree of amnesty for exiles like Dante. He changed their death penalty to that of temporary confinement, provided the exiles put up a cash guarantee and agreed to be 'offered' as penitents to Saint John by the bishop. Dante responded in forceful terms to 'a Florentine friend' that he would not return disgraced in the eyes of his fellow-citizens.[28] In his notes to *Exiles* (where Joyce too imagined himself returning home) he justified his title by claiming that a 'nation exacts a penance from those who dared to leave her payable on return' (149) (*114*). He was convinced, as he told Alfred Kerr, that his countrymen 'grudged my not concealing what I had seen' when writing *Ulysses*: 'In short, some were enraged by the realistic picture, others by the style. They all took revenge.'[29] Joyce too yearned up to nearly the end of his life for recognition of his work on the part of his compatriots and the Irish government. However the official the gracious recall, of Dublin's Dante never materialised. and Joyce interpreted their roles to be in a certain sense and both could have repeated the words of Jesus: 'It is ʌɪɪ ɪus own country, in his own home, that a prophet goes unhonoured.' (Matthew 13: 57).

2 'Creeping Jesus'

In his notes for *Stephen Hero* Joyce indicated that Blake and Dante were his 'two interpreters'. And he placed the epithet 'Creeping Jesus', borrowed from 'The Everlasting Gospel', beside their names.[30] In the fragments of this poem which survive, Blake addresses orthodox believers with indignation: 'The Vision of Christ that thou dost see / Is my Vision's Greatest Enemy.' By this he meant that the image of a gentle and humble Jesus, whom he referred to as the 'AntiChrist, Creeping Jesus', was a false one. He envisaged the true Jesus to be a revolutionary saviour who challenged authority, 'used the Elders and Priests like Dogs', cursed the rulers before the people, and 'His Seventy Disciples sent Against Religion & Government'.[31] Jesus is represented as an anarch, and this interpretation is in direct contrast to Dante's. Blake, whom Joyce considered to be 'the most enlightened of Western poets',[32] provided, in effect, the necessary antidote to the 'unfortunate prejudices' of Dante; that of the individual challenging not only conventional institutions but also the intellectual framework on which they were based.

In his lecture on Blake delivered in Trieste in 1912, Joyce declared that there was a distinct difference between 'that undisciplined and visionary heresiarch and those most orthodox church philosophers', Francisco Suarez and Don Giovanni Mariana de Talavera.[33] Stephen mentions Suarez in *A Portrait* as the Jesuit theologian who apologised for the apparent discourtesy Jesus showed his mother in public (246) (*242*). And he refers to Mariana de Talavera as the author of a sinister defence of tyrannicide (250) (*246*), as Joyce does in commenting on Blake. Joyce perceived a discrepancy between preaching the word of Jesus to the masses and endeavouring at the same time to construct a moral defence for killing.[34] To which display of cruel logic Joyce contrasts Blake's non-violent 'spiritual rebellion against the powers of this world'. He cites as an example Blake's rejection of the position of drawing master to the royal family because of the adverse effects which the artificial atmosphere of the court might have had on his art. Joyce was also moved by Blake's sensitive social conscience, as evidenced in the instances of his magnanimous concern for the poor.[35]

Blake's spiritual revolt against all authorities and institutions consisted in what he termed mental warfare on them. This action, he claimed, would unfasten the 'mind-forg'd manacles' manifested in every cry of fear. Blake insisted, moreover, that intellectual war is a force that 'shall in the end annihilate' kings and wars.[36] Nowhere is this belief made more emphatic than in the preface to 'Milton' where Blake urges the young men of the new age to 'Rouze up . . . set your foreheads against the ignorant Hirelings! For we have Hirelings in the Camp, the Court and the University, who would, if they could, for ever depress Mental and prolong Corporeal War.' And in order to build the new Jerusalem he proclaims 'I will not cease from Mental Fight.'[37] In 'Circe', after Bloom declares the new Bloomusalem, Stephen employs Blakean strategy by asserting that he must kill the priest and king through the agency of his artistic mind.[38] For Blake the struggle between liberty and tyranny, as represented by the fiery creature Orc and the grim old Giant Urizen, was a central one. In 'The Marriage of Heaven and Hell' this struggle is expressed in the antinomies of Artists or Prophets (the devils) and Priests (the angels). The Priests are upholders of a legal or institutionalised version of Jesus' message. Blake claimed that the restrictive laws decreed by the Church were inherited by the State, which enforced them in human codes.[39] Church and State were interdependent forces. The Artists, being Prophets, possess the true revolutionary message and aim to liberate the individual's mind from its bondage to Church and State. This was the liberty of conscience that Joyce deemed imperative for the artist. Dante had become his own priest and king, but his creative imagination still conformed to political and moral laws instituted by those authorities. Blake, on the other hand, averred in *Jerusalem*, 'I know of no other Christianity and of no other Gospel than the liberty both of body and mind to exercise the Divine Arts of Imagination.'[40] He overcame the twofold tyranny of Church and State by stressing, like Joyce, the need for the imagination to impose its own order on life. Joyce affirmed with Los that the business of artists is to create: 'I must Create a System or be enslav'd by another Man's.' The ideal of service to the eternal imagination had replaced Dante's service to the glory of God.

3   The Impossibilities of Siegfried Bakoonin

Not all writers Joyce admired abided by Los's dictum. Reduced to inactivity by exile, Dante pursued his political ideals with his pen. The Roman Empire he sought to rebuild was to be pacific rather than expansive. D'Annunzio, who considered himself to be Dante's successor, took a different view. He held that the poet was of prime importance in society, an artistic *sovrouomo*, and therefore above ordinary morality in his quest for beauty. This belief led him to see his mission as the harbinger of a new national conscience, a new Italy. The revival of a Roman Empire, to 'see in all men of foreign blood the reincarnation of barbarians', was to be achieved under the leadership of the poet himself and his band of followers. D'Annunzio translated this aesthetic ideal into political reality when he set out to capture Fiume for Italy in 1919 and succeeded in ruling that city for a year. Perhaps with these events in mind, Joyce described D'Annunzio's ideas about patriotism as 'semi-fanatic'.[41]

If Mr Duffy in 'A Painful Case' displays a D'Annunzian scorn for the common herd, his politics are not entirely those of Joyce. His refusal to 'compete with phrase-mongers' (123) (*111*) recalls Stephen's statement that 'phrases of the platform' do not befit the artist. But his break with socialism is Stanislaus' position, and his distrust of politicians is akin to Nietzsche's attitude as expressed in *The Will to Power*:

> Democracy represents the disbelief in all great men and in all elite societies: everybody is everybody else's equal. 'At bottom we are all herd and mob.'
>
> I am opposed to Socialism because it dreams ingenuously of 'goodness, truth, beauty, and equal rights' (anarchy pursues the same ideal, but in a more brutal fashion).
>
> I am opposed to parliamentary government and the power of the press, because they are the means whereby cattle become masters.[42]

Joyce, on the other hand, although opposed to parliamentarianism, sustained his interest in socialism on the continent and approached the anarchist position as his break with God and State became more pronounced.

D'Annunzio may have counted himself worthy of carrying on the tradition of Dante, but Joyce put Ibsen forward as the true successor to 'the first poet of the Europeans.' For it was here, as Stephen says in

Stephen Hero (46) (*41*), 'as only to such purpose in Dante, a human personality had been found united with the artistic manner which was itself almost a natural phenomenon: and the spirit of the time united one more readily with the Norwegian than with the Florentine'. Stephen discerns the very spirit of Ibsen himself moving behind his theory of the impersonal manner of the artist. In his review of 'Catilina', however, Joyce points out that since the women in the play are absolute types the ending savours of dogma, 'a most proper thing in a priest but a most improper in a poet.' Yet he praises his Norwegian master for not yielding to the hysterical demands that war, statecraft and religion made on art.[43] Joyce probably meant that the drama centres on the struggle within the individual since none of Catilina's political opponents appears on stage. In *The League of Youth* Ibsen renounced political favouritism by satirising both the Liberals and Conservatives, just as Dante had reproached the Guelfs and Ghibellines. In *An Enemy of the People*, which expressed Ibsen's disillusionment with party politics, Dr Stockmann proclaimed that 'the srongest man in the world is he who stands most alone', and his political solitude resembles Dante's position as a one-man party. Ibsen, like Flaubert, represented for Joyce a model for literary as opposed to political commitment. It was this stance as an 'unprejudiced observer', and not that of a 'convinced' nationalist,[44] that Joyce adopted in his articles on Ireland for *Il Piccolo della sera*.

Neither artist, however, proved to be truly 'unprejudiced'. Joyce clearly supported the radical Sinn Féin movement over the Irish parliamentary party in his articles. In his portrayal of Catilina Ibsen discounted Cicero's orations against the Roman conspirator, showing sympathy for the rebel over the politician. In his preface Ibsen makes it clear that the uprisings of 1848 in Hungary and elsewhere in Europe had a great effect on him during the writing of the play. Similarly, *Brand* was inspired by his anger at Norway's failure to aid Denmark in her war with Prussia in 1864. When the people of the community, whose compromising spirit Brand has been trying to reform, turn against him and drive him out into the snow in the final act, the outlaw declares 'I will fly my flag myself'. Ibsen castigates Norway's neutrality in *Peer Gynt* too, where Peer confides to the traveller Cotton, 'The art of success is to stand free / And uncommitted amid the snares of life' and states that his theory is a 'national inheritance'. When Ibsen was accused of becoming conservative he responded with the poem 'To My Friend the Revolutionary Orator', where he claimed that the only true revolution was the Deluge. But it was not complete since Noah escaped in his Ark. Ironically, Ibsen tells the orator to flood the world with revolutionary chatter, while he will gladly torpedo the Ark. In *Stephen Hero* (215) (*210*), Stephen, another revolutionary, advises his mother to answer the priest who asks for his where-abouts, 'I don't know father. I asked him and he said I was to tell the priest he was making a torpedo.'[45] Both Ibsen and Joyce stress the right of the individual to rebel against troll nationalism or chauvinism.

When Shaw identified 'Ibsenism' with socialism in *The Quin-tessence of Ibsenism* (1891), Ibsen did not object and expressed surprise that he might have arrived at conclusions through his art similar to those the Social Democrats had reached through scientific research.[46] Joyce confided to Stanislaus that 'I fancy I[bsen]'s attitude towards literature and socialism somewhat resembled mine.'[47] In another letter he stated his belief that Ibsen, like Hauptmann, stood apart from the herd of writers because of his political aptitude.[48] (Hauptmann too was a socialist.) In *Ulysses* Stephen is the rebel and Bloom the utopian dreamer. As a young man Peer Gynt becomes an outlaw when he carries off Ingrid, who is destined to be the bride of another. His great ambition is to be Emperor. In the fourth act this dream is fulfilled when Peer, now middle-aged, is hailed as Prophet and Master by a chorus of girls. Gazing out over a desert in Morocco (IV. v.), Peer lets his plans for natural, cultural, and social regener-ation be known:

> And in the midst of my sea, on a rich oasis,
> I shall personally propagate the Norwegian race.
> The blood of our Northern valleys is – well, nearly royal,
> And a little Arab mixture will do the rest.
> Around a bay on rising sand
> I'll found my capital, Peeropolis.
> The world's degenerate. Now comes the turn
> Of Gyntiana, my land!

Ibsen is alluding to the ideal Norwegian community, Oleana, founded in 1852 by his old Chief Ole Bull in Pennsylvania, on the model recommended by the French socialists.[49] Joyce, like Ibsen, supported Utopian ideals but felt that they must be ridiculed. In 'Circe' Bloom is presented with the freedom of the city of Dublin and is proclaimed the 'little father' of the new Bloomusalem in the

Nova Hibernia of the future. He appears for his coronation on a milkwhite horse which is 'richly caparisoned' *(481; 603)*. Peer's horse is also 'richly caparisoned' (IV. v.), and is described by Anitra, the daughter of a Bedouin chieftain, as being 'white as the milk / That flows in the river of Paradise' (IV. vi.). Bloom's bitter definition of love between a man and a woman as 'a cork and bottle' *(499; 619)* is borrowed from Peer's description of Anitra sleeping:

> Hush! A sound! As of a cork
> From a bottle gaily springing!
> Now again! And yet again!
> Sighs of passion? Love's sweet song?
> No, it is the sound of snoring.
> Heavenly sound! Anitra sleeps!

Faust too, as a decrepit old man, takes over the reigns of power, controlling lands and peoples, and establishes a vast land reclamation project that will provide homes and sources of livelihood for millions. Like Peer, Bloom explains his schemes for social regeneration *(489–90; 610)*, and his political platform is also based on socialist ideals.

Although Ibsen's sympathy for socialism confirmed Joyce in his convictions as a socialistic artist, Shaw's analysis of *An Enemy of the People* could not have been totally convincing. When Dr Stockmann decides to become a political loner and turns his back on 'the damned compact Liberal majority', Shaw claims that these remarks are not disparaging of parliaments and democracy. They are simply 'a wholesome reduction of them to their real place in the social economy as pure machinery'. Nor should Ibsen's position be confounded with Anarchism or 'the idealization of the repudiation of Governments', Shaw warns us.[50] Georg Brandes, whose work Joyce was acquainted with, maintained that 'Ibsen's whole character presupposes a distrust and ill-will towards parliamentarianism', and that he was 'an extreme opponent of the sharply defined modern idea of the State'.[51] Ibsen's political ideals, Brandes says, were akin to those publicly proclaimed by the Paris Commune, whose essence was its rebellion against the State according to Kropotkin, and his anarchistic tendencies are evident in a letter written in 1871 where he averred that the State is the curse of the individual.[52] Ibsen did not especially welcome outward, violent changes. He desired instead, as he stated in another letter to Brandes, 'a revolution of the spirit of man',[53] an internal change enabling him to develop all the fruitful possibilities of his nature. Joyce, like Ibsen, claimed that the State exerted a negative influence on the individual, and reduced human pursuit to the purely materialistic level.[54] The artist for Joyce too enlarged the human perspective to include the spiritual – he must reshape men's minds, not by violently imposing a new shape, but by awakening a sense of liberty in them.

There exists an apparent inconsistency, however, in Ibsen's argument as presented in *An Enemy of the People*. Although he did not wish to identify himself with the character of Dr Stockmann, Ibsen is in basic agreement with his hero on the ideological issues. Dr Stockmann wants to make his children free men, but he says they will achieve freedom only by becoming *Aristocrats*. 'The masses are nothing but raw material which may, some day, be refined into individuals', he declares.[55] The minority, not the majority, is always right. Ibsen made it clear that he did not mean by the minority those political reactionaries belonging to a party. He meant rather the minority 'which forges ahead in territory which the majority has not yet reached', those most 'closely attuned to the future'.[56] The artist, then, by forging ahead into unknown territory elevates the masses to individuals. Joyce made a similar claim. The epigraph of *A Portrait of the Artist* is 'Et ignotas animum dimittit in artes' ('applying his mind to obscure arts') and by making forays into the forbidden and unknown aspects of mind and body, Stephen identifies his mission with Ovid's Daedalus as that of 'the artist forging anew in his workshop out of the sluggish matter of the earth a new soaring impalpable imperishable being' (173) (*169*). In his early essay on 'Drama and Life', Joyce (perhaps with Ibsen's argument in mind) admitted as irrefutable truth Mr Beerbohm Tree's contention that 'art cannot be governed by the insincerity of the compact majority.'[57] In a letter written from Rome to Stanislaus, he clarified his political position by alluding to Ibsen's play:

> you seem unable to share my detestation of the stupid, dishonest, tyrannical and cowardly burgher class. The people are brutalised and cunning. But at least they are capable of some honesty in these countries: or, at least, they will move because it is their interest to do so. I am a stranger to them, and a prey for them often: but, in the sense of the word as I use it now, I am not an enemy of the people.[58]

Joyce conceived of his art as elevating both patricians and the masses to individuals. The anarchistic state of mind, moreover, does not cancel out the 'aristocratic' character of the avant-garde, as Renato Poggioli has pointed out, since it 'presupposes the individualistic revolt of the 'unique' *against* society in the largest sense' and yet 'presupposes solidarity *within* a society in the restricted sense of that word – that is to say, solidarity within the community of rebels and libertarians'.[59]

Shaw regarded anarchism as impractical, and he expressed this view in a paper read to the Fabian Society entitled *The Impossibilities of Anarchism* in October 1891. Joyce took a genuine interest in the arguments for and against anarchism. Shaw's essay was reprinted as *Fabian Tract* number 45, and Joyce had this tract as well as those dating from 1884 to 1913 in his library. The distinction between the socialists and the anarchists, according to Shaw, rests in their attitude to the State. The anarchist distrusts State action and, by his advocacy of the prerogative of individuals, he proposes to restrict the one and to extend the other. The Fabian, on the other hand, proposes to democratise the State and places his reliance on it as an efficient instrument in organising the primary industries on which people's lives and liberties depend.

Shaw expressed admiration for Benjamin Tucker, to whose journal, *Liberty*, he had contributed original articles. Tucker viewed the problem as one of authority versus liberty. The State socialists, he argued, dwelt on the fact that the individual would be allowed a much larger liberty in their system than he now enjoys. But the crux of the matter is that he would only be allowed it; he could not claim it as his own. In his view no rightful authority can be external to individual consent.

This controversy obviously stimulated Joyce's interest since the only political philosophy he ever spoke of favourably was Tucker's. He probably would have sided with the American anarchist since in his review of the *Shewing-Up of Blanco Posnet*,[60] he chided Shaw for championing all the progressive movements in art and in politics, and questioned the purity of his motives.

Shaw reiterated his arguments against anarchism and in favour of Social Democracy in *The Perfect Wagnerite*, a book Joyce also read. Shaw interpreted *The Ring* as a socialist tract heralding the passing away of the capitalist order, and claimed that Siegfried was 'a totally unmoral person, a born anarchist, the ideal of Bakoonin, an anticipation of the 'overman' of Nietzsche'.[61] If his analysis seems far-fetched, Shaw says, it should be remembered that Wagner actually went out with Bakunin in the 1849 rebellion at Dresden, that he was wanted by the police, and that he also wrote revolutionary pamphlets. But Shaw warned those readers who found themselves attracted by 'Siegfried Bakoonin's anarchism that 'applied to the industrial or political machinery of society, anarchy must always reduce itself speedily to absurdity' and urged them to read *The Impossibilities of Anarchism.*[62]

Wagner conceived of Siegfried as the new type of man who would emerge after the successful revolution he had pinned his hopes on. From 1849 to 1852 he wrote prose volumes on social and artistic revolution, including the tracts 'Art and Revolution' and 'The Art-work of the future'. Joyce had these revolutionary pieces in his library. Wagner believed that revolution in the political order would countenance revolution in art. He declared that the Folk was the *only* artist.[63] Such a contention opposed Ibsen's view of the artist as an aristocrat and isolationist. Joyce seemed to have sided with Ibsen in 'The Day of the Rabblement'. Yet in his essay on 'Drama and Life' he recognised that drama fulfilled this communal role and he urged his countrymen to 'criticize in the manner of free people, as a free race, recking little of ferula and formula. The Folk is, I believe, able to do so much'.[64] As Synge said in his preface to *The Playboy of the Western World*. 'All art is collaboration.' For Joyce the artist and the citizen can co-operate with each other unwittingly, while still remaining sceptical of the community.

Stephen identifies his mission with that of Siegfried in *A Portrait* when he is about to tell Cranly he will not serve his home, his country and his Church. He then hears the bird call from *Siegfried* and then wonders how he could hit the conscience of the patricians of Ireland (242) (*238*). Siegfried forges a new sword, Nothung, in Mimmy's smithy, a cave, in order to 'hew the way of his own will through religions and governments and plutocracies and all the other devices of the kingdom of the fears of the unheroic'.[65] Stephen, as has become clear, allows himself the non-violent arms of silence, exile, and cunning and forges his art in the smithy of his soul. (Carlyle had said that Dante's *Divine Comedy* 'has all been as if molten, in the hottest furnace of his soul'.)[66]★ He tempers his anarchistic heroic action with a basic pacifism.

★ Carlyle also saw in Dante 'The craftsman there, the smith with that metal of his, with these tools, with these cunning methods' (*On Heroes, Hero-Worship, and the Heroic in History* (London, 1926), vol. I, pp. 119–20).

In 'Circe', however, Stephen's attitude changes somewhat. When his mother orders him to repent, Stephen commits his only *violent* act of the day by flourishing his ashplant, *Nothung*, and smashing the chandelier: '*Time's livid final flame leaps and, in the following darkness, ruin of all space, shattered glass and toppling masonry*' (*583; 683*). This scene might be interpreted as mock-heroic, but it is of symbolic import to Stephen. Earlier in the day he remembered Kevin Egan's attempt on Clerkenwell prison: 'he prowled . . . under the walls of Clerkenwell and, crouching, saw a flame of vengeance hurl them upward in the fog. Shattered glass and toppling masonry' (*43; 54*). Stephen now links his act with those of Irish revolutionaries against the stranglehold of British power. By so doing he also destroys his mother's spirit, and that of the Church, which is attempting to dominate him. He emancipates himself from a sweet yoke on his artistic spirit. The bondage of Church and State, of time and space, is broken by his revolutionary act. For one brief moment he joins with Bakunin in believing that 'the urge to destroy is also a creative urge.' Stephen's physical retaliation, however, is made to be innocuous when compared to the action of the British soldiers. Stephen regains his composure and declares mental warfare on those institutions and his temporary allegiance to Siegfried Bakoonin's methods ends. But the anarchist spirit remains. In his 'Preface for Politicians' to *John Bull's Other Island* Shaw had stated that in Ireland the Protestant is theoretically an anarchist and a rebel, whereas the Catholic is conservative, a supporter of Church and State, an obeyer.[67] Joyce demonstrated that the Catholic hero could be anarchistic and dissident too.

In this context Joyce agrees with Wagner when he says that modern art is of necessity revolutionary:

Art remains in its essence what it ever was: we have only to say, that it is not present in our modern public system. It lives, however, and has ever lived in the individual conscience, as the one, fair, indivisible Art. Thus the only difference is this: with the Greeks it lived in the public conscience, whereas today it lives alone in the conscience of private persons, in the public *un*conscience recking nothing of it. Therefore in its flowering time the Grecian art was *conservative* because it was a worthy and adequate expression of the public conscience; with us, true Art is *revolutionary* because its very existence is opposed to the ruling spirit of the community.[68]

Stephen's art is opposed to the ruling spirit of the community and since the public conscience dwells within him alone, the conscience of his race which he wishes to forge is as yet *uncreated*.

4 Literature and the Conscience

The conspiratorial will did not arise out of an intellectual vacuum. Stephen, it seems, is competing with George Moore who, after a quarter of a century's absence, resettled in Ireland. He explained his motives for doing so in a passage from his autobiographical *Hail and Farewell!* (1914). In *Vale* (1914) he described how the rewriting of Edward Martyn's *The Tale of a Town* had awakened the dormant Irishman in him. The Boer War had transformed his love of England to hate, and 'a voice heard on three different occasions had bidden me pack my portmanteau and return to Ireland.' He now took an interest in the Gaelic movement, and exhorted his countrymen to speak and write Irish. Like Joyce, Moore considered Catholicism a greater tyranny than the British occupation of Ireland. As a result, he left Catholicism for Protestantism and ironically envisioned himself in a Messianic role, the instrument chosen to redeem Ireland from Catholicism. On his return to Ireland he had expected to be acclaimed the spokesman of the national conscience:

> I walked across the greensward afraid to leave the garden, and to heighten my inspiration I looked toward the old apple-tree, remembering that many had striven to draw forth the sword that Wotan had stuck into the tree about which Hunding had built his hut. Parnell, like Sigmund, had drawn it forth, but Wotan had allowed Hunding to strike him with his spear. And the allegory becoming clearer I asked myself if I were Siegfried, son of Sigmund slain by Hunding, and if it were my fate to reforge the sword that lay broken in halves in Mimi's cave.
>
> It seemed to me that the garden filled with tremendous music, out of which came a phrase glittering like a sword suddenly drawn forth from its sheath and raised defiantly to the sun.[69]

Moore claims, therefore, that *he* is the Irish Siegfried and successor to Parnell. Since his words have gone unheeded, he concludes that his mission in Ireland is over and decides to leave for the Continent:

> And it was borne in upon me at the same time that a sacrifice was

demanded of me, by whom I knew not, nor for what purpose, but I felt I must leave my native land and my friends for the sake of a book; a work of liberation I divined it to be – liberation from ritual and priests, a book of precept and example, a turning point in Ireland's destiny, and yet I prayed that I might be spared the pain of writing it and permitted instead to acquire the Clos St Georges, a wife and a son. But no man escapes his fate. Something was propelling me out of Ireland, whither I was not sure. I must yield to instinct, I said to AE. He was deeply moved.[70]

Stephen, however, counters some of Moore's moves. He disapproves of the Gaelic revival and, when he is asked by Cranly in *A Portrait* whether he intends to become a Protestant, he answers unequivocally: 'I said I had lost the faith . . . but not that I had lost selfrespect. What kind of liberation would that be to forsake an absurdity which is logical and coherent and to embrace one which is illogical and incoherent?' (248) (*243–4*). On the other hand, both Stephen and Moore agree on the necessity of self-imposed exile in order to forge the national conscience. Moore departs in February, although he would have preferred to do so in May,[71] but Stephen succeeds in leaving by the end of April. He too singles himself out as Parnell's successor. Moore, in stressing that one must choose between literature and dogma, predicts his book will achieve the spiritual liberation of Ireland and thereby mark a turning point in the national destiny. Joyce shared this lofty purpose and expressed the same confidence in literature as a liberating agent, but he laid prior claim to it since he had announced this motive for *Dubliners* in a letter to Grant Richards in 1906.

Joyce stressed this literary rivalry in *Ulysses*. In the library scene Dr Sigerson's avowal that 'Our national epic has yet to be written' and that 'Moore is the man for it' (*192; 246*) is ironically inserted as part of the gossip about members of the Celtic revival. Joyce once claimed that Ireland was an 'untilled field', in allusion to the book of short stories by Moore.[72] In the first piece of *The Untilled Field*, entitled 'In the Clay', Rodney, a sculptor, flouts the Celtic renaissance, since he had always 'looked upon Dublin as a place to escape from' in order to cultivate his art.[73] The theme of escape is constant in Joyce, especially in 'Eveline' and 'A Little Cloud'. Little Chandler agrees that 'There is no doubt about it: if you wanted to succeed you had to go away. You could do nothing in Dublin' (79) (*73*). He dreams of becoming a poet and of being recognised by English critics 'as one of the Celtic school by reason of the melancholy tone of his poems'. Joyce underlines the irony of Little Chandler's (and Moore's) longing for exile at the same time as longing to appeal to 'a little circle of kindred minds':

> He began to invent phrases from notices which his book would get. *Mr Chandler has the gift of easy and graceful verse. . . . A wistful sadness pervades these poems. . . . The Celtic note.* It was a pity his name was not more Irish-looking. Perhaps it would be better to insert his mother's name before the surname: Thomas Malone Chandler, or better still: T. Malone Chandler. (80) (*74*)

In Moore's story, 'The Wild Goose', Ned Carmady decides that he must get away from the 'mean ineffectual atmosphere' of Dublin, from the 'wailing of an abandoned race'. He insists that he must flee from Ireland's 'soul-sickness'.[74] This was the spiritual 'paralysis' Joyce spoke of in *Dubliners* and from which Stephen liberates himself in *A Portrait of the Artist*. In 'The Way Back', Rodney reappears as a character and states wryly, 'Ireland has always struck me . . . as a place that God had intended to do something with; but he changed his mind and that change of mind happened about a thousand years ago.'[75] In *A Portrait*, after Stephen expounds his theory of the god-like artist, it is Lynch who asks surlily, 'What do you mean . . . by prating about beauty and imagination in this miserable Godforsaken island? No wonder the artist retired within or behind his handiwork after having perpetrated this country' (219) (*215*). But it is Joyce instead of Moore who is writing Ireland's national epic. In *Ulysses* Joyce, like Hamlet, '*se promène, lisant au livre de lui-même.*'

The downfall of Parnell not only engendered the artistic souls of Joyce and Moore, but it also marked the beginning of the quest for Ireland's national identity. Writing in 1899 on 'The Literary Movement in Ireland', Yeats affirmed, 'Politics are, indeed, the forge in which nations are made, and the smith has been so long busy making Ireland according to His will that she may well have some important destiny.'[76] He saw hope where Moore saw only hopelessness in Ireland. He explained the aim of the new movement in his essay on *Poetry and Tradition* (1907): 'We were to forge in Ireland a new sword on our old traditional anvil for that great battle that must in the end re-establish the old, confident, joyous world.'[77] Yeats made an important distinction between the old and the new poetry:

> The poetry that comes out of the old wisdom must turn always to

religion and to the law of the hidden world, while the poetry of the new wisdom must not forget politics and the law of the visible world; and between these poetries there cannot be any lasting peace.[78]

The poet was now the 'divine' smith who, by forging a new sword in the manner of Siegfried, would re-establish that grand destiny envisaged by Parnell.

As a young man Joyce questioned Yeats's method in his endeavour to define the national soul. But Yeats was not as deceived as Joyce made him out to be. In his first meeting with the poet in 1902 Joyce objected to Yeats's concern with politics.[79] Yet when Yeats first drew up his plans for the creation of a new intellectual movement he made it a prime target to fight against the lingering influence of Young Ireland:

> Young Ireland had sought a nation unified by political doctrine alone, a subservient art and letters aiding and abetting. The movement of thought . . . had created a new instrument of Irish politics. . . . To recommend this method of writing as literature without much reservation and discrimination I contended was to be deceived or to practise deception.[80]

Poetry was not to be subservient to nationalism or to be an instrument for Irish politics – a principle that Joyce also vigorously upheld. In this regard, the statement made by the old Fenian, John O'Leary, that 'There are things a man must not do to save a Nation' impressed Yeats and was in keeping with Joyce's own attitude on this question. When asked what things O'Leary replied, 'To cry in public', but Yeats thought he would have added, if pressed, 'To write oratorical or insincere verse.'[81]

Yeats's criterion for judging good art was the same as Joyce's. It was not moral or political but aesthetic. This canon drew the same charge of amorality against it as Joyce's did at University College. On this point Yeats entered into an argument with the pseudony-mous columnist of the *United Irishman*, 'Trial', in an article on *Literature and the Conscience* in 1901:

> A phrase in my letter to the *Freeman's Journal* about the proposed clerical censorship of the National Theatre has caused a good deal of misunderstanding. 'Trial', for instance, objects to my description of literature as 'the principal voice of the conscience', and himself defines literature as 'any piece of writing which in

point of form is likely to secure permanence.' If 'Trial' will recall
the names of a few masterpieces he is much too intelligent not to
see that his description is inadequate. Let him recall to mind 'Don
Quixote', or 'Hamlet', or 'Faust', or Tolstoi's 'War and Peace' and
'Anna Karenina', or almost any play by Ibsen, his 'Enemy of the
People' let us say. If he will do so, he will understand why
literature seems to me, as indeed it seems to most critics of
literature, to be 'the principal voice of the conscience'. A great
writer will devote years, perhaps the greater part of a lifetime, to
the study of the moral issues raised by a single event, by a single
group of characters. He will not bemoralise his characters, but he
will show, as no other can show, how they act and think and
endure under the weight of that destiny which is divine justice. No
lawgiver, however prudent, no preacher however lofty, can
devote to life so ample and so patient a treatment. It is for this
reason that men of genius frequently have to combat against the
moral codes of their time, and are yet pronounced right by
history. 'Trial' will recall many examples, of which the most
recent is Ibsen. A play or a novel necessarily describes people in
their relation to one another, and is, therefore, frequently
concerned with the conscience in the ordinary sense of that word,
but even lyric poetry is the voice of what metaphysicians call
innate knowledge, that is to say, of conscience, for it expresses the
relation of the soul to eternal beauty and truth as no other writing
can express it. That apparently misleading sentence of mine was,
indeed, but an echo of a sentence of Verhaeren's, the famous
Belgian poet. He says that a masterpiece is a portion of the
conscience of the world. An essay on poetry by Shelley and certain
essays by Schopenhauer are probably the best things that have
been written on the subject of modern writers, but Mr George
Santayana has written a book called 'The Sense of Beauty', which
deals profoundly with the whole philosophy of aesthetics.
P.S. I must add a sentence or two to what I have said about the
conscience. It is made sensitive and powerful by religion, but its
dealings with the complexities of life are regulated by literature.
'Trial' spoke of a book which discusses problems of the hour and
yet seems to him at once literature and iniquitous. He is certainly
mistaken. Literature, when it is really literature, does not deal
with problems of the hour, but problems of the soul and the
character.[82]

A writer will study the moral issues of a given situation, but will not judge his characters by the ordinary moral codes of society. Conscience did not mean what the empiricist philosopher Alexander Bain described as 'an imitation within ourselves of the government without us'. Balzac's country doctor marked out the priest as the 'conscience' of society, and related how in feudal times the priest was king, pontiff, and judge all rolled into one.[83] Literature, however, proclaims its morality independent of the special moralities of churches and parliaments. A writer offers an ampler vision of life than that promulgated by the representatives of Church and State, and in this sense it can be said that literature regulates the dealings of conscience with the complexity of life by creating different standards by which conduct can or might be judged. Literature is the principal voice of the conscience since it expresses the relation of the soul, be it individual or national, to beauty and truth. This was almost undoubtedly what Joyce understood conscience to mean. The literary class was, as 'Trial' pointed out in a column appearing a week after Yeats's article, distinct from the rest of society, independent of it, and with a special message to communicate. When Joyce wrote to Nora from Dublin in 1912 he humbly recognised that he was one of the writers engaged in giving Ireland the voice of its conscience:

> The *Abbey Theatre* will be open and they will give plays of Yeats and Synge. You have a right to be there because you are my bride: and I am one of the writers of this generation who are perhaps creating at last a conscience in the soul of this wretched race.[84]

But Stephen's claim at the end of *A Portrait* is individualised and decisive. He admits no success on the part of his contemporaries in forging the national soul. The conscience is as yet *uncreated* because Ireland has been too inward-looking. The new Ireland Joyce conceived of must first become European. Moore had succumbed to Protestantism, or what Stephen considered to be self-deceptive liberation. The conscience Yeats expressed was like that of Michael Robartes, the relation of the soul of the race to a retrospective, or nostalgic beauty. Joyce desired instead to relate the individual soul and that of his race to a beauty which lay in the future. In order to accomplish this end he must leave Ireland, in the words of Robert Hand, 'to seek in other lands that food of the spirit by which a nation of beings is sustained in life'. Joyce's art is revolutionary in the Wagnerian sense, but it is also in accordance with Yeats's definition of its being independent of both Church and State. He had taken

Yeats's doctrine to the limit. Was this the reason which led Yeats to confide to Mrs Olivia Shakespeare, in a letter written after *Ulysses* had been published, that if Joyce returned to Ireland 'I shall have to hide him from the politicians, who are scarce ready for his doctrine.'[85]

5 The Soul of the Artist under Anarchism

The politicians would have been scarce ready for Joyce's 'doctrine' when he first left Ireland. He made a striking statement of his intellectual revolt in a letter of August 1904 to Nora:

> My mind rejects the whole present social order and Christianity – home, the recognised virtues, classes of life, and religious doctrines. How could I like the idea of home? My home was simply a middle-class affair ruined by spendthrift habits which I have inherited. My mother was slowly killed, I think, by my father's ill-treatment, by years of trouble, and by my cynical frankness of conduct. When I looked on her face as she lay in the coffin – a face grey and wasted with cancer – I understood that I was looking at the face of a victim and I cursed the system which had made her a victim. . . .
>
> Six years ago I left the Catholic Church, hating it most fervently. I found it impossible for me to remain in it on account of the impulses of my nature. I made secret war upon it when I was a student and declined to accept the positions it offered me. By doing this I made myself a beggar but I retained my pride. Now I make open war upon it by what I write and say and do. I cannot enter the social order except as a vagabond.[86]

Joyce indicated in another letter to Nora that self-reliance was the only weapon at his disposal for his struggle: 'It seemed to me that I was fighting a battle with every religious and social force in Ireland and that I had nothing to rely on but myself.'[87] 'Civilisation may be said indeed to be the creation of its outlaws', as Stephen affirms in *Stephen Hero* (183) (*178*). Religious protest against the existing order breeds the inevitable political heresy. Joyce rejected all social ties manifested in the tyrannies of the Church, the family and the nation. This principle is taken a step further in *Exiles* (112) (*87*) where Robert describes Richard's longing to be delivered from *every* law and bond.

When Stephen gives his views on the eternal affirmation of the spirit of man in literature in *Ulysses* (*666; 777*), therefore, he does not admit the validity of Madame de Staël's statement that literature had ceased to be an art and had become instead an instrument or 'a weapon in the service of the spirit of man'.[88] Joyce, as has become clear, did not sanction the use of art as a vehicle for revolutionary propaganda. This perhaps explains why he completely deleted the socialistic ending of 'A Portrait of the Artist'. The excision did not mean that he no longer espoused those principles which he had enunciated, but rather that perhaps he felt the original peroration to be too impersonal, and wished instead to strike a more individual note.

Although Joyce refused to assign politics an overt role in art he considered artistic activity indispensable because, as Stephen says in *Stephen Hero*, 'The poet is the intense centre of the life of his age to which he stands in relation than which none can be more vital' (85) (80). Every age, therefore, derives its sustenance from its poets and philosophers. Stephen here paraphrases Shelley's statement, 'Poets are the unacknowledged legislators of the world.' Shelley's radical aesthetics included an anarchistic love of freedom: 'The abolition of personal slavery is the basis of the highest political hope that it can enter into the mind of man to conceive.'* In *The Defence of Poetry* he proclaimed that 'poets are hierophants of an unapprehended inspiration' (or priests of the eternal imagination) whose mission consisted in awakening and liberating the mind and the imagination of men from its enslavement. He describes this political ideal in *Prometheus Unbound*:

> The loathsome mask has fallen, the Man remains, –
> Sceptreless, free, uncircumscribed, – but man:
> Equal, unclassed, tribeless and nationless,
> Exempt from awe, worship, degree, the King
> Over himself.

This statement differs from Dante's when he is made king over himself by Virgil. Shelley's Promethean man pays no homage to any external moral or political authority; rather, he rules 'the empire of himself' as Shelley says in his sonnet on 'Political Greatness'. Shem is condemned for similar attitudes, for being an 'anarch, egoarch, hiresiarch'.

If the only indication Joyce ever gave of a political outlook was

---

* This statement is from Shelley's *Discourse on the Manners of the Antient Greeks Relative to the Subject of Love.*

with reference to Tucker, he found the most complete expression of the anarchistic ideal for artists in Oscar Wilde's *The Soul of Man under Socialism*. Joyce's statement just before leaving Rome that 'The interest that I took in socialism and the rest has left me'[89] cannot be taken at face value because later, in 1909, he felt Wilde's tract was so important as to warrant its translation into Italian.[90] It may be argued that Wilde is speaking of socialism and not anarchism, but, as Hesketh Pearson points out, Wilde's 'whole trend of thought was antagonistic to the Webb-Shavian deification of the state'.[91] On one occasion in Paris during the 1890s Wilde declared himself openly to be an anarchist.[92] Later, in *De Profundis*, he stated that Kropotkin's life was 'one of the most perfect lives I have come across in my own experience' and described him as 'a man with the soul of that beautiful white Christ that seems coming out of Russia'.[93] Kropotkin viewed anarchism as a species of socialism and he, along with Bakunin and Proudhon, considered himself a socialist.

Wilde begins his essay[94] by asserting that the chief advantage to be gained from socialism is that it would relieve man from the necessity of living for others since private property would be abolished. This action would enable each member of society to share in the general prosperity. Property, moreover, hinders individual development for 'The true perfection of man lies, not in what man has, but in what man is.' The true artist is he who believes 'absolutely in himself, because he is absolutely himself'. Isolation is therefore essential as the true artist takes no notice whatsoever of the public, which Wilde refers to as the 'monster'. This statement concurs with that made by Joyce with reference to Bruno in *The Day of the Rabblement*.

Socialism is of value but inadequate since it does not permit 'the full development of Life to its highest mode of perfection'. Wilde objects to many of the socialistic theories on the same ground as the anarchists, namely that they are 'authoritarian' and based on compulsion. If future governments are to wield economic power as present ones wield political power then 'the last state of man will be worse than the first'. Recalling Bakunin and anticipating Stephen's 'non serviam', Wilde states that disobedience is man's original virtue. Authority and compulsion are therefore out of the question as 'all association must be quite voluntary'. Through socialism man is to attain a healthy Individualism. As a result, the State is to give up all ideas of government.

This Individualism is however not egoistic in the Stirneresque sense, but rather unselfish and unaffected. The individualist sympathises with 'the entirety of life, not with life's sores and maladies merely, but with life's joy and beauty and energy and health and freedom'. Joyce said as much in his essay on the literary influence of the Renaissance: 'If the Renaissance did nothing else, it would have done much in creating ourselves and in our art the sense of compassion for each thing that lives and hopes and dies and deludes itself.'[95] Individualism was a virtue he had admired greatly in Ibsen. The most intense mood of Individualism according to Wilde is art. He maintains, moreover, that it is the only real mode of Individualism:

> Crime, under certain conditions, may seem to have created
> Individualism, must take cognisance of other people and interfere
> with them. It belongs to the sphere of action. But alone, without
> any reference to his neighbours, without any interference the artist
> can fashion a beautiful thing.

Aristotle too in his *Nicomachean Ethics* (VI. 3) had asserted, 'Art, being concerned with making, is not concerned with action.' Action, moreover, is the recognised area of the State's influence. The artist can be said to be the most intensive non-invasive individual, in Tucker's words, since his liberty of action does not conflict with other people's liberty of action.

But if Individualism is to be attained, Wilde continues, then there should be no such thing as governing mankind. All modes of government, whether despotism, oligarchy or democracy, are failures. Wilde enumerates three kinds of despots. The Prince tyrannises over the body, while the Pope tyrannises over the soul. And he says the People tyrannise over the body and soul alike. Wilde then declares that the best form of government for the artist is no government, for all authority over him and his art is absurd. These statements reflect Stephen's position and that of Joyce in his letters to Nora.

Wilde's exposition probably swayed Joyce. Wilde's claim was that the greatest leeway afforded the artist was Individualism or anarchism. Anarchism aimed at the utmost possible freedom of the individual compatible with social life. Only by eliminating the threefold tyranny over the individual could the artist's personality be freed and enable him to come into his own. Wilde made explicit what is only implicit in Joyce. Of more importance, was that Joyce probably realised for the first time in Wilde's tract that his demand for absolute freedom to accomplish his aesthetic aims could be made consonant with the political views of Tucker, who stressed respect for individual liberties.

6   Finnegans Wake: 'Anarxaquy' and the Eternal Struggle

In exile, if not already in Ireland, Joyce identified his artistic vocation *directly* with anarchism. He announced this affiliation in an amusing letter to Stanislaus from Rome in 1907:

> [Scene: draughty little stone-flagged room, chest of drawers to left, on which are the remains of lunch, in the centre, a small table on which are *writing materials* (*He* never forgot them) and a salt-cellar: in the background, small-sized bed. A young man with snivelling nose sits at the little table; on the bed sit a madonna and plaintive infant. It is a January day. Title of the above:] *The Anarchist.*[96]

It is the only political epiphany Joyce recorded, except for the scene in *A Portrait* where the young artist focuses on Parnell's death. The sudden, unexpected title of the piece captures a memorable phase of Joyce's political mind. If he had not supplied the title for us, it would have been impossible to realise the connection unaided. There is, of course, implicit irony in the title and we know that Joyce was not incapable of satirising himself in his most serious moments. The simple domestic setting does not offer the slightest indication of subversive activity. Yet for Joyce the connection came easily. The alliance between literature and anarchism had become marked in the 1880s and 1890s, particularly among the Decadents, the forerunners of the dadaists and surrealists. Joyce, however, rejected their libertarian urge for violence and destruction. His anarchism was pacific and had a benign aspect from which a 'sane and joyful spirit issues forth'. His statement made a few months later about his dwindling interest in socialism, therefore, should be examined closely:

> The interest I took in socialism and the rest has left me. I have gradually slid down until I have ceased to take any interest in any subject. I look at God and his theatre through the eyes of my fellow-clerks so that nothing surprises, moves, excites or disgusts me.

His apathy covers the *whole* range of his previous concerns, not exclusively the political. It is difficult to believe his lethargy, a loss of *all* interest in *all* subjects, to be more than momentary. In the political sphere, as I have already pointed out, he set out to translate Wilde's tract a few years later. In the same letter, in fact, Joyce qualified his sweeping remarks:

> Yet I have certain ideas I would like to give form to: not as a doctrine but as the continuation of the expression of myself which I now see I began in *Chamber Music*. These ideas or instincts or intuitions or impulses may be purely personal. I have no wish to codify myself as anarchist or socialist or reactionary.[97]

One who rejects the whole social order can scarcely be called a *reactionary*. These ideas, it should be duly emphasised, *may* be purely personal or indeed they may be part of a larger context. The difference is that now Joyce will no longer codify or arrange them so as to form a *doctrine*, as he had been doing previously in his letters to Stanislaus. Self-expression or artistic Individualism, however, is not incompatible with the anarchistic ideal, as we have seen.

With *Finnegans Wake* Joyce embarked on his boldest experiment of self-expression. After 1922 his country had become for him 'Our island, Rome and duty', as he says in the *Wake* (374). In his efforts to rid Ireland of its spiritual yoke Moore claimed that *Hail and Farewell!* was nevertheless a 'sacred book'. Dante, when the orthodoxy of his faith had been challenged, had Virgil confer the mitre upon him, and also spoke of his work as the *'poema sacro'*. Joyce constructed his book by employing the same means the Church had in founding its own edifice. As he told Frank Budgen, 'The Holy Roman Catholic Church was built on a pun. It ought to be good enough for me.'[98] He intended to beat Rome at its own game.

Joyce wrote *Finnegans Wake* with a 'pelagiarist pen'; that is, he 'piously forged' (182) or re-forged the national conscience but in a decidedly heretical manner, thereby attesting to the French proverb, 'à force de forger on devient forgeron.' Like Shem he is the 'national apostate' come to cure Ireland of its national malady, Catholicism. In *A Portrait* Joyce had shown himself to be a 'subtle heresiarch' by using Aquinas, the Church's greatest philosopher, against the Church and its censorship. Here he is less subtle. The case of the individual against authority is highlighted in the fable of the Mookse and the Gripes. Joyce suspected that Wyndham Lewis's position in attacking him in *Time and Western Man* approached that of the Church.[99] As the Mookse in the tale, Lewis appears at one point in the full attire of the 'supremest poncif', or supreme pontiff, exhorting subordinate rulers to 'Gather behind me, satraps' (154). But the Joyce-like Gripes refuses to submit to either the alleged temporal or spiritual power of the Mookse, who now assumes the name of a particular English pope, 'our once in only Bragspear' (152), 'Adrian (that was the Mookse now's assumptinome)' (153). Joyce once again underlines the collusion of the Church and British State against Ireland before independence. At the same time he will not put up with Lewis's pontificating in the arts, or his preten-tiousness – 'poncif' being the French equivalent of kitsch.

Joyce's presentation of religion in *Finnegans Wake* is similar to that in *Ulysses*. Helmut Bonheim has documented the many insults hurled at God in the form of distorted locutions.[100] God is invariably a conservative force and his human failings and qualities of lowness and lewdness are not those commonly attributed to Him. Bonheim also argues that a general theme of *Finnegans Wake* is that 'Man's birthright . . . is to seek freedom from oppression, oppression of any kind' and to disobey tyrants.[101] This theme is in keeping with Joyce's anarchistic temperament (although Bonheim denies it is so) since Bakunin had declared that the desire to rebel is one of man's most precious qualities. Bernard Benstock interprets the essence of the antitheism in the *Wake* to be represented in the attitude, 'Should the God of the Roman Catholic – or some composite deity bridging all organised religions – actually exist, Joyce declares himself opposed and sits in judgment of Him.'[102] But this is only to state in a milder form Bakunin's sweeping inversion of Voltaire's dictum: 'If God really existed it would be necessary to abolish him.'

Nor is this anarchistic view incompatible with Vico's view of history. Vico had proclaimed that 'the world of civil society has certainly been made by men, and that its principles are therefore to be found within the modifications of our own human mind.'[103] Vico's was a humanist, not a transcendental reading of history. Bakunin stretched the Vichian perspective further by maintaining that the true goal of history, contrary to the idealist Hegelian view, is our humanisation and deliverance: 'the triumph of humanity, the object and significance of history, can be realised only through liberty'.[104]

The triumph of humanity is represented in the *Wake* by the rising of all Finnegans. Maria Jolas detected Joyce's revolutionary theme in the missing apostrophe of the title and claimed that Joyce had enunciated his belief in the destiny of humble people: ' "Watch out", he said, not only to England's ruling classes, but to ruling classes everywhere, "Finnegans (do) wake."'[105] Perhaps Joyce's theme is not as overtly political, but such a view is consistent with Vico's contention that the individual and the universal cannot be treated as distinct from each other.

Marxist critics have misconstrued Joyce's position as merely factitious unconventionality. At the Congress of Writers in Kharkov in 1933, Karl Radek accused him of lacking a 'social conscience'. Joyce discussed this attack with Eugene Jolas, and he pointed out in reply that all his characters – starting with those in *Dubliners* through to those in *Finnegans Wake* – belonged to 'the lower middle classes, and even the working class, and they are all quite poor'.[106] He stressed too that he had represented the predicament of the lower classes with understanding.[107] George Lukács, a more recent critic, carried the Marxist argument a step further. He criticised Joyce for treating only the superficial aspects of life, and for discarding social reality. 'If Joyce had set Napoleon on the toilet of the petit bourgeois Bloom,' Lukács hypothesised, 'he would merely have emphasised what was common to both Napoleon and Bloom.'[108] But Lukács has misunderstood. A major conviction of Joyce is that political mythmaking tends to place leaders on pedestals, and to forget that they are susceptible to the same needs and desires as other people. (Bloom thinks of Parnell, for instance, as 'the idol with the feet of clay'.) As a result, Joyce was all for deflating grandiosity in his usual comical manner, as when in 'Cyclops' (*325; 422*) the English are described as 'a race of mighty heroes, rulers of the waves, who sit on thrones of alabaster silent as the deathless gods.' Napoleon would not have escaped this comic treatment either. Lukács failed to realise that defecation can be made a form of satire, and that, for Joyce, human processes – that is, both physical and mental acts – are interrelated. No other writer had been willing to present men in this way. To relate Napoleon and Bloom is an important perspective that literature can offer, by preventing us from assuming that the one is all grandeur, and the other all triviality. Joyce's desire to remove distinctions between men is not only humorous then. It is political as well. In discussing *Stephen Hero*, Joyce had pointed out, in a letter to Stanislaus, that his hero was not an aristocrat like Lermontov's.[109] If his heroes are difficult to admire it is because his work was the result of rigorous self-examination and written without any vain, romantic desire to arouse sympathy. He endeavoured to help men see themselves as they are. For him, as for the character in

Hauptmann's *The Rats* (1911), 'Before art as before the law all men are equal.'

Ultimately it was people rather than political parties or States which mattered. As Frank Budgen perceived, *Finnegans Wake* affirms the spirit of the city through all changing political circumstances:

> Vico's theory of cyclic evolution, which allows for identity of personality in change and for recurrence in progression might well appeal to the poet who dressed up the archer king of Ithaca in a black suit and bowler hat and sent him out on a quest for advertisements, or whose H.C.E. rules the city whatever party is in power. And Bruno's theory of duality and identity of contraries must have needed little demonstration to the individualist who refused to serve and became his own taskmaster, to the exile who took his city into exile with him.[110]

Joyce, like Dante before him, gave the keys of his native city to the readers of his work. Vico's and Bruno's theories are not at variance with Joyce's individualist position. Bakunin pointed out that the first attack upon the omnipotence of Church and State came from 'the *renaissance* of the free mind in the fifteenth century, which produced heroes like Vanini, Giordano Bruno, and Galileo'.[111] Joyce expressed a similar attitude in his essay written in Padua on 'The Universal Literary Influence of the Renaissance'. If the 'great rebels of the Renaissance' struggled against absolutism it was not because the system itself was foreign to it: 'The yoke was sweet and light; but it was a yoke'.[112]

As Joyce makes clear, *any* external system burdens the human spirit simply because it is a yoke and therefore tyranny. He told Georges Borach, 'As an artist I am against every state' because 'The state is concentric, man is eccentric. Thence arises an eternal struggle.'[113] What Joyce meant was that the State has a common centre whereas man is not placed centrally within its orbit but rather deviates from it. Throughout history the individual maintains an eternal struggle (or what Blake called 'mental fight') against the State. So as the Vichian cycles of mankind undergo successive governments (monarchic, aristocratic and democratic), the artist is not subject to their laws, but only to those laws of his own being. In a conversation with Arthur Power Joyce confirmed this conspiratorial aspect of the literary artist:

When we are living a normal life, we are living a conventional one, following a pattern which has been laid out by other people in another generation, an objective pattern imposed on us by church and state. But a writer must maintain a continual struggle against the objective: that is his function. The eternal qualities are the imagination and the sexual instinct, and the formal life tries to suppress both. Out of this present conflict arise the phenomena of modern life.[114]

Joyce did not hold that the best political system was the democratic one;[115] he was sceptical of all political structures. In *Finnegans Wake* sleep is the great anarchiser,[116] and a peaceful one at that.* National boundaries traced out in the daytime world disappear, and the eternal imagination conquers both time and space, or priest and king.

7 The Reaction to Fascism

Joyce avowed, 'I don't take Vico's speculations literally; I use his cycles as a trellis.'[117] The *New Science* provided a structural apparatus for *Finnegans Wake* rather than a philosophical confirmation of his views. In his introduction to *The Words upon the Window-pane* (1931), Yeats allowed that Joyce was 'expounding or symbolizing' it, but he ascribed to the work of the Neapolitan philosopher a different purport:

> Students of contemporary Italy, where Vico's thought is current through its influence upon Croce and Gentile, think it created or in part created the present government of one man surrounded by such able assistants as Vico foresaw.[118]

In a letter to Harriet Shaw Weaver of 1 February 1927 about the protest against the piracy of *Ulysses*, Joyce said, 'I feel honoured by many of the signatures and humiliated by some, those of Gentile, Einstein and Croce especially. It is curious too on account of

---

* Joyce's aversion to aggressiveness, turbulence, violence of any kind was quite deeply felt. 'Birth and death are sufficiently violent for me,' he said. He was not only dismayed by the thought of crime, he had no interest in it, and said he found this a handicap in writing *Work in Progress*; a book that dealt with the night life of humanity, should, he felt, have some reference to crime in it, but he could not bring himself to put any in it' (Padraic Colum, *Our Friend James Joyce*, p. 184).

Vico.'[119] Yeats had read Croce's *Philosophy of Giambattista Vico* in 1924,[120] but he now took an interest in the Fascist interpretation of Vico as advanced by Giovanni Gentile, Mussolini's Minister for Education, and other Italian idealists. Vico's thinking tended to be anti-democratic, for he believed that popular governments inevitably breed the greatest tyrannies. In Ireland Yeats believed for a while that his own anti-democratic ideals were embodied by General O'Duffy's 'Blueshirts', and he composed a few marching songs for them. In *Finnegans Wake* the Irish Fascist leader is referred to uncomplimentarily as 'the O'Daffy' (84). And Dolph tells Kev, in their moment of reconciliation, 'In effect I could engage in an energument over you till you were republicly royally too bally prussic blue in the shirt after' (305). For Joyce, who was like Tucker and Earwicker 'anarchistically respectful of the liberties of the noninvasive individual', totalitarianism represented the opposite pole to freedom.

In the 1920s and 1930s European intellectuals generally expressed dissatisfaction with parliamentary democracy, claiming that it meant in effect rule by vested interests or rule through corruption. Many turned to Fascism, or the rule of the Few, as a viable alternative to representative government. Shaw, for example, believed that the future lay with Mussolini and Stalin. In the *Art of Being Ruled* (1926) Wyndham Lewis presented his critique of western democracies, and also a detailed analysis of socialist theory as expounded by Marx, Proudhon, Fourier and others. In examining these political creeds he registered his hasty endorsement of Fascism: 'for anglosaxon countries as they are constituted to-day some modified forms of fascism would probably be the best.'[121] It was in this book also that he first launched his attack on Joyce, which he later elaborated and incorporated in the section entitled an 'Analysis of the Mind of James Joyce' in *Time and Western Man* in 1927. Lewis claimed that *Ulysses* was a time-book, originating from Bergson and Einstein who substituted a flux for physical objects. This classification carried political connotations for Lewis, since he believed that science stood for the theory of collective life, and art for that of the individual life. The revolutionary state of mind may have become 'instinctive', he feared, mainly because science had conditioned men to an acceptance of change. In both his books Lewis alleged that science was

---

* In a letter of 16 January 1921 (III, p. 150) to Miss Weaver, Joyce singled out only Einstein's signature as giving him great honour.

manipulating the passions of the mob. He now described Joyce as 'the poet of the shabby-genteel, impoverished intellectualism of Dublin. His world is the small middle-class one.'[122] Joyce resented this criticism and he has Professor Jones, Lewis's counterpart in the *Wake*, deliver his sermon to 'muddlecrass pupils' (152). He interpreted Lewis's jibe to be Fascist-orientated, and the portrait of Professor Jones is appropriately militaristic:*

> this soldier-author-batman for all his commontoryism is just another of those souftsiezed bubbles who never quite got the sandhurst out of his eyes so that the champaign he draws for us is as flop as a plankrieg. (162)

What Lewis detected in Joyce's verbal anarchy (as well as in Gertrude Stein's) as 'the sign of the herd-mind' was inaccurate if not mistaken. Joyce's style was not disorderly but it displayed what Herbert Gorman described (in a passage Joyce did not delete) as 'the anarchistic conception of the unfettered mind':

> a feeling that the perfect freedom in life with the absolute minimum of restraining laws was an ideal devoutly to be desired, a feeling that was, of course, no more socialism than it was capitalism. But it naturally followed that no favoured class should have privileges denied a more unfortunate class, that freedom – freedom of the intelligence, freedom of the artistic urge – should be the common property of all, beggars as well as Edwardian noblemen and purse-pound landowners. From this anarchistic conception of the unfettered mind it was but a step to the theory of an economic equality, to a world where hardships engendered by class distinctions and the unfair distribution of the riches of the earth no longer existed. Joyce, lacking or ignoring an exact knowledge of socialism, made that step. But it would be absurd to insist that he was a Marxian or that he acquiesced in any degree to the principle that individual freedom should be subordinated to the interests of the community. He despised the bourgeois class as a class and there is no doubt he knew that his true ideal was an intellectual plane of living unattainable by the mass of mankind. It was pleasant to dream about but all the realities were against it. His intellectual anarchy, then, had little or nothing to do with Karl Marx.[123]

---

* Lewis fought in World War I.

Joyce believed in individualism, but in an individualism that would be accessible to all, not one in which man sacrificed his precious freedom to a clique or to one-man rule.

Professor Jones demonstrates his anti-Semitic tendencies by dismissing the works of 'Bitchson' (Bergson) and 'Winestain' (Einstein) as having no merit and he also attacks the anthropologist 'Loewy-Brueller' (Levy-Bruhl) for having written a book entitled '*Why I am not born like a Gentileman*' (150). The pun includes a play on the words 'gentleman', 'gentile' (as opposed to Jew) and perhaps also Giovanni Gentile. Lewis generously praised Hitler in 1931, but he later retracted most of his views in *The Hitler Cult* (1939). In his *Guide to Kulchur*, Ezra Pound termed Lewis's 'discovery' of Hitler superior to his own 'discovery' of Mussolini. Pound combined a zealous support of Fascism with an offensive anti-Semitism. Joyce, who had regarded Gogarty's and Griffith's remarks on the Jews with extreme disgust, found Pound's comments equally repugnant. As early as 1928 he told Harriet Shaw Weaver by letter, 'the more I hear of the political, philosophical, ethical zeal and labours of the brilliant members of Pound's big brass band the more I wonder why I was ever let into it "with my magic flute".'[124] In 1934 Joyce again informed her, 'I am afraid poor Mr Hitler-Missler will soon have few admirers in Europe apart from your nieces and my nephews, Masters W. Lewis and E. Pound.'[125] He responded in *Wakese* to Mussolini's invasion of Ethiopia in October 1935 in a letter to Helen Joyce: 'May the 17 devils take Muscoloni and the Alibiscindians! Why don't they make Pound commander-in-chief for Bagonghi and elect me as Negus of Amblyopia?'[126]★

Although Joyce refused to make any pronouncements on Hitler and Mussolini in public, his comments from these letters indicate his aversion to the new form of tyranny. In February 1940, there appeared in *Prospettive*, a Fascist periodical published in Rome, the Italian translation of *Anna Livia Plurabelle*, made chiefly by Joyce and Nino Frank, but which was signed by Ettore Settani. Joyce's consent to have his work published in *Prospettive* might be interpreted as an indication of political affiliation. This is a misconstrual however. The editor, Curzio Malaparte, confined his remarks to a literary appreciation of Joyce's works; he made no political comments whatsoever.[127] Decades earlier, Joyce had been taken for a Unionist because he wrote reviews for the *Daily Express*. Now he apparently

---

★ In *Finnegans Wake* (237.03) 'muscalone pistil' may disguise an allusion to Mussolini.

preferred to have his work published in a Fascist periodical, rather than not to have it published at all. In 1934, Ennio Giorgianni, in his Fascist-inspired *Inchiesta su James Joyce*, claimed that, in attacking Irish nationalism and the Catholic Church, Joyce had embraced the 'internationalism' preached by the Jews.[128] So his international outlook did not endear Joyce to Fascists. Joyce was not indifferent to this war's outcome either. Privately, he informed friends such as Padraic Colum of his stand on the European crisis: 'He spoke in a measured way, condemning Mussolini's Italy for putting the squeeze on France, stating his absolute confidence in the French army. France, because it was rational, was for him Europe's highest civilisation. 'Where else', he asked, 'can you go out to dinner and have a cardinal on one side of you and a commissar on the other?'[129] He still marvelled, however, as to how such an intelligent nation as France could have conceived of such a war.[130] He did not condone the activities of either side in helping to ferment hostilities: 'every time I turn on the radio I hear some British politician mumbling inanities or his German cousin shouting and yelling like a mad-man.'[131] He now emphasised the humour of *Finnegans Wake* as a counteracting agent to the bombing in places like Spain.[132] He also spoke of his sympathetic treatment of the Jews in *Ulysses* and its strong anti-totalitarian character in a letter to a young Harvard student who had complained of Joyce's attitude towards his race.[133] Joyce confirmed his views by helping several Jews to escape from Nazi persecution to Ireland, the United States and England.[134] Phillip Herring has objected that it is pointless to refer to Joyce's action for these Jewish acquaintances, since he could not 'identify with the oppressed rabblement anywhere', and he has registered his distress over Joyce's 'inherent lack of interest in the human condition'.[135] I find it remarkable, however, that in an age in which those big words *engagement* and *commitment* made so many European intellectuals unhappy, Joyce's only commitment took the form of humanitarian action so typical of Bloom. At the crucial moment, Joyce had repaid Alfred Hunter's gesture towards him of over thirty years before.

The key to Joyce's politics is the statement he made to Georges Borach in 1918: 'As an artist, I attach no importance to political conformity.'[136] That Joyce was not a systematic thinker should not surprise us: the politics of most writers defy a strict coherence. In Joyce's case, his heterodox politics can be explained by the wide range of writers who influenced his views. The principal models in literature are, as we have seen, Dante, Blake, Ibsen, Wilde and Shelley. Joyce inherited from Dante the sense of moral and political intrepidity of the artist who, in rejecting all party affiliation, constitutes a party by himself. From Blake Joyce learned to combat tyranny through the imagination, and to assert the liberty of mind and body. In Ibsen Joyce found not only the independence of the modern artist who stands alone politically, but one who reinforced his own socialistic views as well. Although he shared with his literary compatriots, Yeats and Moore, the motive of creating a national conscience, Joyce was more radical than his predecessors. For Joyce, the freeing of the individual was the main issue, indeed the only one. His political ideal of release from all external constraint – which he had formed by reading the anarchists, and Tucker in particular – went hand in hand with his artistic ideal of the right to unfold one's talent in full freedom. Joyce discovered that Wilde affirmed these twin ideals in *The Soul of Man under Socialism*. Insofar as it is possible to pin Joyce down to a political label, that of 'libertarian' comes closest to describing his position. What Joyce proposed to achieve in his art was a political vision which consisted of a socialism without Marx, and an anarchism without violence. Even so, Joyce found this perspective to be limiting. Fortified by his own conviction and that of Shelley's – that the artist is the central man of his age – Joyce aspired at first to be European, and later, more grandly, to be 'Europasianized Afferyank'. That this was his final aim is indicated by the curious comment he made to Max Eastman on his use of so many river names in *Anna Livia Plurabelle*: 'he liked to think how some day, way off in Tibet or Somaliland, some boy or girl in reading that little book would be pleased to come upon the name of his or her home river.'[137] Implicit in this desire to be all-embracing, to reach all men through art, is the underlying conviction of the kinship of men. Human kinship in turn implies that a larger ideal than appears on the surface is at work in Joyce. Bloom comes closest to stating it in 'Cyclops' when he stands his ground against the invective of the Citizen and announces, without being doctrinaire, that love, not hatred, is the aim of life. The simplicity of this demand, and the tautological parable ('Love loves to love love') which follows, does not, as is sometimes maintained, reduce the authority or genuineness of Bloom's testament, even if Joyce allows it to be mocked. The attempt of the two narrators in 'Cyclops' at mockery – by either sentimentalising or coarsening the meaning of love – is unconvincing. The point is that Bloom's message is stated directly only once in *Ulysses*, and it is reasserted in an anonymous way as the 'word known to all men' (*49; 61/581; 682*) which Stephen yearns for. Joyce never discloses his humanistic perspective flatly, but keeps it in parenthesis, as if fearful that he might be considered soft or sentimental.★ In *Stephen Hero* Joyce had indicated that this diffidence before absolute statements characterised the modern artist. What Joyce is implying, without celebrating it, is that (even in the 'reconciliation of opposites') the recognition of human kinship should be the cause and end of freedom, and that freedom without affection is meaningless.

Joyce's saving quality as an artist was that he distinguished, as Pound did not, between the aesthetic and the political. As a young man he told Padraic Colum, 'I distrust all enthusiasms.'[138] He later interpreted these enthusiasms to be Cyclopian attitudes. At the same time he made it his express purpose to refrain from indulging in political commentary. Such had not been the practice of Eliot, Lewis or Yeats. Typical of Joyce's attitude was his indignant refusal to answer a questionnaire on the Spanish War sent to him by Nancy Cunard: 'No! I won't answer it because it is politics. Now politics are getting into everything.'[139] As a consequence, his noncommitment caused misunderstanding in some quarters. Irving Babbitt saw that the only alternatives for modern man were between being a Bolshevist or a Jesuit.[140] Joyce was accused of being both and more. In a letter to Harriet Shaw Weaver he noted that in the opinion of some he was 'a crafty simulating and dissimulating Ulysses-like type', a '"jejune jesuit", selfish and cynical.'[141] In 1920 Joyce wrote down an elaborate list of all the rumours circulating about him in a letter to Stanislaus:

> That I was sent to Ireland 8 years ago
> by the Austrian F.O. (report of Maunsel and Co)
> That I made money during the war as a Brit. gov.
> spy (report of friends and relatives in Dublin)
> That *Ulysses* was a pre-arranged pro–German code
> (report of Brit. war censor subsequently scouted
> by literary experts! . . .)

★ It was probably for this reason that Joyce declared bluntly to Frank Budgen that Shelley's *Prometheus Unbound* seemed to him to be 'the Schwärmerei of a young Jew' (*JJMU*, p. 13). Still, Joyce ranked Shelley along with Shakespeare and Wordsworth as the three great poets in English (II, p. 90).

That I was a Sinn Fein emissary in Switzerland and
the English Players a blind (report of one of the
English actors of my company, paid by me)
. . . .
That I am a violent bolshevist propagandist (report
of yourself for purposes of discussion)[142]

Many of these political labels are transferred to Shem and Earwicker
in the *Wake*. Joyce, however, sought the simplest liberation of an
emotion and by extension the liberation of the people. He contented
himself in being, in the words he applied to Mangan, the spiritual
focus of his time, and refused 'to prostitute himself to the rabble or to
make himself the loud-speaker of politicians.' As he told Alfred
Kerr, 'it's a mark of morality not only to say what one thinks is true –
but to create a work of art with the utmost sacrifice.'[143] That his
motives were indirect reflected his desire not to coerce other
individuals into accepting his point of view and not to interfere with
their liberty.* The Dedalean policy of silence, exile, and cunning had
stood him in good stead.

---

* Although he does not approach his readers directly, Joyce nevertheless imposes
demands on them, demands he perhaps underestimated. With *Finnegans Wake* in
particular the reader is forced to enter into a compact with Joyce, to meet him on his
own terms (though, to a certain extent, this can be said of all writers). Joyce would
doubtless have answered that his ideas are simple and only his technique complex. But
a paradox of Joyce's politics remains that although he holds out liberty for all, his
work has not reached a general audience.

Notes

1 Old Ireland

1 Roland McHugh, *The Sigla of Finnegans Wake* (London, 1976), p. 35. See also these early reviews: 'Scientist of Letters', *New Republic* CIV (20 January 1941), p. 7; Stephen Spender, *Listener* (23 January 1941); Max Lerner, *New Republic* CVII (28 September 1942), p. 386. Typical of recent comments are Lionel Trilling, *Beyond Culture* (New York, 1965), pp. 166–7; and William Chace, *The Political Identities of Ezra Pound and T. S. Eliot* (Stanford University Press, 1973), p. xv.
2 II, p. 362.
3 *JJMU*, p. 191.
4 *Claybook for James Joyce*, trans. Georges Markow-Totevy (London, 1958), p. 96.
5 *JJ*, p. 710.
6 *Drama and Life* in *CW*, p. 45.
7 'Ireland, Island of Saints and Sages' in *CW*, p. 162.
8 *CW*, p. 227.
9 Ibid., p. 194.
10 Ibid., p. 226.
11 Ibid., pp. 225–6.
12 *CW*, p. 227.
13 Ibid., p. 227.
14 F. S. L. Lyons, *Charles Stewart Parnell* (London, 1977), pp. 611–14 and 621.
15 Robert Dahl, *Modern Political Analysis* (Englewood Cliffs, N.J., 1970), p. 6.
16 See *CW*, pp. 154–74. Other quotes from this lecture in this section which are not footnoted are from this text.
17 Ibid., p. 162.
18 Michael Dolley, *Anglo-Norman Ireland* (Dublin, 1972), pp. 62–5.
19 II, p. 187.
20 Quoted in Dorothy Macardle, *The Irish Republic* (New York, 1965), p. 40.
21 'Fenianism' (1907) in *CW*, p. 189.
22 See *CW*, pp. 73–83, 175–86.
23 *CW*, p. 189.
24 III, p. 264.
25 *CW*, pp. 189–92.
26 Ibid., p. 189.
27 C. P. Curran, *James Joyce Remembered* (London, 1968), p. 63.

28 *CW*, p. 173.
29 Ibid., p. 193.
30 *Charles Stewart Parnell*, pp. 572–5.
31 *CW*, p. 228.
32 Ibid., p. 213.
33 Ibid., p. 196.
34 Ibid., p. 228.
35 Conor Cruise O'Brien, *Parnell and his Party* (Oxford, 1957), p. 290.
36 'Gas from a Burner' in *CW*, p. 243.
37 *CW*, p. 228.
38 *CW*, p. 152.
39 *The Autobiography of William Butler Yeats* (New York, 1969), p. 211. See *JJ*, p. 784 fn. 8.
40 *The Dramatic Works of Gerhart Hauptmann*, ed. Ludwig Lewisohn (London, 1914), vol. III, p. 528.
41 *Parnell and his Party*, pp. 284 and 297.
42 Patrick J. Walsh, *William J. Walsh: Archbishop of Dublin* (Dublin, 1928), p. 313.
43 *Charles Stewart Parnell*, pp. 482–6, and 512–15.
44 Patrick J. Walsh, pp. 409 and 424.
45 F. S. L. Lyons, 'James Joyce's Dublin', *Twentieth Century Studies* 4 (1970), p. 14.
46 Emmet Larkin, 'Launching the Attack: Part II of the Roman Catholic Hierarchy and the Destruction of Parnellism', *Review of Politics* XXVIII (July 1966), p. 360.
47 Ibid., p. 366.
48 *CW*, p. 196.
49 Ibid., p. 209 and 211.
50 'James Joyce's Dublin', pp. 15–16.
51 *The Autobiography of William Butler Yeats*, p. 133.
52 Ibid., p. 378.
53 Introduction to *The Words upon the Windowpane* (1931) in *Explorations* (London, 1962), p. 343. See also 'The Irish Literary Theatre' (1899) in *Uncollected Prose by W. B. Yeats*, ed. John P. Frayne and Colton Johnson (London, 1975), vol. II, p. 162.
54 *Letters to the New Island*, ed. Horace Reynolds (Cambridge, Mass., 1934), p. 155.
55 William Dawson, 'Arthur Clery 1879–1932', *Studies* 22 (1933), p. 81.
56 *CW*, pp. 161–2.
57 Brian Inglis, 'Moran of the *Leader* and Ryan of the *Irish Peasant*' in *The Shaping of Modern Ireland*, ed. Conor Cruise O'Brien (London, 1960), p. 109.
58 II, p. 260.
59 *Arthur Griffith: Journalist and Statesman* (Dublin, 1922), p. 18.
60 *UI*, 4 March 1899.
61 Donal McCartney, 'The Political Use of History in the Work of Arthur Griffith', *Journal of Contemporary History* 8 (1973), p. 8.
62 *UI*, 14 October 1905.
63 *CW*, pp. 188–9.
64 *The Autobiography of William Butler Yeats*, pp. 278–9.
65 *CW*, pp. 69–72.
66 *UI*, 2 November 1901.
67 William Rooney, *Poems and Ballads* (Dublin: *United Irishman*, 1902), p. ix.
68 See *CW*, pp. 84–7.
69 *Poems and Ballads*, p. xi.

70 *CW*, pp. 102–5.
71 *UI*, 31 October 1903.
72 *CW*, p. 185.
73 'The Literary Movement in Ireland' in *Ideals in Ireland*, ed. Lady Gregory (London, 1901), p. 90.
74 *Recollections of James Joyce*, trans. Ellsworth Mason (New York, 1950), p. 16.
75 Eugene Sheehy, *May It Please the Court* (Dublin, 1951), p. 35.
76 Ibid., p. 32.
77 Ibid., p. 34.
78 *JJ*, p. 146.
79 'The Trieste Notebook' in *The Workshop of Daedalus*, ed. Robert Scholes and Richard M. Kain (Evanston, Ill., 1965), p. 95.
80 *CW*, pp. 149–52.
81 II, p. 43.
82 *JJ*, pp. 169–71.
83 *James Joyce Remembered*, p. 78.
84 I, p. 53.
85 *JJ*, p. 81.
86 II, p. 111.
87 *A Hero of Our Time*, trans. Philip Longworth (London, 1964), p. 68.
88 *CW*, p. 127.
89 *Recollections of James Joyce*, p. 15.
90 *The Complete Dublin Diary of Stanislaus Joyce*, ed. George Healy (Ithaca, New York, 1971), p. 2 fn.
91 Ibid., p. 54.

2 Young Europe

1 Italo Svevo, *James Joyce*, trans. Stanislaus Joyce (San Francisco, 1969).
2 *Giacomo Joyce* (London, 1968), p. 8.
3 II, p. 89.
4 Richard Ellmann, *Yeats: The Man and the Masks* (New York, 1948), p. 112.
5 *JJ*, p. 12.
6 Quoted in Denis Mack Smith, *Italy: A Modern History* (Ann Arbor, Michigan, 1969), p. 190.
7 II, p. 159.
8 Ibid., p. 152.
9 'L'Invulnerabile', *Il Piccolo della sera*, 13 March 1905; 'I Veri contendenti', 25 March 1905; 'Sul Mare', 26 April 1905.
10 'Verrà la rivoluzione in Russia?', 17 May 1905; 'La Russia in Rivolta', 26 October 1905; 'La Difficoltà della pacificazione in Russia', 8 November 1905; 'La Rivoluzione in Russia', 31 December 1905.
11 'Riflessioni finali', 25 June 1906.
12 Piero Treves, 'Ferrero dans son temps et le nôtre' in *Cahiers Vilfredo Pareto* IX (1966), p. 37.
13 'La Conferenza polemica di Guglielmo Ferrero sulla filosofia della storia', November 1910.
14 *CW*, p. 155.

15 II, p. 190.

16 Ibid., p. 190.

17 Information from Mrs Ferrero Raditsa.

18 II, p. 201.

19 Giovanni Busino, 'Quelques Remarques sur la place de Guglielmo Ferrero dans l'histoire des idées sociales et politiques' in *Cahiers Vilfredo Pareto* IX (1966), p. 196.

20 *L'Europa giovane* (Milan, 1897), pp. 190–4.

21 II, p. 190.

22 *L'Europa giovane*, pp. 5–6, 9–11, 159–62.

23 *CW*, pp. 223–8.

24 II, p. 212. Stanislaus said that 'the idea for "Two Gallants" came from the mention of the relations between Porthos and the wife of a tradesman in *The Three Muskateers* which my brother found in Ferrero's *Europa Giovane*' ('The Background to *Dubliners*', *Listener* 51 (25 March 1954), p. 527). I have been unable to find, however, the particular passage in Ferrero's book which Stanislaus mentioned.

25 II, pp. 132–3.

26 *L'Europa giovane*, p. 31.

27 Ibid., pp. 163–70.

28 *Dubliners*, pp. 53–4.

29 *L'Europa giovane*, p. 418.

30 *CW*, p. 168.

31 See Marvin Magalaner, 'The Anti-Semitic Limerick Incidents and Joyce's "Bloomsday"', *PMLA* 68 (1953), pp. 1219–1223.

32 II, p. 190.

33 *L'Europa giovane*, pp. 409–13.

34 *Opere edite ed inedite di Carlo Cattaneo*, ed. Agostino Bertane (Florence, 1908), vol. IV, p. 156.

35 II, p. 84.

36 *L'Europa giovane*, p. 357.

37 II, p. 190.

38 *L'Europa giovane*, pp. 90–7, 359.

39 II, p. 309.

40 Ibid., p. 183.

41 Herbert Gorman, *James Joyce: A Definitive Biography* (London, 1941), p. 183.

42 II, p. 183.

43 Ibid., pp. 187–8.

44 Dora Marucco, *Arturo Labriola e il sindacalismo rivoluzionario in Italia*, (Torino, 1970), p. 42.

45 Ibid., pp. 154–5.

46 II, p. 174.

47 Ibid., p. 187.

48 Roberto Michels, *Storia critica del movimento socialista italiano* (Florence, 1921), p. 319.

49 Ibid., p. 321.

50 II, p. 202.

51 Ibid., p. 174.

52 *Avanti!*, 2 September 1906.

53 Ibid., 2 September 1906.

54 Ibid., 7 October 1906.
55 II, p. 173.
56 Ibid., p. 174.
57 *Avanti!*, 9 October 1906.
58 Ibid., 11 October 1906.
59 II, p. 183.
60 Gaetano Arfé, *Storia dell'Avanti!* (Rome, 1956), p. 66.
61 II, p. 197.
62 See especially Hélène Cixous, *The Exile of James Joyce* (London, 1976), pp. 200–1. Joyce is here presented as a socialist 'poseur'.
63 II, p. 174.
64 Ibid., p. 148.

3 Perspectives: Socialism and Anarchism

1 In *The Workshop of Daedalus*, pp. 56–74.
2 *The Portable Walt Whitman*, ed. Mark van Doren (New York, 1973), p. 17.
3 Richard Ellmann, *The Consciousness of Joyce*, (London, 1977), p. 77.
4 *The Portable Walt Whitman*, pp. 245–6.
5 Ibid., p. 330.
6 Renato Poggioli, *The Theory of the Avant-Garde*, trans. Gerald Fitzgerald (Cambridge, Mass., 1968), pp. 9–11 and 94–101.
7 *The Consciousness of Joyce*, p. 78.
8 Edmund Wilson, *To the Finland Station* (Garden City, New York, 1953), p. 331.
9 *The Anarchists*, ed. Irving L. Horowitz (New York, 1964), p. 16.
10 *James Joyce: A definitive biography*, p. 183 fn.
11 Quoted in Irving L. Horowitz, *The Anarchists*, p. 54.
12 John Stuart Mill, *On Liberty*, ed. Gertrude Himmelfarb (Harmondsworth, 1974), p. 187.
13 Arthur Lehning, 'Anarchism', in *Dictionary of the History of Ideas*, ed. Philip P. Wiener (New York, 1973), vol. I, pp. 70ff.
14 See Frank Budgen, *JJMU*, p. 192; *JJ*, p. 147.
15 Jacob Schwartz at a meeting of the *James Joyce Society* recorded by *Folkways Records*, 1960 (Gotham Book Mart).
16 Quoted in James J. Martin, *Men Against the State* (De Kalb, Ill., 1953), p. 209.
17 Benjamin Tucker, *Instead of a Book By a Man Too Busy to Write One* (New York, 1969), p. 414.
18 Mikhail Bakunin, *God and the State* (New York, 1970), p. 17.
19 *CW*, pp. 17–24.
20 *JJMU*, p. 192.
21 *Instead of a Book*, p. 23.
22 Max Stirner, *The Ego and His Own*, tr. Steven Byington (New York, 1973), p. 24.
23 II, p. 205.
24 I, p. 52.
25 II, pp. 80–1.
26 *Instead of a Book*, p. 24.
27 Ibid., p. 24.
28 Quoted in *Men Against the State*, p. 244.

29   *The Ego and His Own*, p. 316.
30   Ibid., pp. 3–4.
31   II, p. 151.
32   Stanislaus Joyce, *Dublin Diary*, ed. Healey, George Harris (Cornell U.P. 1971), p. 54.
33   *The Statesman's Book of John of Salisbury*, trans. John Dickensen (New York, 1963), p. xxi.
34   Michael Davitt, *The Fall of Feudalism in Ireland (Or the Story of the Land League Revolution)* (London, 1904), p. xvii.
35   George Moore, *Parnell and His Island* (London, 1887), see especially p. 132.
36   *Instead of a Book*, p. 414.
37   *The Fall of Feudalism*, pp. 50, 52.
38   F. Sheehy-Skeffington, *Michael Davitt* (London, 1967), pp. 206–7.
39   *The Fall of Feudalism*, pp. 403–407.
40   Ibid., p. 401.
41   *Dublin Diary*, p. 55.
42   *CW*, p. 195.
43   *Theory of the Avant-Garde*, p. 119.
44   II, p. 160.
45   *Callista: A Sketch of the Third Century* (London, 1962), pp. 31–3.
46   II, pp. 111 and 134.
47   I, p. 364.
48   *Essays and Letters*, trans. Aylmer Maude (London, 1904), p. 340. See *The Personal Library of James Joyce*, Thomas E. Connolly (University of Buffalo, 1955), p. 40.
49   II, p. 106.
50   *JJMU*, p. 21.
51   II, p. 90.
52   Ibid., p. 134.
53   Quoted in *JJ*, p. 520.
54   Stanislaus Joyce, 'The Background to *Dubliners*', *Listener* 51 (25 March 1954), p. 526.
55   See Marvin Magalaner, *Time of Apprenticeship: The Fiction of Young James Joyce* (London, 1959), pp. 135–7.
56   *CW*, p. 83.
57   I, pp. 62–3.
58   *CW*, p. 179.
59   Ibid., pp. 190–1.
60   Ibid., p. 105.
61   *God and the State*, p. 24.
62   Ibid., pp. 9–10.
63   George Woodcock, *Anarchism* (Harmondsworth, 1975), p. 28.
64   See Lionel Trilling, *The Liberal Imagination* (Harmondsworth, 1970), pp. 83–4.
65   Johann Most, *The Beast of Property* (International Working Men's Association, 1884), p. 38.
66   Robert Adams, *Surface and Symbol: The Consistency of James Joyce's 'Ulysses'* (New York, 1967), p. 138.
67   Johann Most, *The Deistic Pestilence* (Hull, 1902), pp. 14–15.
68   *Instead of a Book*, pp. 393–404.
69   *God and the State*, pp. 11, 25–6.

70 As pointed out in *The Consciousness of Joyce*, p. 83.

71 *God and the State*, p. 59.

72 *Joyce's 'Ulysses' Notesheets in the British Museum*, ed. Phillip Herring (Charlottesville, Virginia, 1972), p. 120.

73 *What is Property?* trans. Benj. R. Tucker (New York, 1970), pp. 49–50.

74 *Joyce's 'Ulysses' Notesheets*, pp. 120, 396.

75 Errico Malatesta, *Anarchy* (London, 1974), p. 53.

76 *Instead of a Book*, p. 14.

77 Quoted in Paul Eltzbacher, *Anarchism*, trans. Steven T. Byington (New York, 1908), p. 240.

78 *CW*, p. 200.

79 *Joyce's 'Ulysses' Notesheets*, p. 87.

80 *Instead of a Book*, p. 140.

81 *CW*, p. 171.

82 *Joyce's 'Ulysses' Notesheets*, p. 120.

83 Ibid., p. 120.

84 Weldon Thornton, *Allusions in Ulysses* (University of North Carolina Press, 1968), p. 328.

85 *CW*, p. 173.

86 *Daniel Defoe*, trans. Joseph Prescott (Buffalo, 1964), p. 24.

87 *God and the State*, pp. 43–4.

88 *Selected Writings on Anarchism and Revolution*, ed. Martin A. Miller (Cambridge, Mass., 1970), pp. 119–32.

89 *The Great French Revolution* (New York, 1927), vol. I, p. 59.

90 *The Conquest of Bread*, ed. Paul Avrich (New York, 1972), p. 63.

91 George Woodcock, *Anarchism*, p. 152.

92 *Critique of the Gotha Programme*, p. 17.

93 *Joyce's 'Ulysses' Notesheets*, p. 87.

94 *Instead of a Book*, p. 404.

95 *The Conquest of Bread*, p. 142.

96 *Joyce's 'Ulysses' Notesheets*, p. 86.

97 *Fields, Factories and Workshops* (London, 1913).

98 'A Portrait of James Joyce', *New Republic* LXVI (13 May 1931), p. 347.

4 The National Scene

1 Quoted by Isaiah Berlin, 'Fathers and Children' in *Fathers and Sons* (Harmondsworth, 1976), p. 41.

2 II, p. 154.

3 *MBK*, p. 80.

4 Thomas Kettle, *The Ways of War* (London, 1917), p. 24.

5 See *JJ*, pp. 271–2.

6 Ibid., p. 64.

7 See Herbert Gorman, op. cit., p. 135 and *Stephen Hero*, p. 58 (*53*).

8 Thomas Kettle, *The Day's Burden* (Dublin, 1910), p. ix.

9 *JJ*, p. 520.

10 II, p. 148.

11 *JJ*, pp. 72–3.

12 II, p. 223.
13 *Leader*, 22 June 1907.
14 'A Book of Songs', *Nation* I (22 June 1907).
15 These have been collected under the title of *The Idea of a Nation* (Dublin, 1907).
16 Ibid., pp. 1–2.
17 Ibid., pp. 8–13.
18 II, p. 158.
19 *MBK*, p. 173.
20 II, p. 158.
21 *UI*, 6 October 1900.
22 Donal McCartney, 'The Political Use of History in the Work of Arthur Griffith', *Journal of Contemporary History* 8 (1973), p. 12.
23 'Would the "Hungarian Policy" Work?', *New Ireland Review* 22 (February 1905), p. 328.
24 *UI*, 11 February 1905.
25 *New Ireland Review*, p. 322.
26 Robert Tracy, 'Leopold Bloom Fourfold: A Hungarian-Hebraic-Hellenic-Hibernian Hero', *Massachusetts Review* 6 (1965), pp. 523–38.
27 Tracy claims that this crown does not exist and that here Joyce is reproducing Griffith's error. But Weldon Thornton has established that it does exist. See *Allusions in Ulysses*, p. 375.
28 Richard Davis, *Arthur Griffith and Non-Violent Sinn Fein* (Dublin, 1974), p. 92.
29 See *Surface and Symbol*, pp. 100–104.
30 Bernard Benstock, 'Arthur Griffith in *Ulysses*: The Explosion of a Myth', *English Language Notes* 4 (1966–7), pp. 123–8.
31 *UI*, 23 July 1904.
32 Richard Davis, op. cit., p. 116.
33 William Dawson, 'Arthur Clery, 1879–1932', *Studies* 22 (1933), p. 82.
34 *Nationist: A Weekly Review of Irish Thought and Affairs*, 21 September 1905.
35 Ibid., 21 September 1905.
36 II, p. 158.
37 Ibid., p. 153.
38 Ibid., p. 147 fn.
39 *SF*, 4 August 1906.
40 *Dialogues of the Day*, 4 August 1906, p. 38.
41 *UI*, 14 June 1902.
42 *SF*, 8 September 1906.
43 II, p. 167.
44 Ibid., p. 260.
45 Ibid., p. 187.
46 Ibid., p. 187.
47 *MBK*, pp. 173–4.
48 R. M. Henry, *The Evolution of Sinn Fein* (Dublin, 1920), p. 60.
49 II, p. 187.
50 *UI*, 3 February 1900.
51 Ibid., 9 June 1900 and 18 April 1903.
52 Ibid., 2 July 1904.
53 Richard Davis, p. 109.
54 *Arthur Griffith: A Study of the Origin of the Sinn Fein Movement* (Dublin, n.d.), p. 3.

55 *UI*, 4 and 11 January 1902; 17 January 1903.
56 *James Connolly: Selected Writings*, ed. Beresford Ellis (Harmondsworth, 1973), p. 15.
57 II, p. 166.
58 Herbert Gorman, op. cit., p. 183 fn.
59 II, p. 71.
60 *MBK*, p. 174.
61 *JJ*, p. 147.
62 II, p. 167.
63 Ibid., p. 187.
64 *James Connolly: Selected Writings*, pp. 42–3.
65 *SF*, 26 February 1907.
66 II, pp. 208–9.
67 *SF*, 26 February 1910.
68 *UI*, 24 October 1903.
69 II, p. 187.
70 Ibid., p. 164.
71 *SF*, 15 September 1906.
72 II, p. 171.
73 Ibid., p. 191.
74 *SF*, 10 November 1906.
75 II, p. 189.
76 Ibid., p. 198 fn.
77 *SF*, 15 September 1906.
78 II, p. 192.
79 Ibid., p. 189.
80 *SF*, 24 November and 1 December 1906.
81 *UI*, 23 April 1904.
82 Ibid., 28 May 1904.
83 Ibid., 28 May 1904.
84 Nakum Sokolow, 'The New Jew: A Sketch' in *Zionism and the Jewish Future*, ed. H. Sacher (London, 1916), p. 220.
85 Ulick O'Connor, *Oliver St John Gogarty: A Poet and His Time* (London, 1964), pp. 61–2.
86 Ibid., p. 63.
87 *JJ*, p. 178.
88 *UI*, 9 December 1905.
89 *Oliver St John Gogarty*, p. 97.
90 II, p. 148.
91 Richard Davis, p. 29.
92 II, p. 205.
93 Richard Davis, p. 122.
94 *Republic*, 28 February 1907.
95 Ibid., 14 March 1907.
96 Ibid., 21 March 1907.
97 Ibid., 7 March 1907.
98 Ibid., 28 March 1907.
99 *CW*, p. 191.

100 Herbert Spencer, *The Study of Sociology* (University of Michigan Press, 1961), pp. 186–7.
101 *In Dark and Evil Days* (Dublin, 1916), p. 225. Joyce had this book in his library.
102 *Tom O'Kelly* (Dublin, 1905), pp. 224–7. Joyce had this book in his library.
103 *JJMU*, p. 156.
104 II, p. 316.
105 *SF*, 13 April 1907.
106 Ibid., 15 January 1910.
107 Ibid., 11 June 1910.
108 *CW*, p. 193.
109 *SF*, 11 May 1907.
110 *CW*, p. 195.
111 *SF*, 15 December 1906.
112 *CW*,p. 196.
113 *UI*, 6 June 1906.
114 *CW*, p. 198.
115 Ibid., p. 200.
116 *SF*, 24 August 1907.
117 *JJ*, p. 529.
118 *CW*, p. 198.
119 II, p. 157.
120 Ibid., p. 287.
121 *SF*, 1 April 1911.
122 Ibid., 27 April 1912.
123 Ibid., 4 May 1912.
124 *CW*, p. 224.
125 *SF*, 5 May 1906.
126 Ibid., 17 October 1908.
127 Ibid., 8 June 1912.
128 II, p. 187.
129 *UI*, 2 March 1902.
130 Quoted in Padraic Colum, *Arthur Griffith* (Dublin, 1959), p. 99.
131 'Is the Gaelic League a Progessive Force?' in *Dana* (November 1904), pp. 216–17.
132 *JJMU*, p. 183.
133 *Political Writings and Speeches* (Dublin, 1922), p. 70.
134 Ibid., pp. 70–1.
135 *Freeman's Journal*, 1 June 1907.
136 *MBK*, p. 80.
137 Quoted in *JJ*, p. 340.
138 II, p. 315.
139 *Republic*, 24 January 1907.
140 Ibid., 31 January 1907.
141 Ibid., 11 April 1907.
142 Quoted in Edmund Curtis, *A History of Ireland* (London, 1973), p. 381.
143 E. R. Norman, *The Catholic Church and Irish Politics in the 1860s* (Dundalk, 1965), pp. 16–17.
144 Georges Borach, 'Conversations with James Joyce', trans. Joseph Prescott, *College English*, vol. 15, 6 (March 1954), p. 326.

145 II, p. 439.
146 *JJMU*, p. 346.
147 Ibid., p. 202.
148 Padraic Colum, 'A Portrait of James Joyce', *New Republic* LXVI (31 May 1931), p. 347.
149 Frank Budgen, *Myselves When Young* (London, 1970), p. 198.
150 Padraic Colum, 'A Portrait of James Joyce', p. 347.
151 *MBK*, p. 124.
152 William Gaunt, *The March of the Moderns* (London, 1949), p. 200.
153 *The Ways of War*, p. 5.
154 A. R. Orage, *An Englishman Talks it Out with an Irishman* (Dublin, 1918), pp. 15 and 8.
155 *SF*, 8 August 1914.
156 Ibid., 3 October 1914.
157 *JJ*, p. 455.
158 *International Review*, vol. I, 4 (10 August 1915).
159 Ibid., vol. I, 2 (5 July 1915).
160 *JJMU*, p. 29.
161 *International Review*, vol. I, 6 (5 October 1915).
162 Ibid.
163 *Collected Letters of D. H. Lawrence*, ed. Harry T. Moore (London, 1965), vol. I, p. 367.
164 *Collected Letters of D. H. Lawrence*, vol. I, p. 491.
165 *International Review*, vol. I, 9 (15 December 1915).
166 Bertrand Russell, *Principles of Social Reconstruction* (London, 1917), pp. 22–3 and 48.
167 *CW*, pp. 246–8.
168 *JJ*, p. 225.
169 *Principles of Social Reconstruction*, p. 134.
170. Letter to me, July 1975.
171 II, p. 89.
172 *Anarchy*, p. 18.
173 *The Conquest of Bread*, p. 31.
174 *Myselves When Young*, p. 198.
175 I, p. 364.
176 *International Review*, vol. II, 6 (31 May 1916).
177 Jacob Schwartz at a meeting of the *James Joyce Society* recorded by *Folkways Records*, 1960. (Gotham Book Mart).
178 II, pp. 106–7.
179 *Illustrated London News*, 2 September 1905, p. 323.
180 *The Times*, 29 August 1905.
181 *What is Property?* (New York, 1970), p. 275.
182 *The Soul of Man Under Socialism* in *Complete Works of Oscar Wilde* (London, 1971), p. 1099.
183 *Anarchism*, p. 30.
184 *The Kingdom of God and Peace Essays*, trans. Aylmer Maude (London, 1974), p. 552.
185 Ibid., p. 547.
186 *The Times*, 29 August 1905.

187 *Joyce's 'Ulysses' Notesheets*, pp. 16–17.
188 'Conversations with James Joyce', p. 326.
189 *The Soul of Man Under Socialism*, p. 1099.
190 *JJ*, p. 486.
191 Ernest J. Simmons, *Tolstoy* (London, 1973), p. 217.
192 *CW*, pp. 93–4.
193 Richard Davis, pp. 91–2.
194 *Instead of a Book*, p. 23.
195 Paul Eltzbacher, *Anarchism*, pp. 185–7.
196 *Instead of a Book*, p. 365.
197 'Conversation with James Joyce', p. 325.
198 *JJMU*, p. 171.
199 Stanislaus Joyce, 'Early Memories of James Joyce', *Listener* 41 (26 May 1949), p. 897. See also *Recollections of James Joyce*, p. 30.
200 F. S. L. Lyons, *Ireland since the Famine* (Glasgow, 1974), p. 381.
201 Richard Davis, p. 73.
202 See Herbert Gorman, p. 232. See also *JJ*, pp. 412 and 788 fn. 22.
203 I, p. 118.
204 *Ireland since the Famine*, p. 133.
205 Ibid., p. 384.
206 I, p. 357.
207 III, p. 16.
208 Quoted in *JJ*, p. 623.
209 I, p. 185.
210 Ibid., pp. 189–90.
211 Ibid., p. 191.
212 Samuel Smiles, *Self-Help* (London, 1968), p. 11.
213 *JJMU*, p. 155.
214 Richard Ellmann, *The Consciousness of Joyce*, pp. 89 and 141.
215 Valery Larbaud, 'A Propos de James Joyce et *Ulysses*: Réponse à M. Ernest Boyd'. *Nouvelle revue française* XXIV (January 1925), p. 9 fn.
216 Valery Larbaud, *Nouvelle revue française* XXIII (January–June 1922), pp. 388–9.
217 II, p. 187.
218 I, p. 54 fn.
219 *SF*, 25 October 1913.
220 John Mitchel, *Jail Journal* (Dublin, 1913), pp. xiv–xv.
221 George Lyons, *Some Recollections of Arthur Griffith and His Times* (Dublin, 1923), p. 43.
222 Arthur Power, *Conversation with James Joyce* (London, 1974), p. 65.
223 III, p. 45.
224 I, p. 181.
225 III, p. 61.
226 Andrew Cass (pseudonym of John Garvin), 'Childe Horrid's Pilgrimace', *Envoy* (April 1951), p. 30.
227 Joseph Campbell and Henry Morton Robinson, *A Skeleton Key to Finnegans Wake* (New York, 1969), p. 33.
228 Andrew Cass, *Irish Times* 26 April 1947.
229 John Garvin, *James Joyce's Disunited Kingdom* (London, 1976), p. 190.
230 Ibid., p. 147.

231 *JJ*, p. 558.
232 Michael Collins, *The Path to Freedom* (Cork, 1968), pp. 38–9. Originally published in 1922.
233 Ibid., p. 44.
234 Ibid., p. 46.
235 *James Joyce's Disunited Kingdom*, pp. 142–3.
236 Ibid., p. 138.
237 I, p. 235.
238 Wyndham Lewis, *Time and Western Man* (London, 1927), p. 91.
239 'Early Memories of James Joyce', p. 896.
240 *The Path to Freedom*, p. 38.
241 *Ireland since the Famine*, p. 538.
242 Roland MacHugh, 'Recipis for the Price of the Coffin' in *A Conceptual Guide to Finnegans Wake*, ed. Michael H. Begnal and Fritz Senn (London, 1974), p. 28. Also *James Joyce's Disunited Kingdom*, p. 183.
243 Margery Forester, *Michael Collins: The Lost Leader* (London, 1972), p. 346. Nathan Halper originally identified the first two parts of the quote in 'The Date of Earwicker's Dream', p. 82.
244 I, p. 395.
245 *Our Friend James Joyce*, (London, 1959), p. 168.
246 III, pp. 330 and 370.
247 I, p. 311.
248 *James Joyce*.
249 *The Joyce We Knew*, ed. Ulick O'Connor (Cork, 1967), p. 35.

5 Literary Politics

1 *The Divine Comedy*, trans. John D. Sinclair. 3 vols. (London, 1971). Subsequent quotes will all be from this edition.
2 George Moore, *Evelyn Innes* (London, 1898), p. 124.
3 II, p. 122.
4 Quoted in *JJ*, p. 520.
5 Herbert Gorman, p. 74.
6 *Dante's Vita Nuova: A Translation and an Essay*, Mark Musa (Indiana University Press, 1973), p. 104.
7 II, p. 134.
8 *MBK*, p. 121.
9 I, pp. 62–4.
10 II, p. 134.
11 Ibid., p. 134.
12 I, p. 73.
13 *Recollections of James Joyce*, p. 9.
14 *JJ*, p. 227.
15 *JJMU*, pp. 351–2.
16 William Barry, *The Papacy and Modern Times* (London, 1911), pp. 251–2.
17 Walter Ullmann, *Medieval Political Thought* (Harmondsworth, 1975), p. 30.
18 *JJMU*, p. 192.
19 *The Consciousness of Joyce*, p. 80.

20 *Myselves When Young*, p. 198.
21 *CW*, p. 101.
22 Ibid., p. 184.
23 Ibid., p. 100.
24 *Workshop of Daedalus*, p. 100.
25 'The Universal Literary Influence of the Renaissance' in *Journal of Modern Literature*, 5 (February 1976), p. 16.
26 *CW*, p. 82.
27 II, p. 166.
28 *Dantis Alagherii Epistolae*, ed. Paget Toynbee (Oxford, 1966), p. 159.
29 Alfred Kerr 'Joyce in England', trans. Joseph Prescott, in *A James Joyce Miscellany*, ed. Marvin Magalaner (New York, 1957), p. 41.
30 *Workshop of Daedalus*, p. 72.
31 *Blake: Complete Writings*, ed. Geoffrey Keynes (Oxford, 1971), pp. 748–59.
32 *CW*, p. 75.
33 Ibid., p. 216.
34 'The Universal Literary Influence of the Renaissance', p. 17.
35 *CW*, pp. 215–16.
36 'Annotations to Bacon', Keynes, p. 407.
37 Ibid., pp. 480–1.
38 *JJ*, p. 381.
39 'Annotations to Bishop Watson's "Apology for the Bible"' in William Blake, *Complete Writings*, ed. Geoffrey Keynes (Oxford, 1971). See also Peter F. Fisher, *The Valley of Vision: Blake as Prophet and Revolutionary* (Toronto, 1961), p. 159.
40 Keynes, pp. 716–17.
41 *JJ*, p. 673 fn.
42 *The Will to Power*, trans. A. M. Ludovici (London, 1910), vol. II, p. 206.
43 *CW*, pp. 100–1.
44 Ibid., p. 163.
45 B. J. Tysdahl, *Joyce and Ibsen* (New York, 1968), pp. 139–41.
46 Michael Meyer, *Henrik Ibsen: The Top of a Cold Mountain 1883–1906* (London, 1971), p. 150.
47 II, p. 183.
48 Ibid., p. 86.
49 *Peer Gynt*, trans. Michael Meyer (London, 1973), p. 21. All translations are taken from this edition.
50 George Bernard Shaw, *The Quintessence of Ibsenism* (London, 1922), pp. 93–4.
51 Georg Brandes, *Henrik Ibsen and Björnstjerne Björnsen* (London, 1879), pp. 57–8.
52 Ibid., p. 59.
53 Brandes, p. 56.
54 'Conversations with James Joyce', p. 326.
55 *An Enemy of the People*, trans. Michael Meyer (London, 1974), p. 74.
56 Michael Meyer, *Henrik Ibsen: The Farewell to Poetry 1864–1882* (London, 1971), p. 309.
57 *CW*, p. 44.
58 II, p. 158.
59 *Theory of the Avant-Garde*, pp. 30–1.
60 *CW*, p. 208.
61 *The Perfect Wagnerite* (London, 1898), p. 48.

62 Ibid., pp. 77–9.
63 *Prose Works*, trans. W. A. Ellis (London, 1892), vol. I, p. 207.
64 *CW*, p. 42.
65 *The Perfect Wagnerite*, p. 49.
66 *On Heroes, Hero-Worship, and the Heroic in History*, vol. I, p. 112.
67 *John Bull's Other Island* (London, 1907), p. xix.
68 *Prose Works*, pp. 51–2.
69 *Hail and Farewell!* (London, 1925), vol. II, pp. 380–1.
70 Ibid., p. 434.
71 Ibid., p. 435.
72 Quoted in *JJ*, p. 225.
73 *The Untilled Field* (London, 1903), p. 11.
74 Ibid., p. 388.
75 Ibid., p. 417.
76 *Ideals in Ireland*, ed. Lady Gregory, p. 102.
77 *Essays and Introductions* (New York, 1968), p. 249.
78 *Ideals in Ireland*, pp. 97–8.
79 Richard Ellmann, *The Identity of Yeats* (New York, 1964), p. 87.
80 *The Autobiography of William Butler Yeats*, pp. 136–7.
81 Ibid., p. 143.
82 *UI*, 7 December 1901.
83 *The Country Doctor* (London, 1911), p. 64.
84 II, p. 311.
85 *The Letters of W. B. Yeats*, ed. Allan Wade (London, 1954), p. 698.
86 II, p. 48.
87 Ibid., p. 53.
88 *On Literature Considered in its Relations with Social Institutions* (1800). Quoted in Renée Winegarten, *Writers and Revolution* (New York, 1974), p. xxiv.
89 II, p. 297.
90 *JJ*, p. 283.
91 *The Life of Oscar Wilde* (London, 1947), p. 158.
92 George Woodcock, p. 285.
93 *Complete Works of Oscar Wilde*, p. 934.
94 Ibid., pp. 1079–1104.
95 'Universal Literary Influence of the Renaissance', p. 18.
96 II, p. 206.
97 Ibid., p. 217.
98 *JJMU*, p. 347.
99 *Our Friend James Joyce*, p. 145.
100 *Joyce's Benefictions* (Berkeley, 1964), pp. 88–111.
101 Ibid., p. 127.
102 *Joyce-Again's Wake* (Seattle, 1965), p. 107.
103 *The New Science of Giambattista Vico*, trans. Thomas Goddard Bergin and Max Harlold Fisch (Ithaca, New York, 1968), para. 331.
104 *God and the State*, pp. 48–9.
105 'Joyce as Revolutionary', *New Republic*, CVII (9 November 1942), p. 613.
106 Eugene Jolas, 'My Friend James Joyce', in *James Joyce: Two Decades of Criticism*, ed. Seon Givens (New York, 1963), p. 14.
107 Eugene Jolas, 'Homage to the Mythmaker', *Transition* (April–May 1938), p. 174.

108 *Writer and Critic* (New York, 1971), p. 180.
109 II, p. 111.
110 *JJMU*, p. 340.
111 *God and the State*, p. 29.
112 'Universal Literary Influence of the Renaissance', p. 15.
113 'Conversations with James Joyce', p. 326.
114 *Conversations with James Joyce*, p. 74.
115 See Richard Ellmann, *Ulysses on the Liffey* (New York, 1972), p. 52, where a different view is put forth; see also *The Consciousness of Joyce* p. 95, where it is maintained that the pun is an 'agent of democracy'.
116 See *JJ*, p. 729, where it is maintained that 'Sleep is the great democratizer'.
117 *Our Friend James Joyce*, p. 123.
118 *Explorations*, pp. 353 and 354.
119 I, p. 249.
120 Joseph Hone, *W. B. Yeats 1865–1939* (London, 1962), p. 368.
121 *Art of Being Ruled*, (London, 1926), p. 369.
122 *Time and Western Man*, p. 93.
123 Herbert Gorman, p. 183.
124 I, p. 277.
125 III, p. 311.
126 I, p. 301.
127 See the articles by Malaparte in the 15 February 1940 issue of *Prospettive*.
128 See Giovanni Cianci, *La Fortuna di Joyce in Italia* (Bari, 1974), p. 80.
129 *Our Friend James Joyce*, p. 232.
130 Maria Jolas, 'Joyce en 1939–1940', *Mercure de France*, CCCIX (1950), p. 52.
131 I, p. 367.
132 *JJ*, p. 706.
133 Ibid., p. 722.
134 See III, pp. 424, 430, 432, 436; *JJMU*, p. 346; *JJ*, p. 722.
135 'Joyce's Politics' in *New Light on Joyce from the Dublin Symposium*, ed. Fritz Senn (Indiana University Press, 1972), p. 13.
136 'Conversations with James Joyce', p. 326.
137 *JJ*, p. 610 fn.
138 *The Joyce We Knew*, ed. Ulick O'Connor (Cork, 1967), p. 66.
139 *JJ*, pp. 716–17.
140 Quoted in William Chace, *The Political Identities of Ezra Pound and T. S. Eliot*, p. 48.
141 III, p. 166.
142 Ibid., p. 22.
143 Alfred Kerr, 'Joyce in England', p. 39.

Index